PELICAN BOOKS

A718

THE PYRAMID CLIMBERS

Vance Packard was born at Grandville Summit,
Pennsylvania, in 1914. He has earned his living by
writing ever since he graduated from Columbia
School of Journalism over twenty years ago, and has
worked for a number of American newspapers, the
most recent being *Collier's*.

Since Mr Packard's speciality was and is human
behaviour, his interests led him straight to the work
being done by the Institute for Motivational Research
in New York State and to articles and speeches made
by motivational research people throughout America.
The Hidden Persuaders, *The Status Seekers*, and
The Waste Makers are all published in Pelicans. His
latest book, *The Pyramid Climbers*, was published in
1963.

Mr Packard lives in New Canaan, Connecticut, and
teaches a course of magazine writing at New York
University. He is married and has three children.

VANCE PACKARD

The Pyramid
Climbers

PENGUIN BOOKS

Penguin Books Ltd, Harmondsworth, Middlesex, England
Penguin Books Pty Ltd, Ringwood, Victoria, Australia

—

First published in the U.S.A. 1962
First published in Great Britain by Longmans, Green 1963
Published in Pelican Books 1965

—

Copyright © Vance Packard, 1962

—

Made and printed in Great Britain by
Cox and Wyman Ltd,
London, Reading, and Fakenham
Set in Monotype Times

*To those in the business world whose generosity
and cheerful candour contributed so much
to this exploration*

If a man reaches the top, he is not going to tell you how he really got there.

   – A senior executive of a very large U.S. corporation

Contents

Acknowledgements

I am indebted to a great many people who took time from busy schedules to share with me the benefit of their experience in assessing and observing modern executives. A few cannot be identified, either because of their positions or because of the nature of their contributions. And a complete listing of the other people to whom I became indebted in the course of this exploration would fill a number of pages. I do wish, however, particularly to express my gratitude to the following executives, management consultants, executive-search specialists, behavioural scientists, appraisal specialists, and other authorities on executive life:

Dr Chris Argyris, Frederick G. Atkinson, Dr Jerome C. Beam, Harold Bixler, Lawrence Bloomgarden, Sid Boyden, Dr Leland P. Bradford, Albert Brown, Carter Burgess, Frank Canny, Dr James N. Farr, George Fry, Dr Frederick J. Gaudet, John L. Handy, Ed Hergenrather, William A. Hertan, Wardwell Howell, Dr Eugene E. Jennings, Dr Harry Levinson, Robert Lounsbury, Dr Robert N. McMurry, Dr John R. Martin, Robert F. Moore, Dr Charles A. Myers, Johnson O'Connor, Edward Reynolds, Charles D. Scribner, Everett Smith, Roger Sonnabend, Lyle M. Spencer, Harold Stieglitz, Dr Lewis B. Ward, King Whitney, Jr, S. Vincent Wilking, John H. Williams, Robert V. L. Wright. It is safe to assume that some of these people will not concur with all of the thoughts advanced in this book.

I am especially indebted to nine of the above who were among the dozen knowledgeable people who read this book in manuscript. All offered valuable criticisms and suggestions.

My indebtedness extends also to friends outside the business world who offered criticism from the layman's point of view. These included Jane and Edward Eager, Kay and John Tebbel, Audrey and William Roos, Audrey and Lester Cooper, and that sharpest of critics, my wife Virginia. And finally I wish to thank Marion Fuller, Ann Bridgeman, Judith Gilman, and Marion Harding for their help in the final stages of preparing the manuscript.

VANCE PACKARD

New Canaan, Connecticut
2 September 1962

PART 1

MEN AGAINST THE MODERN PYRAMIDS

CHAPTER 1

The Bitch-Goddess Raises Her Demands

Success – 'the bitch-goddess, Success' in William James's phrase – demands strange sacrifices from those who worship her. Aldous Huxley

We are about to enter a veiled and curious world. The object of this exploration is to bring back relevant information about the breed of people who climb modern pyramids.

Members of this breed are the hustling, well-packaged executives who pitch their camps on ever higher ledges of the pyramids of business power. They devote their adult lives to assaulting the slippery, crevice-ridden slopes of the pyramids in the hope of arriving at a peak, or at least a ledge near a peak. They learn the secret lore of negotiating difficult passages. They sharpen some very special traits, such as maze-brightness, which help them survive and advance.

Their desire is to be touched by Success, the goddess who stands guard on the mist-covered peaks. Success permits only a few select climbers to enter her cloud clubs. She has been known to be both feather-headed and ruthless in her choices. She keeps changing the requirements she expects of a climber as he progresses towards her realm. Lately she has become much more exacting in what she requires of the candidate.

How does one please the bitch-goddess Success? To put it more politely: How are the future leaders of major enterprises assessed, sifted, groomed, and finally chosen? Which are the candidates who tend to 'top out' at an early stage of the climb towards success? How do the more adept manage to work their way up to positions near those mist-covered peaks? What, in short, is the process of success? And what are the implications of the present process for the men involved – and for the rest of us?

This exploration might reasonably be viewed as a new phase of a continuing investigation, a further endeavour to discern what is happening to the individual in the face of the new kinds of pressures generated by our violently changing world. In this instance the individual is the rising executive who may, for better or worse, come to have considerable influence upon society at large.

Primarily our focus will be on the rising executive of the medium-to-large-size U.S. profit-making institution. I have also consulted executives of small companies, executives of universities and of government (where there are also pyramids), and executives in countries outside the United States, for purposes of comparison.

This process of success in the sixties merits our concern as well as our curiosity. Corporations are becoming more and more important in the lives of most of us; and more and more young Americans are committing their aspirations to these institutions. Increasingly we live in a corporate society. Business executives are seen as our foremost social models if not our leading heroes. They enjoy the greatest material rewards we can offer, and some of the greatest rewards of prestige. (In Great Britain and France business executives enjoy far less prestige.)

One of the easiest ways to sell homes in the United States at practically any level above that of the working class is to call them 'executive' houses. A Long Island developer offering houses that he labels 'Executive Suites' bills them as 'the summit of luxury for the Top Level Executive' and promises that their dimensions will 'reflect your own success'. In at least seven cities there are now hotels or motels called 'The Executive' or 'Executive House' or 'The Executive Inn'. Albert of Fifth Avenue, New York, features the 'Executive Haircut' in his advertisements. My own wife Virginia keeps track of our social engagements in a book labelled *The Executive's Appointment Calendar*. She can't remember where she got it.

The librarian at the Harvard Graduate School of Business Administration told me, with some amazement, that the library's journal containing synopses of technical articles on management had been turning up in the anteroom of a dentist's office. The title of the journal – *The Executive*.

The power of the executives who reach points near the top of major corporations is already tremendous, and will increase considerably as their far-flung organizations continue to grow in size and as the fruits of exploding technology flow into their hands.

Few of us would disagree when Crawford H. Greenewalt, chairman of Du Pont, states: 'Whatever he is, the business-man is the product and pilot of the system under which most of us earn our livings.' And it might be added that the tens of millions of Americans who work under the direction of an executive well know that his impact on their life can be massive, especially if he is afflicted with the emotional fractures frequently associated with the climbing process. Further, the notions of executives on what is appropriate and estimable in behaviour and aspirations colour the attitudes of the rest of us. Robert Lounsbury, the thoughtful general counsel of Kennecott Copper, commented to me: 'The executive class is transmitting an attitude to society which has a profound impact upon society itself.'

The demand for executives is rising, and apparently will continue to rise for several years, despite the fact that automation is finally starting to take over many of such lower decision-making functions as inventory control. Though some would disagree, *Nation's Business* puts the need at 50 per cent more executives by 1970.

Changes are occurring in the kinds of management skills called for in the breed that will succeed in the future. For one thing we are only beginning to visualize the probable impact on the American economy of the new European unity which is emerging. Soon U.S. businessmen will be facing the prospect of an economy that has become second-largest in a number of respects. Both the competition and the new markets that European unity promises – plus the need of U.S. companies to expand significantly to develop world markets – call for new imaginative kinds of business leadership. There is grave doubt that American industry has been developing enough of the kind of leaders who will be competent to guide their enterprises effectively in this new environment. Management experts concede that a serious 'managerial lag' is developing between the challenges emerging and the skills available to cope with them. Some call this lag the single greatest problem facing free enterprise in the United States.

Another development which is producing a change in requirements is the rush to diversify. Increasingly, companies are becoming constellations of enterprises. In the large, highly diversified company, it is now unlikely that you will find an executive near the top who has an immense detailed grasp of all aspects of producing and selling all his company's products. I found that some executives were not even able to list with confidence all the products their company now makes. This change has tended to denigrate special knowledge, at least near the top, and to emphasize instead all-purpose administrative skills – and 'personality'.

There appears to be a growing conviction that corporate profits in the future will depend relatively less on materials, money, and labour, and relatively more on 'management', than in the past. Consequently industry is focusing an immense amount of attention on the calibre of its management personnel, often spending up to $50,000 to recruit and break in a moderately high-level executive.

This corporate interest in managers has brought about a fantastic proliferation in the consulting firms that specialize in helping companies choose, groom, and assess executives and semi-executives. The Manhattan telephone directory lists forty-seven firms starting with the word *Executive* and twenty-seven starting with *Management*.

Perhaps a word ought to be said at this point about my own procedure in this exploration. I sought to look at the rising executive from a wide range of vantage points. Thus the approach might, hopefully, be called eclectic.

The aim has been to try to bring together as comprehensive

– and unvarnished – a picture as possible of what it takes in the way of skills, commitments, strategies, physique, mental state, observance of rules, education, background, and so on, to get ahead in the modern corporation. In the process I have explored a number of intriguing possibilities for improving the calibre of executives and their environment.

I talked first of all with a great many people who have devoted their careers to evaluating executives. There were talks with most of the nation's leading executive recruiters and with a few executive coaches (a speciality in this area). There were talks with officials of most of the leading psychological-testing and psychological-consulting firms that specialize in executive appraisal. One unforgettable day I spent several hours in the company of aspiring executives submitting to a battery of psychological tests designed to assess my own executive potential. And I spent another day sitting in with a number of corporate personnel directors as they were counselled by psychologists on how to spot the good and bad prospects among would-be executives.

There were, too, sessions with officials of several of the larger management-consulting firms and with officials of the nation's two leading management associations.

Quite a few fascinating hours were spent at clinics where executives are counselled or assessed. In one instance I sat in while six psychiatrists at Gracie Square Hospital in New York compared notes on the inner world of the executive. There was a visit to the Menninger Foundation in Topeka, Kansas, where many executives come for seminars. And there were talks with the medical directors of clinics that specialize in executive check-ups.

People on university staffs who have been trying to understand the executive breed were a very helpful source of insights. I had consultations with staff members of several of the graduate schools which offer strong programmes in executive training.

A most important category of informants, of course, were successful executives themselves. I talked with scores of top-level executives of sizeable corporations, including a couple of dozen presidents. Also, I was fortunate in having been invited to participate in a number of executive seminars in the United States and Europe and to spend evenings as the guest of management groups and their wives. Some of the encounters have left vivid impressions. I treasure the memory of a number of over-stimulated tycoons in Oklahoma leaping fully clothed into a swimming pool. Since starting this project, I have talked to samples of the executive breed from thirty-five states, three Canadian provinces, and twelve countries outside North America.

To complete this summary of sources, there were sessions with such people as the head of a large detective organization which handles many assignments involving executives; with realtors who have specialized in finding proper homes for various levels of executive; with officials who watch the patterns of discrimination in executive suites.

From such talks I filled 167 stenographic notebooks. As for written sources, there were opportunities to examine on a confidential basis many appraisal reports on executives and would-be executives. It was possible to read a number of instruction sheets dealing with executive appraisal, including sheets specifically designed to assess presidential candidates. The reading also included a vast number of published and unpublished studies.

The great majority of business people encountered in my investigation impressed me with their good will, decency, and intelligence. A number were delightful, modest, highly literate individuals with a deep interest in the world beyond their companies' walls. Such an exploration gives one a new awareness that certain of our major corporations possess or have produced some highly admirable leaders, men of breadth, perception and a high sense of responsibility. Such men as Clarence B. Randall, George Romney, Henry Ford II, James C. Worthy, and J. Irwin Miller might be mentioned.

While the primary aim of this exploration was to try to understand the mechanics of success in the modern corporation, some large questions arose about the sanity of it all – and about the reasonableness of some of the new demands made on those who hope to attain high-level success.

Consider the evident manipulation of the ambitious man trying to get ahead in his enterprise. Is all this manipulation necessary to the reasonable functioning of free enterprise in the sixties?

If there is a single dominant conclusion to be made, it is that our aspiring executives (while the most fussed-over segment of our society) are the most manipulated and exploited steady job-holders in the land.

A new kind of gruff paternalism has developed in our large enterprises, an exploitation of leaders rather than labourers. With prosperity, labour has grown independent; most of its paternal direction now comes from union leaders. Labour's leaders have successfully threatened strikes when management has proposed that union members submit to psychological testing. But hundreds of managers and would-be managers meekly submit their fate to such tests – including 'personality' tests – every day, despite mounting criticism of such testing.

The aspiring managers of most large enterprises are fairly constantly being scrutinized, measured, moved about, and pondered. Their rolls of fat and their personal quirks are a matter of deep concern to higher management. In some companies the managers may be directed to have a psychiatric check-up, and in a great many they are 'invited' to submit to psychological check-ups. These aspiring managers are expected to maintain an attitude of piety and total loyalty towards the corporation (an attitude no longer expected of rank-and-file employees). They are expected to move their families to any of the company's 129 branch plants that happens at the moment to need someone with their qualifications.

Some corporate managements worry about a manager if he seems to exhibit an undue sense of humour, if he seems unduly contented, or if he appears to have independent means. And many urge their aspiring executives to be good 'corporate citizens' in the community in their 'free' time.

Executives often discover that their disciplined fidelity to the corporation has been assured by 'lock-in' forms of deferred compensation. They find themselves caught in a web of corporate beneficence. If they decide they would like to break free of their particular employer, they may discover that they stand to lose an appalling amount of money being held for them. A man who had worked for Procter & Gamble said, 'If you work there ten years, you wonder if you can afford to leave.'

The lock-in technique of deferred payment often works to assure that the executives will stand in proper dread of losing their jobs, and so refrain from questioning a superior's judgement in an unpleasant way. Arch Patton, member of the large management-consulting firm of McKinsey & Company, tells of an executive who speculated that he might lose not only his job but also up to $60,000 in deferred pay if he questioned his superior's judgement and fought too hard for his own viewpoint. This, the executive protested, 'puts an unrealistically large premium on a man's honesty'.[1]

Whether all the dehumanizing of the executive's environment which occurs is necessary also seems questionable.

Despite swings in style of theoretical belief in recent decades, from fascination with 'scientific management' through fascination with 'human relations' to the most recent interest in 'participation', there is in actual practice today a startling amount of inhumanity in management thinking about the proper treatment of managers. Presumably this springs from management's inherent thing-mindedness, manufacturing-mindedness, and statistics-mindedness . . . and from its passion for proving somehow that management is a science. At any rate, what has resulted is a proliferation of mechanistic and marketing terms to refer to managers. The good management is often a 'smoothly running machine'. Individual managers often are reduced in management shorthand to blocks on 'blueprints' and become coded units in 'management inventories'. Their salient characteristics may be punched out on I.B.M. cards.

Executive talent is said to be 'stockpiled'. Management personnel are on occasion referred to as 'component parts' of the management machinery.

The outside executive-recruiting firms have gone along in adopting this concept of the non-humanity of managers. One leading recruiter told me that the recruiter's main problem is to discover whether a prospect is 'a successful package'. And a major recruiting firm illustrates the cover of its advertising brochure with a giant, well-punched I.B.M. card. The rather small figure of an executive, with brief-case, stands looking at the punch card – ten times as big as he is – clearly asking himself, 'Do I fit these specifications?'

Management experts frequently start setting their management inventory in order by writing job descriptions which are placed in little black boxes. Then the experts try to find people to fit the 'specifications'. The organizers of modern management yearn for 'scientific proof' in their selection of people. This helps account for the fascination of a good many – but definitely not all – managements with those results of psychological tests which are briskly set forth in percentiles and numerical scores.

Rationality is today considered the supreme virtue in the large corporation. The human managers are expected to be at all times absolutely logical and at no time humanly emotional. Their total absorption is assumed to be with the task at hand; the pretence is maintained that feelings about the fulfilment of the task are either non-existent or cannot be permitted to intrude. Dr Chris Argyris, professor of industrial administration at Yale, points out that in the executive system the expression of feeling becomes so suppressed that superiors often are only vaguely aware of the impact they create on their people when they wield power.

All this masking of feeling and pretence of pure rationality lends an air of stiltedness and juicelessness, an out-of-this-world aridity, to the managerial environs of many corporations.

Much of the non-humane aspect of the corporate treatment of managers was inspired by techniques first developed for the military to categorize officers and men during the three

most recent wars involving the United States. Psychological
testing and periodic rating of officers received a great boost
in all three wars, and many of the corporate personnel
directors and management consultants I encountered reported that they had gained much of their early experience by
categorizing tens of thousands of military men and war-
plant employees during the Second World War. In the war
situation these experts were confronted with great numbers of
suddenly recruited strangers who had somehow to be cate-
gorized swiftly. Further, the totally authoritarian setting
made manhandling seem easy and even natural.

One still hotly debated issue is whether all the de-individualizing of the executive which also frequently occurs is either
wise or necessary. Related to this de-individualizing is the
growing passiveness of the role assigned to executives and the
blurring of individual responsibility.

There is a common assumption that, *vis-à-vis* the company,
a good executive is self-effacing. *Industrial Marketing*, for
example, carried an article that offered this counsel: 'An
important part of the company spirit is the renunciation of
pride of authorship.'

What is the truth in the sixties about the thesis developed –
and roundly denied – in the fifties that corporations want
team-playing conformists? In the early fifties Clark Kerr, the
distinguished economist who is now president of the University of California, warned of 'a tragic decline of the historic
American belief in the independent mind and the independent
spirit' because of the demands for total allegiance to large
organizations. A few years later, in the mid fifties, William H.
Whyte, Jr, described how large organizations – business,
governmental, and educational – were producing a human
(or unhuman) type, the 'organization man'. In the corporations, he contended, the younger, lower-level trainees and
managers were joyously embracing togetherness as a way of
life.

Management people have tended to renounce this view as
distorted. One survey of 160 corporation presidents disclosed
that seven out of ten denied that the organization man existed

in their companies.[2] Later in the report of this particular survey, however, the author noted that the presidents questioned 'would be extremely cautious about promoting the men with uncommon views'. This was at approximately the time Du Pont's President (now Chairman) Greenewalt wrote a book – widely heralded in business circles – extolling the need for 'The Uncommon Man' in industry.

In the last few years a number of penetrating studies have been made by behavioural scientists at such universities as Yale, the University of California, M.I.T., Michigan State, the University of Michigan, and Ohio State which offer new depths of insight and disturbing new ramifications concerning the impact of the organization on the individual.

The challenge modern man faces turns out to be more complicated than merely adjusting to – or coping with – conformity. He must learn to work out a tolerable relationship with the great hierarchical power structures which increasingly dominate our workaday world and establish healthy relationships with the people in the various layers of such hierarchies. Many investigators have been exploring ways to make the impact of these business hierarchies more humane.

A highly placed executive of a major corporation commented to me in the seclusion of his home, 'The most useful service you could perform is to demonstrate what is happening to individual rights and dignity in the modern corporation.'

While I was attending one seminar on executive selection the psychological consultant commented matter-of-factly that corporations today tend to stifle the man who has boldness and initiative. What most startled me was that not one of the executives in the room rose to challenge the statement.

Executives like to think of themselves as tigers, but this image is increasingly fanciful. The roles they play tend more and more to be passive. They are acted upon fully as much as they act. They move from job to job, and even from company to company, with less and less show of self-determination. In this connexion it should be remembered that the executive-recruiting firms are retained by the corporation rather than by the executives and take their fees from the corporation, not the man.

The increasing passiveness of the executive's role possibly shows up also in a study made of promising executives who went back to universities as a part of their executive development. The study revealed that only 12 per cent of the executives questioned had sought the opportunity for study on their own initiative. The rest simply accepted the company's diagnosis that the experience would be good for them.

Such passivity would seem intolerable to a great many small businessmen. Recently I talked with a man who is in a field in which the entrepreneurs are being hard pressed to survive. He is a custom-home builder, a disappearing breed. But when we talked of his tribulations, he reminded me with some pride of what he considered an important fact. He said: 'In my business you at least meet the world on your own terms.'

A final and disturbing question which arises is whether or not corporations are producing a breed of leaders dangerously isolated from the realities of our changing world. This isolation shows in their frequently egocentric view of the society in which they function.

A well-informed executive operating in the Wheeling–Pittsburgh–Youngstown area made a comment about this isolation which did not strike me with full force until after the steel crisis of April 1962. This crisis, you will recall, was triggered when the major producers – in a seemingly innocent, single-minded manner – almost simultaneously raised their prices on an identical basis shortly after the Kennedy administration had helped arrange what many thought was a non-inflationary contract between the steel companies and the union. Federal authorities seeking to head off the price rise and, some would say, save face, responded with an angry vehemence that startled the steelmen and shook the economy. The steel companies, much to their embarrassment, had to back down.

The Pittsburgh executive offering the comment is a supplier to the steel industry, and while he was talking about executives in general he was drawing largely on his close observation for many years of high-level officials in the heavy industries of the area. He said: 'Something needs to be done to end the isolation of the executive from his society. He lives in a little world of his own kind and won't mix. He has little interest in the views of those who do not accept his views. He assumes that anyone who is not in business is no damned good. The executive too often is out of touch with what is happening in society at large.'

With U.S. industry being pushed abruptly into a highly competitive world market, the insulation of the typical U.S. executive represents something of a peril to the nation. The times call for business leaders who are interested in languages, in international political and monetary problems, in the aspirations and behaviour patterns of people in many lands. The new business leaders will often need to think of their market as consisting of people in seventy nations speaking thirty languages.

A good many modern executives are even isolated from developments in their own empires. As all-purpose generalists, they are dependent on specialists or consultants for advice concerning what is going on.

All this isolating, dehumanizing, de-individualizing, and manipulating has a lasting effect on many of the men who experience these conditions. An executive in Chicago said: 'Many executives themselves feel that they have had something destroyed.'

Perhaps we should be heartened by the fact that many leading business heads and theorists are uneasy about the way executives are now being chosen and developed. Philosophic battles are taking shape on what sort of environment the corporation should provide. A number of bold new experiments are being undertaken to produce better corporate leaders, to provide a more humane corporate environment, and to offer more encouragement to the uncommon men of boldness, imagination, and self-reliance.

In the early phases of our exploration of the world of the pyramid climbers, I will examine the process of success as it actually works, and strive to keep comment to a reasonable minimum. Later I will examine possibilities for improving that process and note what in fact is already being done to improve it.

CHAPTER 2

The Pyramids and the Climbers

Teams of labourers built the pyramids and teams of craftsmen the medieval cathedrals. Now, for the first time, however, management itself has become a team effort. Crawford H. Greenewalt, chairman of Du Pont[1]

I met one of Mr Greenewalt's team managers at a Midwestern conference. He was a lean, tense, dynamic man who had obtained his first management post on the company's team in 1941 as a group leader in a chemical laboratory. During the following two decades he moved upwards in responsibility through six positions. When I saw him he was assistant director of a function in one of the company's numerous departments. Although gaining altitude with each move up the ledges of that modern pyramid known as Du Pont, he obviously was still a considerable number of ledges away from the peak.

The number of ledges – or steps – in a company's hierarchy varies of course with the company's size and philosophy of organization. Some like tall, slender pyramids, with only a few people under each leader; others prefer short, squat pyramids. Occasionally one literally sees these modern pyramids in brick and mortar, where the home office occupies a skyscraper with the suites of the highest officers at the pinnacle. In many instances the corporate pyramid is disguised as a University-of-Miami kind of campus with music piped into every section. But no matter what its outer manifestations, the hierarchic structure as diagrammed on paper is the company's hierarchy of power.

The chief executive officer, whether president or chairman of the board, is at the top, and below him are layers of executives and managers with steadily diminishing degrees of power. Directly beneath the president, for example, there may be three executive vice-presidents; one for marketing, another for manufacturing, and one for all administrative services (community relations, law, finance, personnel, public relations, and so on). Under each executive vice-president are from three to a dozen plain vice-presidents. Many are heads of divisions. Under each vice-president dangle a few office directors with their own staffs of assistants. And beneath each office director may be a cluster of managers of operations. And under each operations manager we may find plant managers who, of course, each have their own little hierarchy. Fourteen levels of supervisory personnel are not uncommon; the larger companies may have more than twenty levels. Most of the big companies, however, try to hold the line at between nine and eleven levels.

Each box on the organization chart is likely to be keyed to a job description. This description may cover several pages and list the twenty-six duties and fourteen responsibilities of that particular post. All this charting is considered necessary to hold these modern corporations together. The rationale is best summed up by an Ohio State University professor of business organization:

Organization structure provides an invisible framework by which the work of various individuals is fitted into an effective team. It provides a means for assigning authority and responsibility to individuals, for communicating between experts at various levels and for enforcing accountability.

Each company has its own way of designating the level of any particular individual. At the Bell Laboratories in Murray Hill, N.J., the chief is a one-digit man, the department heads are two-digit men, the unit managers are assigned three digits, and the working scientists four. A major business-machine company devised a system to indicate position on a numerical basis from 001 (technician) up to 089 (chairman of the board), but at this writing has not introduced it.

In small companies there is little need for visible trappings to delineate levels of authority, since everybody knows every-

body (and his job); but as companies have grown to gargantuan size there has been a tendency to seek visual ways of
differentiating the status levels of managers. Company manuals often set up a five-layer model for assigning everything
from office square footage to drapes, carpeting, carafe, telephone stand, and bookcase.

Until a few years ago one of the most dramatic examples of
visual treatment of status levels was along what was known as
'Mahogany Row' in the Firestone Tire & Rubber Company
headquarters in Akron. Officers were located in descending
rank away from Chairman Harvey S. Firestone Jr's office in
progressively smaller quarters. Some distance away the offices
stopped being enclosed by wood and were enclosed by frosted
glass that went to the ceiling. Still farther out, the glass continued to go to the ceiling but was clear. Next came the offices
enclosed only by clear glass rising to just above eye level.
Beyond was the open room.

In the executive dining-room, again, the Chairman sat at
the centre of a horseshoe table with his vice-presidents fanned
out in descending order on either side. Then came the small
round tables, where again distance from Mr Firestone indicated rank.

About 1956, management thinking at Firestone mellowed
and (in the words of one observer) 'came into the twentieth
century'. A decision was made to modernize the executive
suite; it has been modernized up to but not including Mr
Firestone's office, which remains virtually the same as it was
in his father's day. (A grandfather's clock from the family
homestead has in fact been added.) The rest of the executive
suite is now known as 'Teakwood Terrace'. The decor is teak
with Italian marble columns and black Puerto Rican carpeting. The status distinctions of offices within the suite are now
less visible. The main distinction is that the higher-status
officials have an outside view, whereas lower-status officials
mostly have windows with an 'inside' view into the well of the
building. In the dining-room the horseshoe table has been replaced by a more egalitarian circular table. Mr Harvey Firestone habitually sits at the north end of the circle; his brother

Raymond (president) sits at the south end. Officially at least, other officials and visitors may sit where they please.

The point at which supervisory personnel start being 'executives' has never been clearly defined. Some companies arbitrarily draw the line at a $15,000 annual salary; others, more generous, include anyone above first-line supervisors. One informant quipped that an executive at his firm is 'anybody who doesn't belong to a union'. 'Junior executive' was a term invented to give marginal people the benefit of the doubt, but it now appears to be passing out of vogue because it has frequently proved an awkward label. Some men at the 'junior executive' level were sixty-three years old. Perhaps a better label would be 'semi-executive'.

There is general agreement, however, on the three main levels of 'management'. First there is top management, which makes policy; next, middle or administrative management, which carries out policy; and then supervisory management, which has charge of the working force.

Although organization charts represent the official version of the power picture of the company in question, the real-life situation may be considerably different.

The president may be a figurehead, and a third vice-president – through force of personality – may be the real power when important decisions are made. In one Eastern company making packaged foods, with an annual business in excess of twenty million dollars, the fountainhead of power in the company was for years a maiden lady who served as the chairman's secretary. Executives cleared all important matters with her. She sat at the chairman's side at meetings and suggested ways and means of disposing of every important problem that came up. Some of the other executives referred to her – off the premises – as 'executive sweetie'.

Because of the pyramidal nature of the company hierarchy, there are likely to be several disgruntled persons left untapped whenever an opening occurs immediately above them. This fact has not been unnoticed by outside professional recruiters. They try to keep a file of talented job incumbents who may be or become dissatisfied. Harold Bixler of Boyden Associates, the nation's largest executive-search firm, with headquarters in New York, explained the situation in these terms:

'We are always back to the pyramid. This is one reason why people can be moved. If one of four men in a company is promoted to be general manager, the three men who don't get the job may be movable. They may be asking themselves: "Can I grow here, or shall I look elsewhere?" We may know that these three men are all movable because they didn't get the top job. You have the pyramid principle whether you are dealing with clerks or with officers.'

When an opening occurs, perhaps none of the immediate subordinates may be chosen. This is not only because the professional recruiters are eager to supply outside candidates, but also because the corporation is likely to have a central file of punch cards containing the records, special skills, ambitions, and promotability assessment of every manager in the company. The computer may whir up the name of a man in the St Louis office whose punch card indicates he would be a whiz for the Newark spot. (Or maybe – as the joke which was told to me five times goes – his card was stepped on by a guy in golf shoes.)

If a man near the top moves, quits, retires, or gets himself fired, the chain reaction of chair-jumping which follows occasionally reaches all the way down to the office boy. A McGraw-Hill study several years ago concluded that a third of all key men in industry are involved in job changes every year.

The ambitious, zestful young manager who is eager to make a mark may at first find pyramid climbing an exasperating experience. For one thing, he will find himself working in a conflicting value system. He must appear a hot competitor, in keeping with the folklore, yet at the same time – and more important – he must prove himself a hot cooperator. He must spend much of his work week attending committee meetings and conferences. One New York management-consultant firm, Executive Communications, Inc., determined after making a study of meetings held by the nation's hundred top industrial firms that the average company in this group had been holding about two thousand company meetings a year. It was further demonstrated that 90 per cent of meetings were ineffective and that many if not most should never have been called. The conclusion was that the common corporate practice of depending on the group approach was producing widespread 'deliberative paralysis'. Decision-making and creativity, it was concluded, are best approached on an individual basis.

The young man on the pyramid may also find that despite the fact that his name is on the door as the man in charge of a major operation – and despite the fact that he shuffles through a vast amount of paperwork every day – he is doing very little real decision-making. Companies vary on this, depending in part on how fluid operations are, but in many companies the jobs are so structured that risk-taking decisions are made only by the very top officers.

Dr Robert McMurry, the psychoanalytically oriented psychologist who heads the management consulting firm The McMurry Company (national headquarters in Chicago), snorts whenever he hears about the grave risk-taking responsibility of the rising big-company executive. He says:

'We have been through a couple of two-billion-dollar organizations. You just don't realize the degree of structure that exists there. You have a great big guy making sixty thousand dollars a year in a vast office. Actually, he is making no risk-taking decisions at all. Say he is in charge of purchasing. His job is ninety per cent structured. He has no voice in the specifications of the materials he buys, he can only select certain approved vendors, he can only approve prices within a pre-established range. . . .'

McMurry told of studying the operations of the manager of a two-million-dollar supermarket affiliated with a chain. McMurry asked: 'How much do you think he is authorized to spend without approval? Guess. . . . Ten dollars!' He added: 'When I point out things like this to people in management, it drives them wild because by implication it disparages their own positions.'

Dr McMurry makes a distinction between risk-taking decisions and what he calls problem-solving decisions. Many executives at lower levels do have to solve problems, such as unsnarling a delay in production. 'There is little risk in solving a problem wrong,' he explained. 'On the other hand, when you must act on the basis of few known facts – as when you must decide whether to defy the union – you are making a risk-taking decision.'

At the lower levels of management, people on the pyramids – especially those in such staff jobs as personnel or public relations – may be able to lead the amicable, protected, unchallenging life that some observers have described as characteristic in large corporations. Coffee breaks provide the main excitement. But the men who hope to move into the upper levels are likely to find that the going can get extremely rough. The competitors are likely to become involved in what sociologist Melville Dalton, after a study of management hierarchies, called 'a general conflict system'.

Dr Eugene E. Jennings, psychologist at Michigan State's Graduate School of Business Administration, observes that when you get within three layers of the top you come into what he calls 'the bowling alley' and are in constant peril of being knocked out of competition.

Economic conditions of the moment (over which the executive has no control) can ease or heighten the perils of climbing. A high-level financial executive of a large textile organization said:

'Lots of successful men have great illusions as to why they have been successful. Some don't realize they were plain lucky. In our own company a pretty fair amount of the important advances have depended upon the condition of the textile market at the time the man made the move. If the market is bullish you can make a lot of mistakes and the market covers them. But if there is a down trend, every false move you make is doubled.'

Although it is seldom admitted, many men who reach the peaks of their pyramids owe their success at some stage to the sheer luck of being in the right spot at the right time. One chairman who is candid on this score is dynamic, amiable

Carter L. Burgess, who was president of Trans World Airlines before he was forty and later became president of American Machine & Foundry.

During the Second World War Burgess was serving as an M.P. second lieutenant, patrolling in the Washington beer and red-light district. One afternoon during a free period he walked up the hill to headquarters to see if he had any mail. An officer stuck his head out the window and hollered: 'Hey, have you got a good uniform?' Burgess said he did and the man ordered him to report at once to do guard duty for the first joint meeting of Winston Churchill and F. D. Roosevelt. The officer was grabbing any passing M.P. more than six feet tall.

Soon thereafter Burgess was working regularly with the Combined Chiefs of Staff, where he developed a warm friendship with the late General Walter Bedell Smith. To make a long story short, years later General Smith was vice-chairman of A.M.F. when Burgess was brought into the presidency.

The success cult is so strong in modern business that every man on the pyramids is assumed to have his eye on the peak. (This is less true in Europe, where a more limited ambition is considered honourable.) Such an expectation, of course, is becoming less and less realistic as the pyramids continue to grow taller and taller. Some of the larger ones have tens of thousands of managers, all presumably straining to move towards the one-man chair at the top. In U.S. society the man who commands a firm with a hundred employees is considered, properly, to be quite a success. But the man who heads a hundred-employee unit in a corporate empire employing a hundred thousand may think of himself as being a long way from success. Worse, his wife may think so too.

By the very nature of things, the great majority of men in the middle ranks of management are never going much farther upwards on their pyramid. There just isn't room. By the age of thirty-five many men are – whether or not they admit it – starting to top out. Any additional moves in the company will be lateral. They've reached the point at which they have been judged non-promotable. C. Wilson Randle, making an analysis of 3,500 executives, reported that only a third were still considered promotable.[2]

Some executives may in fact have climbed beyond their capabilities. Essentially ineffectual, they have by coat-tail-hanging been pulled up to levels of responsibility at which they cannot act effectively. In some of the big private bureaucracies when this happens compassionate colleagues may simply build a wall around such a man so that he can't do too much damage, and they operate – except for the amenities – as if he weren't there.

On the typical pyramid there are usually some managers who openly state that the idea of trying to move any farther upwards does not appeal to them. They share the view of the young executive in Sloan Wilson's *The Man in the Gray Flannel Suit* who announced 'I don't think I'm the kind of guy who should try to be a big executive. . . . I don't think I have the willingness to make the sacrifices.' Some managers point out grimly that the top is where the lightning always strikes. Such attitudes, however, are exceptional. Most men on the pyramids are really trying to advance to higher positions.

In the competition on the pyramids it is still usually possible for two men with completely different personality patterns to be equally effective in moving towards the top – which is cheering. Consider the two titans of the U.S. airline business, C. R. Smith, president of American Airlines, and W. A. Patterson, president of United. In the words of *Fortune*, 'Smith is tall, blunt, fidgety, and capable of profane wrath; Patterson is small, tactful, relaxed, cheery.'

This possibility of radical differences in the successful personality is supported by Dr Lewis Bookwalter Ward, Professor of Business Research at Harvard's Graduate School for Business Administration. He has found that there are 'many different ways of treating people . . . several styles of management'. To illustrate, he cited the cases of two plant superintendents working for a glass company. Both men were turning in top performances but went about their jobs in completely different ways. This was particularly apparent in the degree to which they inserted themselves into the activity of their subordinates. At one man's plant the subordinates, describing their routines, mentioned conferring with their superintendent one fifth of the time; at the other man's plant the subordinates mentioned conferring with their superintendent on four-fifths of their activity.

Dr Ward described the superintendent who was only one-fifth involved as 'a relaxed character who put his feet on his desk. Nothing disturbed him. He could let go of projects and say, "This is your baby."' The other fellow 'was running in and out of crises, cutting short his vacations, and extremely busy about everything. He talked to three hundred men personally every day and the men knew he cared about them'.

Which was the better boss? It depends, Ward suggested, upon what you want. 'The company's vice-president in charge of manufacturing liked the busier one better because he, the vice-president, could pick up the phone and that man could answer any question on the spot. He was on top of his job. The relaxed man would say "I don't know, but I'll find out."'

Another basis for judging executive effectiveness is the man's record in developing subordinates into men capable of taking charge of other plants. Here the relaxed man shone. Three men from his group were now superintendents at other plants. The busy man had not produced one, and when was asked if he had any subordinates who were now ready for such higher responsibilities, he said no.

The personalities, chances, and ambitions of the competitors may differ, but the essential non-variable is the pyramid. It is always there and its climate, for better or worse, is not going to be changed in a hurry. Those climbers who hope to get near a peak are never permitted to forget the inexorable narrowing of the ledges on the way up. With the conquest of a space on each higher ledge the rigours, tensions, and total demands increase.

PART 2

SCREENING, GROOMING, PRUNING

CHAPTER 3

Some Types That Seldom Survive

One major automobile corporation instructs its college inter-viewers to determine if the applicant 'looks like us'. Lawrence Bloomgarden, Institute of Human Relations

The screening of candidates permitted to enter the competition on the pyramids of business power is considerably more in-tensive than the screening of gladiators for the arenas of ancient Rome. Our modern competitor must have a sound body, cool nerves, passable teeth, and a psyche that can sur-vive the tapping of all manner of little rubber hammers. There are the official specifications for position (these may fill several pages). And then there are the unofficial specifications which may never be acknowledged or even realized. Such un-written knock-out factors often prevent a candidate from making even the so-called first list of serious prospects.

Some years ago an admiring book, *America's Fifty Fore-most Business Leaders*, edited by B. C. Forbes, made this re-markable statement: 'Neither birth nor education, neither nationality nor religion, neither heredity nor environment are passports or obstacles to the highest success in this land of democracy.' Only 'worth', he said, counts.

This happy bit of mythology has rarely fitted the situation that prevails in large business organizations as a whole and it has little relevance in the sixties. One accident of birth alone virtually eliminates from serious consideration half the human race residing within the U.S. – the elimination that occurs when an applicant for a management post is asked to check the appropriate box containing the letter *M* or *F*. A check in the *F* box is usually a knock-out factor.

I am uneasily aware that so far in this book I have used the pronoun *he* exclusively in referring to 'the executive'.

Feminine readers might think me guilty of a male conceit. The *he*, like the word *man*, can of course blanket both sexes in general usage. In the case of writing about the modern executive, however, I am being reasonably precise in using *he* in its specific gender sense. Although nearly four out of ten job-holders in the U.S.A. now are female, women rarely attain the executive suites of substantial corporations except in secretarial capacities. They are perhaps the most discriminated-against of all minority groups in industry. A Harvard doctoral dissertation by David Carson on executive-training programmes for supermarket chains contains this sentence:

The selection process for the executive training programme at [name of chain] was specifically designed for men only, and 'Manpower Inventory' in this company – and in the others included in this study – meant Male only.

In the early fifties the Harvard Business School's division of research sent a research team into ninety-five business organizations to study executive opportunities for women. Its report said: 'Very few women were found to be holding top executive jobs in the sense of corporate officers or senior executives. A number of women in a variety of fields, however, were found in positions of "second in command".' Several executives indicated that this was the highest level a woman could hope to attain in the near future. The prevailing sentiment was expressed by the head of a Chicago management-consulting firm in these terms: 'The highest position that women are going to reach in the foreseeable future in any large numbers is that of assistant to a top executive. This will be primarily an expansion of the secretarial function!'[1]

The shut-out of women is gradually easing. Women who reach the higher levels of sizeable organizations, however, still tend to represent special situations or achieve their success within special fields more open to women than most. Many of the women heading corporations are the widows of former owners. A few others attained their eminence without family connexions but started with the company when it was small. The best opportunities for women to rise to at least the department-head level appear to be in personnel, research, accounting, advertising, publishing, and design. General Foods had a woman as vice-president in early 1962; so did McGraw-Hill and a number of major advertising agencies.

Women are presently considered more acceptable in 'inside' jobs than 'outside' jobs, where they would have to deal with outside business*men*. It is often considered risky to startle this outsider by assigning a woman to deal with him.

One of the best areas of opportunity for women is in department stores, possibly because they sell primarily to women. A vice-president of a large department-store chain advises: 'We had a vice-president in charge of advertising for several years who was a woman at seventy-five thousand a year and she could have stayed. We have a dozen women in the thirty-to-thirty-five-thousand-dollar class.' Women also occasionally hold important positions in banks. One analysis of ninety-four banks in Michigan revealed that women were officers in three of them.

Male executives have developed a number of explanations and rationalizations to account for the prevailing barrier against women. The women are accused both of making too much of the job and of not being sufficiently dedicated to it. One merchandiser who has had considerable experience in dealing with women as executives said: 'Their only defect comes down to an inability to wear epaulets lightly. When they succeed in avoiding this weakness – which perhaps developed out of their struggles to win recognition – our company has no difficulty in keeping young men working under their direction.' (That, of course, was a male talking.) If they are unmarried, the possibility that they will marry and leave represents the kind of major uncontrollable factor that worries many corporate managers. Whether they marry or not, they are less likely than men to strive for the usual reasons of economic anxiety – 'my wife's country-club bill, a house in Scarsdale, two sons in college, and a daughter who expects a five-thousand-dollar wedding in June,' as one middle-aged executive described *his* economic anxieties to me.

One barrier blocking many women from real advancement

in the typical corporation is the fact that in large cities executives are often expected to lunch at an approved local executive club. Many of these will either not permit a woman on the premises or allow them to enter only by a side door. Cleveland Amory reports that New York's Hemisphere Club became the first important executive luncheon club to recognize by its admission policy that executives can be *F* as well as *M*.

A second convenient and widespread way of screening out unlikely candidates among would-be executives is to throw out all applicants who write *None* where the candidate is asked to list his college degree or degrees. This will still eliminate nearly nine out of ten U.S. males.

A college diploma is becoming an almost universal requirement for admission to the management group. Many companies tell clerical and production-line workers that there is room at the top for the best of them. But in recent years only one top manager in ten has come from such a background, and the number will decrease.

In projecting what management will be like in the 1980s, Harold J. Leavitt, professor of industrial administration and psychology at Carnegie Tech, notes:

Apprenticeship as a basis for training managers will be used less and less, since movement up through the line will become increasingly unlikely. Top management training will be taken over increasingly by the universities.[2]

The study of executive training for supermarkets cited earlier has this to say about the role of education:

In general the supermarket trade is changing its approach towards the selection of junior executives from haphazard choice of experienced men from the rank and file to the rational selection of novices who show promise of developing into competent executives. Some companies tend to overlook company employees in their enthusiasm to exploit other sources, such as colleges.

It quoted one executive as offering this explanation:

It's so easy for any young person to attend college today that I wonder about the intelligence and the ambition of those who don't.

This might be considered debatable, despite increased enrolments, in view of the fact that college costs have been rising faster than family income and the fact that two thirds of the brightest young people in the land – those with I.Q.s of higher than 117 – have not had the benefit of a college diploma.

The most startling explanation for the insistence of a diploma was offered by an executive taking part in a round table on executive potential sponsored by the McKinsey Foundation for Management Research. He said: 'We desperately need a means of screening. Education is one quick means of preliminary screening without having to think too much about it.'

About two-thirds of today's present top managers are college graduates and another 10 per cent have spent some time in college. It should be remembered, however, that such men exemplify the opportunities for management training that existed a quarter-century ago. Today the proportion of beginners in management training who have college degrees is closer to 90 per cent.

In 1957 the American Management Association made an analysis of the careers of 335 company presidents to find what clues their careers suggested for ambitious young men now. Conclusion Number 1, according to one account, was: 'Go to college. Princeton if you can make it. But in any case get a sheepskin.' An official of the A.M.A. told me: 'The guy who has just a high-school education is not much in evidence [in executive circles] any more. Most of the guys who come to our meetings and seminars are college graduates.' He felt there had been a clear change in this respect in the past decade. William A. Hertan, president of Executive Manpower Corporation (headquarters New York City), points out that there is now so much stress on the college degree that one candidate in twelve seeking an executive post falsifies his record to give himself a degree.

Entrance requirements aside, the evidence that a man must have a college education to succeed as an executive in many fields of business is somewhat less than overwhelming. In a check I made of some of the spectacular stories of fortune-building through entrepreneurial success in recent years, most of the men had never been near a college. A University of Wyoming sociologist, Dr Edwin G. Flittie, spent a month observing executives at the headquarters of a major utility company in the West. Afterwards he commented:

In some companies advancement beyond a certain point is contingent upon college training. In carefully observing management employees during the interviews I have concluded that those at the level of middle management or above who have had no college training possess as much poise, sophistication and social adeptness as those who possess a college background. Further, the verbal abilities of these people in terms of fluency and proper usage of English are at least equal to those of most of the college-trained people. Certain of these men were almost apologetic in talking to me (a college professor) for their lack of college training. It is my opinion that most of these men are at least as well qualified to perform their jobs as their college-trained associates. I would include several of these 'non-college' managers as among the most outstanding people with whom I had contact.

Certain industries are much more flexible than others about requiring a college diploma. Until recently the railroad industry did not disqualify good prospects because they had no college degrees. Merchandisers have been the least insistent of all about the diploma. They go by results. The man who doesn't produce, and quickly, is out – regardless of his academic pedigree.

U.S. companies are not alone in having upgraded educational requirements for their managers. In the Soviet Union and in France there is a general insistence that management candidates have the equivalent of a college education. Professor David Granick of the University of Wisconsin found that all plant directors on the Leningrad Regional Economic Council were college graduates, as were most of the rest of the council's staff. Russian managers seem to run heavily to engineers. On the other hand, in West Germany, which has been undergoing a sensational business growth, relatively little stress is placed on educational background, according to Professor Granick in his recent report, *The European Business Executive*.

The most formidable educational requirements I've personally encountered operate in Japan. To enter the management of a major company there a man must not only have a college degree but he must also land his job within the first year after graduation. Otherwise he must try a smaller company. Furthermore, nearly three quarters of the men accepted by major companies are graduates of a specific university – the University of Tokyo.

A third general category of people who are often screened out in wholesale lots at an early stage of the selection process are the non-*WASP*s. The non-*WASP*s who survive the preliminary screening usually must have a lot more going for them in the way of qualifications than *WASP* candidates in order to be accepted and to make much headway up the sides of the typical modern business pyramid.

A *WASP* – as originally defined by sociologist Digby Baltzell – is a White Anglo-Saxon Protestant. *WASP*s have traditionally been the in-group of the U.S. business world. They have been the gate-keepers to management of most large industries and financial institutions, notwithstanding the cheery assertion in *America's Fifty Foremost Business Leaders* that 'neither nationality nor religion, neither heredity nor environment' have been obstacles to great success. To a large extent, the *WASP*s still are the in-group, although some moves have recently been made towards less flatly rejecting non-*WASP*s.

An early rationale for confining executive selection to a homogeneous group was developed in the late thirties by telephone executive Chester I. Barnard in his still widely read *The Functions of the Executive* (now in its fourteenth printing). Barnard listed as incentives to get executives to work more smoothly together the possibility of 'communion' and 'social

compatibility' and 'comfort in social relations'. From such
concepts he leaped into the idea that often 'men cannot be
promoted or selected, or even must be relieved because . . .
they "do not fit", even where there is no question of formal
competence. This question of "fitness" involves such matters as education, experience, age, sex, personal distinctions,
prestige, race, nationality, faith, politics, sectional antece-
dents; and such very specific personal traits as manners, speech,
personal appearance, etc.' That was quite a mouthful, and
some believe that whatever his intention, the statements have
had a profound influence in serving to encourage the *WASP*s
in their conviction that fellow *WASP*s make the best colleagues for the executive suite.

One non-*WASP* who usually has difficulty getting a nod
from the gate-keepers of larger enterprises is the Jew. Approximately 8 per cent of the college-trained population of the
United States is Jewish. Against this, consider the fact that
Jews constitute less than one half of 1 per cent of the total
executive personnel in leading American industrial companies.

This startling statistic can scarcely be due to any lack of interest or aptitude on the part of Jewish college graduates. The
world's most famous – and perhaps most difficult – graduate
school for business administration is at Harvard University.
One graduate in seven who emerges from this school is Jewish.
You get quite a different ratio, however, when you look at the
middle-aged managers U.S. industry sends to Harvard each
year to take part in the school's Advanced Management Programme. These are men who are usually being groomed for
important positions. Harvard has no control over the selection of the men who are sent. They are chosen by the participating companies. One person who has watched this
programme at close range for some years estimates that the
proportion of Jewish managers sent to participate has been
about one in two hundred!

An official of the American Jewish Committee who tries to
keep abreast of employment practices affecting executives has
made a study of the management of many major companies.
He reports:

We went over a directory containing the names of two thousand management people at U.S. Steel very thoroughly with knowledge-able people. Even making allowance for questionable cases, we could find only nine or ten Jewish managers there at that time.

A study of the management roster of a paper-making com-pany turned up only one Jewish executive out of 1,500, and he was in research. A detailed study of the 1,028 top officials of Philadelphia's six leading banks revealed that only six were Jewish.

One curious fact is that several of the corporate giants that were pioneered by Jews or got much of their growth under Jewish leadership have gradually fallen into patterns pretty much like those of industry as a whole. The proportion of Jews among the younger executives at Sears, Roebuck and Radio Corporation of America is pretty much like that found in other giant companies. Those present – as in most of the industrial giants – are likely to be mainly clustered in advisory or creative 'inside' staff jobs as in research. They are steered away from the main 'line' of authority posts and from posi-tions calling for a good deal of 'outside contact'. In short, the discriminatory pattern for Jewish executives is much what it is for that other minority group, women executives.

Some fields of industry and finance are much more ex-clusionary than others in regard to Jews. The industries that seem least receptive to the idea that Jews can be executives are automobile manufacturing, commercial banking, insurance, public utilities, and such heavy industries as steel, coal, and oil. An official of the A.J.C. has stated that at the top levels of virtually all of the nation's hundred largest industrial cor-porations – particularly those operating in the steel, auto-motive, chemical, petroleum, and electrical-equipment fields – all levels of management positions remain closed to Jews. A similar situation is found in the fifty largest American financial institutions.[3]

Perhaps as a result of this apparent lack of opportunity on the giant pyramids, especially the more conservative ones, Jews have tended to concentrate in fields that have been fairly recently pioneered, such as mass communications and mass

entertainment, or fields that require an unusual amount of
risk-taking venturesomeness, such as merchandising and investment banking.

In the past year or so, some slight increase in open-mindedness about Jews has been noted in a number of the large industrial companies. And in a few, signs of a new liberalism
have developed which officials of the American Jewish Committee consider most hopeful. American Motors (which has
been headed by George Romney, a Mormon) has been showing a liberal viewpoint towards Jewish managers that is
startling in an industry that has long had a closed mind on the
subject. The leadership at International Business Machines
has advanced a Jew to vice-presidency (research and development) and is taking other steps to shake up old, frozen attitudes. At Reynolds Aluminium the director of research is
Jewish.

Studies are under way at four universities – Harvard, Cornell, Michigan, and California – to try to get a better understanding of the prejudices at work in the selection and
development of managers. (The A.J.C. expects that these
studies will help considerably in bringing about a change of
attitudes.) The Harvard investigators, under Dr Lewis B.
Ward, have been following the careers of twenty-five Jewish
and twenty-five gentile graduates as they progress in forty
different companies.

Dr Ward comments that one significant contrast seems apparent between the companies that do not hire Jewish people
for management and those that do: the companies with no
Jews seem to have more organization-man types and 'put
considerably more store in adjustment and modesty and lack
of troublesomeness. The companies hiring Jewish boys, on
the other hand, are much more tolerant of positive qualities
that might be troublesome, such as intelligence, aggressiveness, and so on. I get the feeling that what they are telling us
is that "we are willing to try to get along with someone that
will not fit into the job easily in order to get a gain in creativity,
motivation and intelligence".' He also noted the paradox that
some of the managements which seem most democratic with

regard to hiring minorities appear to be among the more arbitrary in their treatment of subordinates. There is less emphasis upon keeping subordinates informed and soliciting their opinions before making decisions.

The preference for *WASP*s in most of the major executive suites also affects Catholic candidates – particularly those of Italian or Slavic background – though less drastically. A good example of the difference was reported by Seymour Freedgood when he studied a hundred-odd auto executives living in the Bloomfield Hills area outside Detroit. He reported of these executives: 'In one case out of ten he is a Roman Catholic of Irish or Italian ancestry. None of the hundred top auto executives is a Jew, and no Jewish families live in Bloomfield Hills proper.'[4]

Sociologist Melville Dalton, in his study of informal factors influencing the careers of 226 people on one corporate pyramid, concluded that being Catholic was a real handicap.

An interesting pattern of Protestant–Catholic division can be seen in the insurance companies in Manhattan. They tend to be either predominantly Protestant or predominantly Catholic. This separation is so drastic that the Catholic-dominated companies are clustered in parts of the financial district different from the Protestant-dominated companies. For example, John Street is predominantly Protestant, Maiden Lane predominantly Catholic. William Street is split down the middle on the basis of religious dominance.

The fields in which Catholics appear to be most heavily represented are the railroads and public utilities. Social historian Moses Rischin surmises that the one big reason Catholics are strong in the railroads is that in the early days of the railroads Irish labourers played a major role in their building. In those days it was easier to move up into management from a labouring position. Less stress was placed on proof of education. Dr Rischin attributes the prominence of Catholics in the public utilities field to the Irish role in municipal politics in the years when utilities were being established. 'The political, administrative, and organizational gifts of the Irish proved especially congenial in these fields,' he adds.

A final large group that is eliminated by the *WASP* formula, of course, is the millions of people whose skin happens to be something other than pinkish-beige. The absence of dark-skinned people in the management ranks of major corporations is virtually absolute.

Some of the graduate schools of business administration have had Negro students, but the impression is that virtually all have gone into business for themselves or into Negro-run businesses. Some banks have started hiring Negroes for clerical jobs. In 1961 the first Negro appeared on the floor of the New York Stock Exchange in a role other than that of runner or clerk. He was a customer's man, a difficult and responsible role. Early in 1962 Pepsi-Cola named a Negro, Harvey C. Russell, to a newly created vice-presidency. He has been directing the company's activities in reaching the Negro and Spanish market. As this is written, the New York State Commission against Discrimination has launched a campaign to create a climate in which it will be possible for Negroes to have a chance to become executives in business and industry. But that's about all that can be said for now.

All of these categorical grounds for screening out candidates because of sex, education, religion, race, and ethnic background greatly narrow the field of executive possibilities. These limiting factors also help account for the close and restricted climate in which the candidates who *are* chosen will have to function.

CHAPTER 4

Inspecting the Serious Prospects

We have developed techniques that strip people psychologically naked. These are real powerful instruments in revealing people as they are. Dr Robert N. McMurry

At best, corporations tend to take a good long time making up their minds about anything. When they are confronted with choosing among several candidates who have made the 'short list' for a managerial opening, the deliberations often seem interminable. This is not simply a manifestation of bureaucratic red tape. The company managements want to know in intimate detail what kind of a team-mate they would be getting.

Thus it is that the man who survives preliminary screening is likely to spend many dozens of uneasy hours – spread over weeks – answering questions, filling out forms, and submitting to a variety of inspections.

His résumé and application form will be scrutinized for unexplained gaps in employment record, possible marital failure, executive indebtedness, and any proneness to prevarication. Dr McMurry finds that more than one fourth of all applicants for managerial positions tend to overstate their income by including such fringe items as country-club membership, cars provided to them, and the like. Then they often round off the thousands and add one. A candidate's record is also studied for evidence of undue restlessness. One recruiter explained: 'Let's suppose the record shows the man has changed companies four times in eight years. That is all right for a kid, but not for an older man.'

A company hiring representatives usually wants to know all about the applicant's college record. The forms used by some companies have a line on which to record the candidate's average grade. If he is hired this of course becomes a part of his permanent file.

The college or colleges attended can in some companies be a critical question, even for older men whose college experience is so far in the past that it is a misty memory. John L. Handy, president of the recruiting firm Handy Associates, told me ruefully that 'a company in Indiana wanted a vice-president. They gave us all the specifications and we sent them a man as a try-on candidate. They forgot to tell us he had to be either a Harvard or Yale man'.

Until recently the American Brake Shoe Company was so Yale-oriented in its top management that it sought a Yale image and worked closely with Yale alumni. The Prudential Insurance Company of America reserved most of its top spots for Princeton men. For a time you not only had to be Princeton but preferably a former member of the Princeton football team. Though this strong partiality to Princetonians has eased in recent years, Prudential still has many Princeton men at the top. Wardwell Howell, founder of Ward Howell Associates, executive-recruiting firm, recalls that only recently a New York company seeking an executive specified: 'We will want our man to be a graduate of Princeton.'

The personnel director of one very large corporation in the East made a pilgrimage back to his beloved college fraternity each spring and tapped several graduating brothers as management trainees. After nearly a decade this habit produced such a cell of brothers within the company that even top management took uneasy notice and suggested he find new ways to demonstrate his loyalty to the fraternity.

A *Fortune* survey of 1,700 top executives revealed that close to a third who had attended college had gone to one of five Ivy League colleges. Undoubtedly the proportion would rise if confined to financial men. Of the seven top bankers in Philadelphia, a recent count showed five were Ivy-League graduates. (The other two colleges represented were DePauw and Temple.)

A company looking over prospective managers is also likely to show interest in the man's course of study while at college.

Here an often-noted mythology persists. Company presidents in their public comments, especially convocation speeches, announce that they are now searching for the Broad-Gauge Man and deplore the recent emphasis upon narrow specialization. Their working-level recruiters who visit college campuses continue looking for – and offering the highest pay to – men grounded in such technical specialties as data processing, computer design, or sales and accounting. Companies genuinely interested in the liberally educated man exist, especially in financial fields, but they remain exceptional.

Of *Fortune*'s 1,700 top executives, 85 per cent of those with college backgrounds had majored in 'practical' subjects – pre-law, business, economics, engineering, or science. David Granick, in his studies of European executives, finds that in Russia and Belgium a manager is expected to be an engineer; in Great Britain the talented amateur with a grounding in the arts rather than science is more likely to be esteemed.

A great deal of effort goes into finding ways to get behind the façade of the prospect and to obtain an analysis of the man with his guard down. Two instruments Dr McMurry has developed for getting an unvarnished picture are his 'Patterned Interview Form' and his 'Telephone Check on Executive Applicant'. These forms, completed by the investigator, were developed by The McMurry Company for the Dartnell Corporation and now are widely used throughout industry. The six-page patterned interview for executives includes a twenty-two-item analysis of *each* of the man's last four jobs and includes sections on his schooling, family background, domestic and social position, present financial position, place of residence, and motives for seeking the job (is it prestige, security, or earnings?). Under each line where the interrogator is to indicate the candidate's responses are instructions (in faint orange type) which reveal the real purpose of the question. Thus, when a candidate is asked how his last superior was to work with, the orange type asks 'Did he get along with superior?' And when the man is asked, 'How did you get along with your father?' the unvoiced orange question the interviewer must answer is 'How did he react to authority?'

One question requires that the candidate specify whether he has any source of income other than from his job. The orange type asks: 'Will this other income affect his motivation?' A screening form that has been used by a certain chemical company puts this concern more bluntly: 'Does the applicant have too large an outside income?'

Dr McMurry's telephone check is designed to cope with the fact that former employers and associates are always notorious for putting the best face on a man's record in letters of reference. They may be glad to be rid of the man but they don't want to have on their conscience any damage they've done to his future. In the telephone check, the former associate or boss is asked simply to 'verify' information the candidate has already given the investigators (which sounds easy). Questions begin innocuously, but again there are the orange unvoiced questions. After 'How well did he get along with other people?' comes the orange question 'Is he a troublemaker?' Farther along, the old associate is asked to indicate the candidate's strong and weak points. One of the most illuminating questions, near the end, is 'Would you rehire him?' Dr McMurry commented: 'Often on this there is a long pause and then, "I don't know."'

The most controversial of the probing techniques currently used on candidates for executive jobs are the psychological tests. Investigators in many hundreds of companies use both aptitude and personality tests. The latter are the more intrusive and controversial. Some of the testing is highly sophisticated and is supervised by full-fledged psychiatrists or Ph.D.s in clinical psychology. Much of it is crude and scored by glorified clerks who have picked up a smattering of psychology.

Today any young man who aspires to an executive career must accept the probability that at some point he will have to submit to psychological probing.

Personality-type tests came under criticism back in the mid-fifties, especially after William H. Whyte, Jr, demonstrated in *The Organization Man* that the tests then in use favoured the conformist and that one could cheat by simulating conformity. Many management people are under the impression that all psychological testing has gone into a decline since this early wave of criticism. And in many companies that consider themselves sophisticated or that are humanistically oriented there has indeed been a turning away from testing. But we have the paradox that testing continues to grow in popularity while most of the people in the best position to evaluate testing appear to be taking a distinctly critical view. Perhaps what we are seeing is a normal lag in behaviour between the leaders and followers of trends of business practice. And there are always more followers than leaders. At any rate, by and large testing appears to be more popular than ever as a way to screen hordes of corporate personnel, especially managerial candidates.

Just how widespread is the testing? In January 1961, *Management Review* carried a report of a survey of 852 companies made by the Bureau of Business Research of the University of Texas which showed that 80 per cent of the companies were using tests of some sort on job applicants. This, the report noted, represented a 40 per cent growth in testing within the past decade.

A still more comprehensive study was reported by Harvard's Dr Lewis Ward in 1960. Approximately 1,800 executives took part in his study.[1] He found that, regardless of the opinions of some executives, it was clear that in many companies psychological testing is an important feature of management selection and development today.

Most executives, he discovered, have had direct personal experience with psychological tests. Four out of five had taken one or more psychological tests themselves at some stage in their life. More than half of the executives reported that their companies were then using tests for selecting or promoting, transferring, and developing salaried personnel.

Dr Ward noted that testing appeared to be nearly twice as popular with very large companies as with relatively small ones and then commented: 'Generalizing from our respondents, experience with psychological tests will be part of the common background of the coming generation of executives. Almost every executive under thirty years of age has taken one or more psychological tests.'

Ambitious men at the lower and middle ranks of management seem to be more willing to submit the fate of their careers to a psychologist's report than are other levels of company personnel. One psychologist told me that when he was interviewing a pilot for an airline job the pilot suddenly realized his interrogator was a psychologist and called his union. The management had to instruct him to stop interviewing. Earlier, another airline almost had a strike because pilots discovered the company was using a file of ability tests as a convenient guide in the firing of pilots.

Many people in high executive positions likewise resist test-taking, though they may be quick to order it for subordinates. Sid M. Boyden, founder of Boyden Associates, a search firm that deals chiefly with top-level openings, says he can arrange tests if the client insists, but adds: 'Many of the men we place don't feel that they want to go with a test. They are successful. They say "Here I am." Also, our appraisal techniques obviate the need for supplementary testing that might be required for lower-level employees.'

The large management-consulting firm of George Fry & Associates, headquartered in Chicago, does not encourage such a distinction. Mr Fry told me: 'We submit executives to testing all the way up the line.' This included, he said, forty of the highest-level executives in Chicago.

One night very recently I encountered at a party a casual acquaintance, an advertising executive, who was muttering about psychological testing. It seems that he had just spent fourteen hours taking tests and filling out forms (personality inventory, cultural-values test, and so on) at the direction of a psychiatrist. He was being considered for a top job at another firm. Two weeks earlier, he said, he had had a very long session with another psychiatrist who was probing on behalf of still another company considering him for a job.

This chap had been largely responsible for one of the most successful advertising campaigns of recent years in the toiletries field and he held vice-presidential rank at his present agency. I expressed surprise that a company would insist upon testing 'a man as high as you are.' He replied, 'Oh yes. They do. Even the chairman of the board is tested when reappraisal time comes.' He added: 'Testing is becoming increasingly important in marketing and advertising, especially in the large organizations. You used to have one or two men pretty much running the shop. Now you may have fifteen officers, and each is expected to pass judgement on you. It saves their time if most of the screening and appraising is done by an expert who is briefed on the traits and qualifications the company wants in the job.' And, he added, the testing 'gives them a score to go by.'

In both of his last two sessions with psychiatrists he had been asked to draw pictures. He confided – as if he were the first to discover it – that in responding to such tests 'it is much better to be more normal than off-beat, particularly for an executive.'

I should add that this man did not resent the probing. He had come to expect it as a normal condition of his way of life. Only two things seemed really to annoy him. One was that the last psychiatrist appeared to be worried that he was 'too strong' in a couple of respects in his 'profile'. The other was that no allowance seemed to be made for the mental state of the executive taking these tests. 'The man who has a wealthy wife and fifty thousand dollars in the bank is going to be calmer in this fourteen-hour examination than the man who doesn't know how he's going to pay next month's prep-school bill.'

I learned, however, from my own experience in test-taking, that you can be too calm. The Personnel Laboratory, Inc. (headquarters Stamford, Connecticut), one of the larger and more reputable psychological-testing organizations, kindly permitted me to take an abbreviated battery of its tests for executives in a room in New York City where other would-be managers were being tested. It was arranged that I take the test under a pseudonym, pretending to be a candidate for an executive position in marketing with a cosmetic company that regularly uses the Personnel Laboratory and was in fact looking for someone for the job for which I was being assessed. Actually, they wanted a much younger man.

So it was that one afternoon I found myself drawing pictures of a house, a man, a woman, a tree, and telling stories about my people. My pictures were rendered most tentatively, perhaps because I hadn't drawn a picture of people or trees for twenty-five years that I could recall. Seasoned test-takers are used to drawing pictures. I finished sentences. (To 'My lot in life – ' I answered 'is good,' which happens to be true.) I checked off anything that was bothering me from a list of forty possible complaints, ranging from 'falling through space' and 'germs' to 'feelings of guilt' and 'my enemies'. The only one I checked as even sometimes bothering me was 'my children'. I made up stories about a picture. (This was a so-called projective test. In responding to the murky picture I would presumably be projecting my personality.) I re-arranged pictures in story sequence. I checked drawings that were out of context in picture series. I checked things I would particularly like to do (e.g. 'Be a U.S. Senator'). I checked alternate strategies designed to test my sales judgement and evidently tested very poor, in the bottom 20 per cent. One sales challenge read: 'You've made a presentation and your man is ready to buy. How big an order should you ask for?' I checked 'Just enough not to scare him off.' A true salesman, it turns out, would have checked 'Twice what you expect to get.' I should have known that was the right answer from experience in coping with professionally guided fund-raisers.

I checked questions purportedly testing my general judgement. (In one question I was given four choices on what to do 'if you were in the basement of a theatre and discovered a fire.' I checked 'Endeavour to extinguish it.' I should have checked 'Notify the management.' [It didn't say how big the fire was, which I felt was a crucial consideration.]) In addition, because of my disguise, I had the task of inventing an imaginary life history for the 'Personal Background' section to justify my application for a top-level marketing job. (I was a poor liar. The Manhattan address I gave, it turns out, would have been in the middle of the Hudson River.)

The man next to me was a plump, middle-aged gent being tested for a managerial job on the business side of a New York newspaper. A crisp-mannered blonde woman served as our proctor. Most of the others in the room appeared to be junior-executive types. I took tests for only half a day but the others were in for a full eight hours. They were given speed tests, most of which I was spared. I was told that as a courtesy I was being given the benefit of the doubt about intelligence, and so was not tested for such things as verbal skill, idea fluency, arithmetic reasoning, numbers facility. The young man across the table was obviously getting through speed tests much faster than my middle-aged neighbour.

A week later at the Stamford headquarters of The Personnel Laboratory an awfully nice psychologist (female), who knew my identity, gently gave me the bad news. I would be a poor risk for the job as a marketing executive at the cosmetics company. While I was given credit for sensitivity, perceptiveness, etc. – in 'social insights' I scored a 'very high' 90 per cent – I was much too individualistic in my approach to things. In handling practical situations I lacked 'the kind of thinking that people have who can delegate authority'. Here I gathered she was referring to such things as my effort to put out the fire myself. I showed a lack of patience for day-to-day detail that is desired. I was dismally low in sales judgement. And I didn't seem to have the steam in my boiler – the aggressive, driving energy – that the company wanted in a marketing executive.

The lady psychologist stressed, however, that the results were probably coloured by the fact that I was not really seeking the job. If a job I badly wanted had been at stake, I gathered, I probably would have been more careful. My forms were untidy.

One question in the judgement test was 'If you were bored by the conversation of an acquaintance, would you . . .' There were four possibilities. I checked 'listen with polite but bored attention' as the best response. I should have checked 'listen with feigned interest'.

Also, if I had really plunged wholeheartedly into the tests I might have been more self-revealing. In completing sentences, she noted, I made no complaints and did not get involved in brooding or self-pity. In completing the sentence 'My mother is . . .' I simply wrote 'a fine woman'. And later I said my father was a fine man. In response to the provocative invitation to finish the sentence 'I suffer . . .' I wrote 'from sinus'. The pictures I drew and the stories I made up about them were drab. Perhaps I wasn't in a projective mood.

I floored the poor psychologist with the picture of the house I had tentatively sketched. It was an odd-looking chalet with everything centred upstairs. I had put a small side doorway downstairs but then had drawn an outside stairway leading up to a big second-floor sundeck in front of a huge picture window. Beyond the window obviously was a studio living-room. She said of the house:

'I wish I could understand it better. I do this full of caution.' Then she proceeded to analyse my drawing as 'suggesting that it is not easy for you to develop close relationships with others.'

Quite probably that outside stairway leading up to a second-floor terrace and living centre did look a little fishy to a psychologist watching for aloof, nonsocial types. The fact is that the sketch I drew was of an actual house I had just built on Martha's Vineyard. In this real house I had placed the living-room and sundeck on the second floor, with an outside stairway leading up to them, not because I consciously wish to avoid close relationships but because it is only from the second-floor level that you can look out over the treetops at a 300-degree view of the Atlantic Ocean. Not being an aggressive sort, however, I didn't argue. Anyway, drawing a house was only one item in a large battery of tests.

At any rate, she said, if I were a true marketing-executive type I would have rendered the lines of all my drawings more aggressively. Then she added: 'People are more disturbed about their lives than you indicate here.' She commented that there was considerable evidence of irritability in my response, even though there was no evidence that I was basically an irritable person. She said, 'You were abrupt and didn't finish the endings of many words.' I find that two words I ended rather abruptly were *carelessnes* (explaining things that bothered me in other people) and *sailin* (in listing the only hobby I could think of). She suggested that my irritability might be because I had no reason to be exposed to the tests and that I would have shown more patience if a job had really been at stake.

Ordinarily the psychologists at The Personnel Laboratory never lay eyes on the person who has been tested. King Whitney, Jr, the president, explained: 'We don't want to contaminate the test with subjective impressions.'

He went on to say: 'Success in executive work is affected by many factors that can't be tested. We try to provide clients with useful insights which they can integrate with information they have received from other sources to give an over-all picture.' Some observers claim, however, that clients who hire psychological testers often are so overawed by psychological scores that a poor score becomes a knock-out factor for a prospect.

The Personnel Laboratory ordinarily charges the client about a hundred dollars for a report on an executive under consideration. (Its clients include Canada Dry, Revlon, Schenley.) A few of the psychological testers doing a mass-volume business charge considerably less. Other psychological-consulting firms spend a minimum of two days with an executive, place more reliance on interviewing than on testing, and charge up to $250 per executive. Two highly regarded psychological-consulting firms have almost completely abandoned testing of executives in favour of interviewing.

Judged on a volume basis, the largest testing firm in the country appears to be the Klein Institute for Aptitude Testing, Inc., which reports that it serves 1,100 companies in the U.S. and Canada.

The director of one large testing firm gave me a peek at the inner workings of his plant. He led me down an aisle which was lined on each side with cubby-holes. In each cubby-hole was a slim young man scoring or evaluating test results. As we approached one cubby-hole, the young man leaped to his feet and explained that he was studying a possible departmental sales manager for a large oil company. 'How does he look?' the director asked. The young man beamed happily as he reported: 'Fine prospect. Good sales sense. Lots of vim and vitality.' When the same query was put at another cubbyhole down the line, the young man there, who was considering the test score of a managerial candidate for a large tobacco company, reported: 'He can probably hold down the job, but he'll need strong guidance from above.'

Several psychologists complained to me that literally thousands of practitioners are now hanging out shingles around the country and seeking fees for appraisal work. Many are just out of college and are still considerably short of having Ph.D.s. Also, testing techniques being used in the testing of men for some of the nation's largest companies have come under especially severe scepticism or criticism. Many companies, for example, use a test that simply requires a candidate to pick out adjectives that seem to apply to him with particular force. He purportedly projects his personality by his choices. A large chemical company has been using a personality test that can be evaluated by company personnel without the help of a psychologist.

Many companies have been using simulated stress tests that are certainly dubious in their morality if not their validity. Alan Harrington relates that when he was being considered for a job at his 'crystal palace', an interviewer from the personnel department snapped: 'Why does your left eye deviate when you look at me?' Harrington guessed it was because he'd always had a weak muscle in his left eye. The interviewer beamed: 'Good, you weren't embarrassed!' and apparently made an approving notation.[2] In West Germany there has recently been a good deal of use of handwriting analysis as a guide to hiring. David Granick reports this is often used with candidates at the top level, where it would be embarrassing to ask them to submit to some other sort of test.

Nowadays many of the testers claim that they custom-assemble their testing to the specifications set by each company. They examine the hole before they try to measure pegs. In two reported instances – an oil company and an office-machine company – the testers have been asked to find candidates who have psychological profiles which closely resemble those of men who have already performed well for the company in comparable jobs.

Occasionally, but not usually, candidates for jobs are able to go over the results of testing and other appraisals with the psychologist involved. In the anteroom of one testing firm I saw a large, handsome, misty-eyed man angrily pulling on his hat. He had just been going over his test results. Usually the psychologists state their findings in post-appraisal talks with candidates in a different – and less candid – form than they do to the client. The reports to the companies vary in comprehensiveness. I have a report made by the assessing and recruiting firm of Clark, Channell (headquarters Stamford, Connecticut) after extensive testing and interviewing of a promising candidate for the vice-presidency of a large company. The specifications called for a 'tough but fair' type who could shake up the company and swing an axe when necessary. The report runs six pages, typewritten single-spaced.

First the report summarizes ten of the candidate's positive qualities. They include: 'The capacity to utilize his high level of intelligence without interference from internal or external emotional factors.' (In brief, he can be objective.)

' – A capacity to deal with others firmly without appearing to be unreasonable or rigidly authoritarian.

' – An approach that is generally friendly, personable, and cooperative.

' – A high order of physical energy.'

Then it cites three of his limitations. In some reports the limitations far outnumber the assets. Two of this man's limitations were:

' – He shows an underlying sensitivity that may occasionally keep him from utilizing his effectiveness as quickly as he would if the original reaction were not one based on this sensitive quality.

' – He becomes upset if he feels that the direction from above is not of a consistently high order.'

The report then goes into a detailed breakdown of the conclusions. There is a two-page analysis of his 'aptitudes, skills, and abilities'.

Then there is a page about his 'interests, preferences, and values'. Example:

Here is a man who shows the typical drives of an executive. He is interested in advancement economically and in terms of status. However, these are not forces which are so driving as to be outstanding or unreasonable. They appear to be well controlled and well channelled.

Finally comes a page devoted to his 'personality'. It begins 'No significant deviations from the normal were uncovered. . . .'

Although the use of psychological tests continues to grow every year, there is violent disagreement among psychologists, management consultants, and company executives as to the validity and morality of their use. The outspoken Dr McMurry, after testing executives for more than two decades, now uses tests sparingly and refers to many of the testers as 'burglars'.

Harvard's Dr Ward concluded, after his survey of testing: 'If it were not for the fact that so many large companies continue using tests, one would be tempted to speculate that experience in the use of psychological tests leads to their abandonment. As it is, the evidence does suggest there has been a substantial amount of negative experience on the part of some large companies who have tried testing.' I might add that Dr Ward, who helped pioneer psychological testing in the Air Force and has given tests to hundreds of executives, now indicates that he feels projective-type tests are of very little use in predicting success.

In June 1961, Reed Hunt, president of Crown Zellerbach Corporation, urged that all personality testing be eliminated.

He explained: 'I say this out of a certain amount of self-interest, since I understand there is not a corporation president in the country who could pass one of them or would be in his job today if he had ever taken one.'

Someone should advise Mr Hunt that this is scarcely an accurate or up-to-date viewpoint. In some companies today, as we have seen, even presidents (and chairmen) must submit to testing to get and hold their jobs.

CHAPTER 5

The Wife: Distraction, Detraction, or Asset?

Personnel men and others who hire or supervise executives should take pains to avoid giving the wife who is brought in for an interview the feeling that she is regarded as a 'corporate wife', American Business[1]

The one phase of the total screening process of executive candidates that causes corporate managers to do the most fidgeting and ceiling-gazing when the subject is raised is their scrutiny of the candidate's marital situation. There is a strong tendency to play down this aspect of screening. Crawford Greenewalt, the chairman of Du Pont, has scoffed at the 'curious conviction that the wives of business executives are screened critically as part of the criteria for promotion.' He said that 'at our company . . . such notions are sheer nonsense, and I will venture as a guess that the same can be said for most.'

In sharp contrast we have the report of author Osborn Elliott, made at approximately the same time (1959). He studied the lives and viewpoints of several dozen heads of companies and reported: 'Most of the country's top executives strongly believe that the wife can make or break a man's career, and many of them take pains to look over the wife these days when hiring an executive for a top-level job.'[2]

It is true that the amount of interest shown in a man's marital situation varies with the company, and especially according to the company's geographic location. It is also true, however, that – taken in total – the amount of interest shown in a candidate's marital status is considerable. The chances that a company will look into this aspect of a man's background quite thoroughly are at least fifty-fifty if he is being considered for a fairly high-level job. And the chances appear to be considerably higher for the wives of men in sales, advertising, and marketing for large companies. The marketing journal *Printers' Ink* issued a special report in August 1962 which concluded: 'Although most companies don't publicize the extremes to which they sometimes carry wife analysis, few will consider a man for an important position without first appraising the woman behind him. At one large company, roughly 20 per cent of its otherwise promotable men are passed by just because of their wives.'

The executive-sleuth or -recruiting firms usually run some sort of check on a man's wife as a matter of routine. Apparently they wouldn't feel safe if they didn't, since their own reputations are at stake in making a recommendation. Note these sample views:

An official of Ward Howell Associates: 'With almost any executive job paying over $18,000 the prospective boss wants to meet the wife before he hires the man.'

An official of Boyden Associates: 'In most cases we have to see the wife. . . . The personality of the wife is exceedingly important.'

Hergenrather Associates, the large Western recruiting firm, records for every executive candidate some data about his wife's 'background, college, health'. (Excellent, Good, or Average?) Ed Hergenrather, head of the firm, gave a talk to a seminar for Harvard alumni on 'The Art of Searching for the Right Job or a "Mustard Cutting" Man' and gave this counsel on how to search: 'Meet his wife and family if possible: check her out for drinking, talking, emotional stability.'

The management-consulting firm of George Fry & Associates is so impressed by the importance of the wife that a few years ago it staged a 'clinic' at a resort hotel in Mobile Bay, Alabama, attended by fifty-five businessmen and their wives, who argued into the night on the proper role of the executive wife – and her problems of living with an executive husband. Mr Fry believes that 'a corporation which spends considerable time and money developing and training a young man to be an executive feels obligated to know what kind of wife he has. Educating and interesting the executive's wife in her husband's job is an increasing trend.'

And the printed form of the patterned interview developed by The McMurry Company has several questions designed to probe the marital relationship. One particular interest asks simply: 'Age of wife – ?' The unspoken question in orange type asks: 'Did he marry a mother?'

Some companies refuse to act on a man's employment or promotion until a responsible official or investigator has seen the man's wife. She may be 'brought in', to use the *American Business* phrase, or cheerfully invited to come to the company for a chat. More usually, she is sized up discreetly at a dinner party or during a 'social visit' to her home. One leading recruiter has said that he soured on a prospect when he visited the man's home and found dishes piled high in the sink. A top-level executive living in New Jersey told me that before he was hired in both of his last jobs he and his wife, in formal attire, were taken out to dinner at quietly elegant New York restaurants by the president and the president's wife, and obviously his wife's poise, conversational competence, and correctness of dining behaviour were very much under observation. He felt, incidentally, that his wife performed superbly each time.

In Cleveland, an executive said of a hard-working but rather off-beat colleague: 'Jim's future is fine as long as he stays with Eileen [his wife].' She was apparently considered an attractive and steadying asset to him by the company's top management.

A number of executives working in New York City, however, are convinced that their companies have shown little interest in their marital situation – at least *after* they were hired. The families are too widely dispersed over the boroughs and suburbs. In general, the smaller the city in which the executive works the more intensively will the wife be scrutinized. Ward Howell suggests that the candidate's wife is likely to be an important factor in just about every U.S. city except New York, Los Angeles, Chicago, Philadelphia, and Miami. He pointed out that the wife of a Procter &

Gamble executive in Cincinnati or a Corning Glass executive in Corning 'has to be just about perfect'.

It is literally true – cliché or not – that in smaller cities one's wife simply does not wear a mink coat if the president's wife does not. She does not stand up at a bar to drink, even in a sumptuous cocktail lounge. And even in the larger cities the wife still has to go to the annual party where she should prove herself to be socially gracious and well-spoken, hold her liquor, and show that she is a knowledgeable member of the team, adept at relating to her husband's inferiors and superiors in the proper fashion.

The head of a major consulting firm, speaking of the wives of steel-company officials in an eastern Pennsylvania town, said, 'The wife must meet a specific pattern and belong to a specific ethnic background. It is terribly important that she be Methodist or Lutheran, not Presbyterian or Episcopalian.' (This is the reverse of the more usual pattern.) 'Until recently it was *verboten* to be Catholic. The wife must be a quiet club type, not the aggressive club type.'

This same man pointed out that wives of officials of a pharmaceutical company in New Jersey have made social acceptability in the right circles so important that they have a lot to say about who gets ahead at the company. 'I saw them castrate one vice-president,' he recalls. 'They undermined him and he never knew what hit him. . . . You and your wife either are a part of the inner club or you'll be out, and if you are out you might as well get out of town.'

Recruiter Ashton Dunn (Ashton Dunn Associates, headquarters New York) tells of the frustration he had with an exacting corporate client because of the wife. Dunn was asked to find a marketing executive for this company, which is located in New England. In listing the specifications that must be met, the president explained to Dunn: 'We are Yankees; we are either Harvard or Yale. We are either Congregationalists or Unitarians. We feel that anyone who will be happy with us must match this background.'

Dunn finally found a marketing man with this rare combination and the president was interested. He had, however, one further thought. He proposed that the candidate bring his wife to town for a visit. 'All our wives and ourselves like to get acquainted,' the president explained. So the candidate brought his wife, who came from a small hamlet in upstate New York, to town for what was apparently the final inspection by the top executives and their wives. The candidate lost the job. One major reason was that in the course of the amiable chit-chat the wife had shown ignorance in an inexcusable area. She asked someone what town Yale was located in. Later the president explained to Dunn: 'She could never fit into our way of life.'

Chief executives also use such phrases as 'the business family' and 'our executive family' to justify including the wife in the total picture. If the man to be hired must represent the company in a social way at many functions the wife's social skills are assessed with particular care.

In most cases, however, the uppermost concern of management seems to be with the wife's influence on the stability and usefulness of the man's relationship to the company. The issue of the wife usually becomes critically important only if she is seen as a threat to that stability or usefulness. In short, will she cause trouble by being either a distracting or a detracting influence?

For many executive jobs it is not necessary that the man's wife show up as an attractive asset to her husband, but if she is, so much the better, of course. Four ways that a wife can be sufficiently distracting or detracting to worry the company investigators considering her husband are:

1. Will she have a negative attitude towards the commitments he must make in order to progress with the company?

A high-level executive who was divorced by his wife while working for a large company in New York state confided that it is a terrible handicap to a man if the wife isn't emotionally and psychologically committed to the company. This is not true in Europe and Latin America, where the wife is not expected to have too many ideas about the business. And the director of a psychiatric clinic which has worked with hundreds of executives commented that executives are so tied up in business that unless they have wives who are most understanding and patient, difficulties arise. 'Most of the women want more attention than they get,' he said.

One commitment expected of executives that most sharply challenges the wife is the travelling and moving that have become normal parts of executive life. The wife who is going to feel a nagging resentment because her husband seems to be on a gay whirl of cross-country travelling and entertaining at company expense is, in the company's view, not a good risk. Likewise, the wife who causes trouble when the company proposes to shift her husband to the Sioux City office is not considered a good risk. Management consultant John A. Patton conducted a survey of the attitudes of 4,000 executive wives. He found that 93 per cent said they would never hesitate about moving to another area, at least not if their husbands were offered promotions with the move. Psychologist James F. Bender, a consultant to many corporations, observed that in this age of business mobility the pledge of the biblical Ruth – 'Whither thou goest, I will go' – might well be added to the wedding ceremony.

Some companies are reported to be wary of the wife who has an independent income. The thinking is that this may dampen his ambition, and lessen the willingness of both of them to make the commitment the company may expect.

2. Can the wife behave herself in a way that will not be conspicuous or jarring while in the presence of her husband's colleagues or customers or people in the community important to the company?

This does not mean that the typical wife of an executive must scintillate. In fact, she can be a mouse. But she should never be judged capable of attracting unfavourable notice, whether at a plant-opening ceremony or at the president's annual lawn party. Five kinds of wife that make recruiters especially nervous are those who can't hold liquor (if they drink), those who dress too flamboyantly, those who will be socially aggressive and try to take over the town, those who visibly show their impatience when exposed to a few hours of chit-chat, those who tend to be sexually restless or who think they can improve their husbands' chances by being kittenish with the boss. The worst dread of recruiters, however, is to recommend a man only to learn that his wife tends to get publicly plastered. Such wives, it might be added, are not at all unusual in executive circles.

Self-made men who head their own companies or men who head up family-dominated enterprises seem more tolerant of picturesque behaviour on the part of their wives than are executives on the larger pyramids. I attended a convention of such free-wheeling entrepreneurs in Oklahoma. One vivid memory is a poolside scene late at night when several heads of companies were happily trying to throw a fellow from Texas into the pool with his boots on. The Texan was good-naturedly, and drunkenly, resisting. Amid the hollering, his wife, like a mother moose, came rushing furiously to his rescue. She tore the other men away from her husband and shouted to them: 'You ought to have your goddam heads kicked in.'

Executives I've consulted agree that for a wife to speak so forthrightly at a gathering of pyramid climbers is virtually unthinkable. For that matter, though, it is also hard to conceive of pyramid climbers behaving the way these men did. Incidentally, at the convention in question the Texas couple continued to be among the most popular people there.

3. Will she be a source of distracting harassment to the executive because of the kind of home life she maintains for him?

The people who hire or place executives seem to like to think of the home in idyllic terms, as a peaceful haven where the executive can lick his wounds and recharge his psychic battery. They worry when, in their investigations, they don't find such a haven and wonder if the wife is to blame. An associate of Boyden Associates explained this: 'We've got to be assured when we interview an executive that the home will be free of pressure, that the wife will be sympathetic and understanding and not be grumpy.'

The company worries if it uncovers evidence that the wife is a free spender or a haphazard book-keeper. It does not want its man to be distracted by financial troubles. And it worries if there are signs that the marital relationship is edgy. It assumes that the men who build up a load of frustrations at home are likely to take them out on subordinates at the office.

And the company's top officials may worry about the man whose wife has her own career. Will she, in pursuing her own ambitions, neglect her role as the ever-adoring little lady at the fireside? And will her career prevent her from being a nice asset for the company in community affairs?

4. Is it likely that she would fail to keep up with her husband if he begins moving ahead in the company?

The president of a large New England company mentioned this possibility as a problem he has frequently noticed. The wife who is not as ambitious or as social as her husband, he said, may become unhappy and a drag on her husband. 'If a man advances rapidly in his company he moves into new social circles, and the wife is considered a hazard if she cannot "keep up".'

The corporation, by the way, is four-square in favour of marriage – a solid marriage – for its male executives. If there is evidence that the man has been having marital difficulties this fact raises a question about his stability. The company wants evidence that a candidate is a 'family man'. A man with a wife and three children has got something to drive him on, and in smaller communities having a family is seen as a part of conforming to the local pattern.

A divorced man is likely to find his lack of a wife a serious professional handicap. One divorced male I know, who was being considered for the vice-presidency of another company (a big one), recounts that he was careful to put his divorce on the record at the outset. He recalls: 'Five different people interrogated me on this point and it was my biggest handicap in getting the job.' He finally did get it. One plus in his favour, he feels, is that he had three handsome grown children – to whom he was careful to allude several times.

This man has concluded that the presence of a wife is not a bonus, but the absence of one invokes a negative to be overcome. 'They say "Please give our best regards to dear Mildred",' he commented, 'but they really don't give a damn. They just want to know that you are married.'

The worst status of all is that of a bachelor beyond the age of thirty-six. It is possible to be a bachelor and become president. However, in the American Management Association's survey of 335 presidents, only about 1·5 per cent were bachelors. In general the bachelor is viewed with circumspection, especially if he is not well known to the people appraising him. The investigators wonder why he isn't married. Is it because he isn't virile? Is he old-maidish? Can't he get along with people?

All this, however, should not be taken to mean that the corporation necessarily favours the sublimely happy marriage for its men. Actually, many companies appear wary of hiring a man who seems to attach too great importance to his marriage. They wonder if he is too contented to make a good competitor. And they wonder if in the clinch he would put marriage above job.

The retired head of one very large company told me that the man who goes to the top has got to be slightly dissatisfied with his marriage. The successful climber should not take the defects in his marriage so seriously that it will get in the way of his success, but he should be able to put his marriage 'in neutral' when his job becomes unusually demanding.

Some months ago S. Vincent Wilking, vice-president of the management-consulting firm of Barrington & Company, prepared a checklist for young men hoping to become top-level executives. The first question was: 'If you are under twenty-five, are you married or do you have definite plans for marriage within a year? (*a*) Yes. (*b*) No. (*c*) May get married. (*d*) I'm not sure.'

The best of the first three answers would be *No*. Mr Wilking explained why in these terms: 'Early marriage suggests that family life is quite important to you; and the really successful executive has distressingly little time for his family. If you want a full home life, you'd better be content with a lesser job.'

A senior vice-president of George Fry & Associates drew up a paper entitled 'Mr Executive – A Profile for the Sixties' after his staff had conducted a study of case histories of executives. Here is how he sums up the marital profile of 'Mr Executive':

'He enjoys a family life which is conducive to the maximum utilization of his abilities. His wife and children accept, understand, and have made good adjustment to the demands of his management responsibilities.'

Many wives resent all the scrutiny they get when their husbands are seeking jobs in management, and well they might. *American Business* summed up this resentment on the wife's side by quoting a hypothetical typical wife as saying: 'With my gold band I received another circlet – a ring through my nose with Jim's company holding the guide rope. Naturally I want to help my husband succeed, but I resent being poured into the company mould.'

In the Patton survey of 4,000 executives' wives slightly more than half agreed, when asked whether they felt a company official should interview a man's wife, that a casual meeting was acceptable, but not a formal interview. Some old-fashioned believers in privacy strongly disapproved any official appraisal whatever.

Mrs Elizabeth Harvey, wife of a General Motors executive, was quoted as asserting that such appraisal is 'abhorrent to any sensible woman.' Most, however, felt the wife had little choice but to do whatever seemed to be required – and usually they appear to do it without too much resentment.

The divorced vice-president, mentioned earlier, said of company wives: 'By and large they don't hold back. Often they are more interested than he is in getting ahead, and they do what is necessary.'

CHAPTER 6

The Searchers and Snatchers

We know more damned people who are unhappy. . . . Ward Howell, a leading executive recruiter

If captains of industry indulge in casual profanity when mildly irritated, they are downright blasphemous when they discover that their ranks have just been raided by a new kind of servicing organization, the executive-recruiting firm.

Many corporate managements now like the idea of being able to turn over to these outside recruiters the bothersome details of finding a man they need. The recruiters will purportedly sift the universe of executives and semi-executives and come up with the names of three or four prime prospects who not only could fill the job but are certified, *sub rosa*, as willing to come. Corporate captains are apt to swell with rage, however, when they discover that one of their *own* best men has just jumped ship – and perhaps gone to a rival – through the good offices of a recruiter.

This frequent source of outrage accounts for some of the more uncomplimentary names applied to the raiders – among them body-snatchers, head-hunters, pirates, and flesh-pedlars. An executive who is ambitious to get ahead and not sure what his prospects are at his present company is today likely to have a confidential chat with one of the better of these recruiters to make his potential mobility known. And he will call back to report his progress occasionally, to assure himself that he is constantly – and favourably – in the back of the recruiter's mind and not just another entry fed into the recruiter's computer system.

The demand for the services of these executive-search firms has quadrupled in five years; a few receive fees that total millions of dollars annually.

Ward Howell, lean, amiable, gigantic, with a bloodhound's face and temperament, recalls that when he started his company from a phone booth in 1951 there were five firms in the country doing this kind of work. Now there are fifty-five in New York alone. Mr Howell's is one of at least four now with a staff of more than twenty.

Approximately a third of the nation's larger companies call upon such firms as Howell's to fill some of their openings, according to surveys made by Executive Manpower Corporation, another of the leading search firms. Search firms have also begun appearing in England, Management Selection and Executive Appointments Ltd being two of the first.

Corporate leaders like to imagine that their managers are devoutly loyal to the mother company. That is the situation in Japan, where a man's company becomes his life, but it is far from being the situation in the U.S. Most executives consider themselves movable if the right proposition comes along. Or as recruiter William H. Clark put it, 'Executives will all listen to us when we call up. We ask them if they have a minute and they always have.'

Hergenrather Associates in Los Angeles reports that after *Time* magazine printed a one-sentence mention of its firm it received 250 résumés from executives and would-be executives who specifically mentioned the item. Hergenrather regularly receives about 1,000 résumés a month from executives.

Most of the nation's leading search firms are clustered within rock-throwing distance of Grand Central Station in New York City. Other areas of concentration are Stamford, Connecticut, Chicago, and Los Angeles. Most of the founders of the major recruiting firms formerly served with one of the giant management-consulting firms such as Booz, Allen & Hamilton, or McKinsey & Company before developing their present specialties. Booz, Allen & Hamilton, incidentally, still recruits on a large scale along with all its other activities.

Boyden Associates – founded immediately after the Second World War by Sid Boyden, a lean, vigorous man – now has an entire floor of a Madison Avenue skyscraper and branches in Dallas, Chicago, Cincinnati, Geneva, and San Francisco; other branches are projected. One Boyden official said: 'Right now we are looking for ten presidents to go into jobs that will pay up to $100,000 base, plus a package.' The firm is also looking for general managers and other officer-level men.

At its New York headquarters Boyden maintains the sumptuous atmosphere of an executive suite for the benefit of the dozens of executives who come – sometimes looking around with care to make sure they don't encounter an acquaintance – to visit each day. The visiting executives immediately see that the walls are appropriately dull green, that the chairs are of gleaming red leather, and that the carpeting (of course) is thick and wall-to-wall to provide the properly hushed atmosphere. On the wall to greet them is a reassuring mural based on appropriate recreations for top-level executives (sailing and golfing). Sid Boyden's personal corner office is spacious and commands a view of the New York skyline, as a top-level man's should.

John L. Handy, another leading recruiter, has given his inner sanctum extra touches of gentility to flatter the visiting executive. His elegant 'office' overlooking Park Avenue is deskless and, with its rare china and Queen Anne chairs, has the look of an eighteenth-century parlour. Mr Handy himself, a stately, silver-haired man with a preference for pinstripes, also looks the part of a man at ease with the very highest executives. A graduate of Milton Academy and of Harvard, he is a former master of the Golden Bridge Hounds and was once a dealer in Far Eastern produce. He speaks of himself as now being in the business of 'the redistribution of executive talent'. Ward Howell and William Hertan (who heads Executive Manpower Corporation), on the other hand, maintain offices that are functional and matter-of-fact. Howell estimates that about fifty executives and would-be executives come to his office every day to visit or to leave résumés.

Recruiters have placed men in jobs that pay up to $200,000 a year. Such a *coup* can bring at least $40,000 in fees to the recruiter. Some of the more celebrated moves they have engineered: Howell helped put Dause L. Bibby into the president's chair at Remington Rand; Handy presented Boone Gross to Gillette Company as a possible sales manager and he later became president; Boyden Associates negotiated Thomas Sunderland into the presidency of United Fruit. A major research firm discovered Sherwood Egbert at a Los Angeles company making power tools and brought him into the presidency of Studebaker-Packard during one of its upheavals. This search firm, one of the more dignified, no longer cites this *coup* as the foremost sample of its prowess. Possibly one reason is that a year after he went to Studebaker-Packard Mr Egbert, a hell-for-leather, go-go-go ex-Marine, made the newspapers when he was briefly detained by the law. Pickets interfered with the passage of his car into a strikebound plant operated by his company and he reportedly took off his top-coat and offered to fight the pickets (which just isn't done, at least in Indiana).

Most of the recruiting firms – especially those affiliated with the Association of Executive Recruiting Consultants – receive from the client company a fee equal to approximately 20 per cent of the new executive's guaranteed compensation for the first year. Many are paid a third of their fee each month. They frown on those who offer to search on a contingency basis.

At first glance it must seem wonderful to executives to have the corporation pick up the multi-thousand-dollar tab charged by the recruiter for placing him with the company. Self-reliant executives who like to shape their own destinies (and all who worry about the new impingements on individualism) may, however, feel uneasy about a system which puts the individual executive in a passive role where he is only one possible package being scrutinized by buyer and dealer. Defenders of the present system argue that a mere individual could ill afford – as the corporation well can – to pay one fifth or one fourth of his first year's salary to cover recruiting charges. Certainly he couldn't be expected to pay within one year (at least not without help from the banks, which seem eager to lend to executives). A more reasonable arrangement in terms of giving the executive a greater sense of responsibility for his own fate might be to have the corporation and the individual share all recruiting costs from the time he becomes involved and expresses interest.

The majority of the firms will handle openings in middle management – some will handle an occasional trainee – but, since fees are geared to salary, they all naturally try to handle as many big-paying jobs as possible. Thus it pleases them twice as much to place a man at a $30,000 salary as it does to nail down a $15,000 job.

The great recent growth in the use of such middlemen to handle searches is explained on a number of grounds. In selling themselves to corporate clients, these recruiters can cite the fact that they have a large file of movable executives and would-be executives. Another appeal is that they can be more independent of company pressures and politics. Also they have the time. Searching for – *and* investigating – an executive can be an enormously time-consuming process. But the main consideration is the need for secrecy. Frequently the company seeking an executive has not yet notified the man currently holding the job that his days are numbered. On the candidate's side there is always a need for extreme secrecy if he is currently a corporate executive. He does not dare give his mother company an inkling that he is considering the possibility of running away from home.

One executive who confided to me that he is on the prowl for another job swore me to secrecy and said: 'You have no idea how careful I have to be.' Further, it is simple prudence for the prospect to be secretive about his aspirations because, as in marital wooing, you can scare away a suitor by seeming too eager.

Thus the myth is maintained that the prospect couldn't be happier than where he is – especially if he is near the top of his company. Recruiters fully understand the myths and secrets that must be maintained in making an approach to a high-level man. Often the recruiters profess simply to be seeking the man's advice about possible prospects and only later say brightly: 'By the way, is it conceivable that you could visualize a situation where you might be interested in this opening?' Usually, too, the recruiters try to meet a prospect far away from his office.

To get leads on possible candidates for an opening the recruiters search first of all their own files. The smaller agencies use crude mechanical devices that will drop from their files the names of men who meet elementary specifications. Handy's office, on the other hand, has an I.B.M. system, installed at a cost of $300,000, which can whirl through 100,000 cards to produce an 'ace' for the job in question. Mr Handy divides his 'aces' into 'good', 'very good', and 'best'.

To get leads the recruiters also pore through industrial directories and trade journals and make thousands of telephone calls. They often write letters to every person who might conceivably be able to lead them to a possible candidate.

I first had direct contact with such recruiters in 1959, when I received a letter from one of Mr Handy's scouts. The recruiter was looking for a marketing director for a 'company that manufactures packaged household and cosmetic products and its sales are well in excess of one hundred million dollars annually. . . . The salary and bonus should run to no less than $75,000 plus stock options and other benefits.' He added that any prospects I suggested 'can be assured that our dealings are handled with professional tact and complete confidence.' I was immensely flattered to receive the query but wasn't of much help. I couldn't think of a soul in the field of marketing packaged goods who was, to my mind, worth $75,000 a year plus optional benefits. Perhaps I was overawed by the figure, but after all, it was – as I kept thinking – twice as much as the Chief Justice of the United States was being paid.

Occasionally the best prospects really are coy and must be pursued by the recruiter. Bert Antell of Antell, Wright & Nagel (headquarters New York City) told me that, working in conjunction with a management-consulting firm, he called a man named Bill Lane from thirty-seven cities before he finally interested Mr Lane sufficiently to agree to breakfast with him at the Drake Hotel in Chicago. Mr Lane then permitted himself to be proposed for the presidency of River Brand Rice (Houston) and was accepted. Antell described Lane's appeal in these terms: 'He has personality, drive, enthusiasm and a will to win.' Lane had been executive vice-president of a potato-chip company. I happened to meet Mr Lane subsequently in Oklahoma. He proved to be a surprisingly youthful, mild-mannered man, and he confirmed the long-distance pursuit by Antell. Lane was pleased that he had finally made the move. 'The company I was with,' he explained, 'has since gone through two mergers.'

A few of the search firms use psychological testing and depth-interviewing techniques in appraising prospects, but more commonly they simply accumulate the kinds of facts and impressions that any perceptive layman can handle. The approaches vary in formality. Hertan says: 'We try to get down to the meat of the man. How does he think? What are his mental capabilities and limitations? Where has he failed? Has he had any *general* executive experience? Many men make fine executive vee-pees for manufacturing but are too specialized in their thinking ever to make executive vice-president or general manager of the over-all company.'

Handy, on the other hand, has a thirty-one-item checklist which is filled out in the course of dissecting and appraising each serious candidate. These are the thirty-one items covered: 'Age . . . marital status . . . education . . . chronological record of positions held . . . drive . . . responsibility . . . ability to think . . . ability to communicate . . . ability to get along with people . . . a normal desire to see things go better . . . personality (first and second impressions) . . . mental equipment . . . financial status . . . real estate . . . bonds . . . stocks . . . cash . . . indebtedness . . . mortgages . . . other . . . probable retirement income . . . mental and nervous state . . . ambitions for the next five years . . . ambitions for the next ten years . . . ambitions for the next fifteen years . . . recreation . . . outside studies . . . community activities . . . list of those with whom

you have worked for references ... what are you trying to do?
... what do you want out of life?'

Before a search firm completes its run-down on a candidate
it often does some quiet investigating in the man's neighbour-
hood, or hires a private investigator to bring in a report.
Ex-F.B.I. agents are often favoured for this work and at least
two recruiters have ex-F.B.I. men on their staffs. Such sleuth-
ing is aimed at discovering whether the man has a 'harem
problem' (the recruiters' phrase) or has overextended himself financially. Mr Hertan has concluded that one executive
in six is weak in his credit rating because of his anxiety to
improve his social status. Two 'red flags' that stir recruiter
William Clark to further investigation are evidence of the
possibility that the man 'can't handle liquor' and evidence
that he is vague about dates. Clark wonders whether the
candidate is covering up something. 'It would scare us to
death not to check a man out,' he says.

The practice of bringing executives in from outside to fill
good jobs has pro and con aspects for both the company and
the company's aspiring executives. For the company, the
major appeal of promoting entirely from within is that such a
policy encourages loyalty (and thus enhances the company's
power over its personnel). On the other hand, the company
that promotes entirely from within may find itself with
executives complacently waiting for seniority to lift them
to higher levels. They are running neither hungry nor
scared.

From the viewpoint of the executive, the unpalatable side
of the practice of recruiting from outside is that it can in-
furiate a man to see an outsider getting a job he had expected
to inherit. The attractive side – and this may be the overriding
factor – is that the growth of professional recruiters makes it
easier for the restless executive to see the possibility of getting
out of a frustrating situation into a more congenial one in
another company. This lessens his dependence on the whims
of his own company.

Recruiters find it easiest to raid companies (1) that are in
trouble, (2) that have developed more qualified executives than

they can absorb, and (3) that have not bothered to lock in their executives with pensions and other over-the-horizon rewards. In terms of geography, the search firms find it easiest to recruit men for jobs in the Denver area (at the base of the Rockies), on the West Coast, and in the Northeast. Jobs with Deep South companies are the most difficult to fill, geographically (partly because of the publicity about racial strife). Florida companies are the attractive exception to the Deep South pattern.

Some companies are generous in offering blessings and Godspeed to the executive coveted by another company. This is particularly true when the company has got itself overstaffed with competent executives and desires to thin out all but the top-rated ones. It is also true when the executive is coveted by an important customer. General Electric is one company that has recently shown a good deal of generosity in helping G.E. executives make connexions elsewhere, and quite possibly the reasons given enhance the company's desire to be kindly.

In many companies, however, the managements are deeply resentful when they learn that a recruiter has been trying to lure one of their good men. Howell is one of several recruiters who declared that they had been personally upbraided by company presidents enraged by their roles in luring away good men.

A number of managements profess to be sticklers for etiquette when it comes to 'raiding'. They contend that any outside company or recruiter interested in approaching a job-holding executive must first clear with the man's management before contacting him. Among gentleman slave traders, this is felt to be simple courtesy. Clarence B. Randall, former chairman of Inland Steel, is one industrialist who emphatically disagrees. He feels that such 'clearing' violates the freedom of action of the man involved. He argues that it isn't in keeping with our concept of the worth of the individual 'to bargain about him like a piece of merchandise without his knowledge.'

A great many companies go even further in impinging

upon the individual's freedom to bargain. They arrange anti-raiding pacts. Such pacts – whatever their legality – are such common facts of life that recruiters must take them into account when commissioned to find a man for a company in the oil, chemical, soap, steel, tobacco, tyre, or aircraft industries. In these industries, the pacts are particularly likely to be a factor when it comes to hiring away a man working for a direct competitor or a customer, but often do not apply in raids upon a small company in the industry.

The feeling is that hiring from competitors can result only in a retaliatory pirating, or in demands for higher pay from the executives who might be solicited, or in a possible loss of company know-how. Mr Howell observed: 'When we talk to a company at the start, we ask whether we may look in the logical places for the man needed.'

Many of the recruiters also refrain from raiding certain companies – specifically clients. The code of ethics of the Association of Executive Recruiting Consultants stipulates in Article VI: 'We will not initiate discussion with any member of a client organization regarding employment . . . with another client.' This courtesy has produced some interesting results. A number of corporations have concluded that it is prudent to take out insurance against being raided. They do this by occasionally commissioning one of the larger, more bothersome recruiting firms to find a man for them. This makes them clients of the recruiting firm and thus out of bounds for future raiding.

And so we get the final twist. A number of the recruiting firms now refuse to accept certain of the big, executive-rich companies as clients so that they may be free to continue to raid those companies!

CHAPTER 7

The Earmarking Process

He feels strongly that he can and must 'get ahead' quickly in the organization. . . . He romanticizes the role of the executive and is convinced that his future achievement is assured because he is ambitious. From an unfavourable report on a young manager made to his management by a consulting psychologist[1]

To corporate managements it seems wholly reasonable and natural to take a proprietary attitude towards a new manager since it is quite likely that they spent many thousands of dollars getting him and breaking him in. Acquiring promising college graduates is, of course, cheaper than finding and checking out a full-blown executive, but even college-recruitment programmes are expensive. The investment must be protected by charting the young man's 'development' through intensive training and indoctrination.

Young men headed for executive careers may conclude, quite reasonably, while still in college that working for smaller but growing companies offers more appeal in terms of both environment and opportunity. But when the industrial recruiters begin visiting the campus to interview prospects the young men often find themselves caught up in the competition for bids from the largest, highest-prestige companies.

It is chiefly the large companies – and the electronic companies living off government contracts – that can afford extensive college-recruiting programmes that reach hundreds of campuses. It is also the big companies that can afford to print on high-gloss paper the glowing, illustrated invitations to embark on careers with unlimited opportunities at Consolidated Enterprises. These factors aid the giants in getting first pick of the college crop.

At the large company the recruit fresh from college is usually treated as if he has simply changed classrooms. He will probably be rotated from one job to another with little expectation, at first, that he will make any serious contribution. He is learning. He is getting the over-all view and making himself readily interchangeable. He may be taking company-sponsored courses with other trainees. Later, as at college, he will elect a 'major' and settle down in one spot for more intensive training and perhaps start doing a little real work.

Young men supercharged with ambition to get going may find all the schooling and rotating a bore. Possibly as a response to such feelings a number of companies, including several in the Bell system, have adopted an approach resembling that used at hospitals to train interns. The trainee is put to work soon after employment at a reasonably challenging task under the watchful eye of a 'sponsor'. Management trainees at five of the Bell companies are given a one-week orientation course at the outset of their employment and then are assigned to a district manager for a year. At the end of that year the superiors (managers) sit down and choose from the class of trainees the best third of the group.

The process continues, with special attention in many companies focused on those already considered most promising. Seminars and conferences are particularly favoured as trainee-development media. One authoritative estimate is that two thirds of all managers in U.S. industry are having their 'development' guided, planned, or stimulated by some type of formal management-development programme. General Electric has spent several million dollars on facilities alone for its Management Research and Development Institute on a fifty-five-acre tract overlooking the Hudson at Crotonville, New York. This fascination with 'management development' is not a U.S. monopoly. David Granick reports that, though it is rarely mentioned in France or Belgium, it is 'on everyone's lips in Great Britain'.

Before many months have passed the very junior executive may be rudely jolted despite all the talk of 'management

development'. He may conclude that he has been given a
rough shuffle and that his future progress is not so neatly
mapped as he had assumed it would be from listening to the
college recruiter and the orientation coaches. To his dismay
he may find himself assigned to a remote spot under a boss
who mumbles instructions and is much too busy and harried
to pay much attention to him. Or he may find himself under
a boss who loathes hotshots from the business schools who
are still, to his mind, wet behind the ears.

This, of course, is life, but the typical passive trainee who
has been guided from point to point through college and the
company's training programme is often ill prepared for it.
Investigators at Carnegie Tech's School of Industrial Administration who carefully studied the early progress of three
young men found that this lack of loving care was the new
men's major surprise. The instructions they got from their
bosses were likely to be hurried, incomplete, and sometimes
garbled.

Perhaps a year later these bosses would be expected to sit
down and make their reports on how their juniors had performed, which brings us safely back again to the more formal
aspects of 'development'. The young man is not completely
lost after all – if he gets a good report card. The report card,
as at school, will probably add up to a numerical score. Corporate personnel officials have become dependent on such
scores because the scores give them something more than
judgement to which to cling.

As company managements in recent years have found
themselves dealing more and more with managers and
managers-to-be who are virtual strangers – a result of expansion, deploying, and merging – they have turned increasingly to appraisal forms for rating these managers and
would-be managers. The use of such devices has increased
spectacularly within the past decade, particularly among the
larger companies. A majority of the giant companies now
score their managers periodically on some sort of report card.
Assessment of the executive is known variously as an 'audit',
'review', 'appraisal', or 'evaluation'. Some companies call

the total result of all the grading of managers their 'Man-power Inventory'. Quite commonly the rating sheets on a man are filled out by his superiors, though in some instances outside professionals are brought into the operation.

I have been able to see a number of the rating sheets used by company personnel to grade a man and sample sheets on men who were rated high and low. In one eye-opening instance I inspected the complete packet of samples and forms used at one of the nation's leading communications corporations for periodic assessment of its managers in one area.

In the appraisal form I studied, the manager was to be rated not only on his performance but (more important – judging from the attention given them) also on personal factors such as 'Manners', 'Appearance', 'Habits', 'Health', 'Character', 'Open-mindedness – acceptance of ideas and reaction to criticism'. The rater was further instructed to check either *yes* or *no* after 'Potential for Positions of Greater Responsibility'. How this was checked could seal a man's fate in the company file, and he might never know what – or who – hit him.

I came next to the sample form which illustrated how a rating should be executed. This involved a plant manager who had been recommended as a candidate for the company's advanced-management programme. He obviously was a comer; we'll call him Mr Blank.

What kind of man was this ideal Mr Blank? Under 'Outside professional, community, service and business activities' was noted with evident admiration the fact that he was a director of a local bank, current chairman of the United Fund Drive, past president of the local Kiwanis, and treasurer of a local country club. His off-duty life was clearly solid and strenuous.

Under 'Personal performance' it emerged that Mr Blank was 'exceptionally loyal' to the company but that he 'needs to avoid being curt and cold with subordinates.' He was 'open-minded in soliciting ideas and suggestions' from home-office officials. 'However, he does not solicit or accept ideas from his own staff.' Clearly Mr Blank was upward-oriented in his open-mindedness. Under 'Development needs and suggestions' the rater proposed that Mr Blank needed not only to become more 'open-minded' but to get a better grip on his emotions 'in connexion with matters pertaining to organization changes and job irregularities.' Corporate managements tend to admire the man who is unruffled by aggravations created by others in the company.

I picked up another form. This one showed how the superiors-sitting-in-judgement then draw up a 'Development Programme' for our man. It suggested how the news is to be broken to the man that he is doing fine in some respects but needs beefing up in others. The man may be commended for the fact that in the year since the last appraisal 'he has made good progress in developing a less reserved and more friendly manner.' As for improvement still needed, he is to be told that he needs to learn 'to respond more positively, calmly and realistically to organization changes and job irregularities.' Back, then, to the corporation's impatience with the man who shows impatience.

Our man under development is to be admonished to catch himself 'when he is about to respond negatively and emotionally in these situations. . . .'

Finally there was a sample of a most interesting form used to draw up the ideal 'Man Specification' for each managerial post in the division. The sample I saw was for a manager in charge of mechanical buying. Under 'Personal habits', the ideal specification called for an employee who has 'conventional personal habits and a pleasing personality'. Under ideal 'attitude', I discovered that he should be 'enthusiastic about the company and his work. Very cooperative. . . . Willingly accept criticism and job irregularities.'

In short, our ideal man is flexible, amenable, amiable, conventional, predictable.

Two personnel officials of General Electric detailed in the journal *Personnel* in 1959 how they went about conducting a manpower audit at a Cincinnati plant. They showed how they listed each man's assets and liabilities. Under assets, for example, they listed 'loyal to company' and under liabilities they mentioned 'does not always appear to be aggressive'. The most portentous of the points to be checked, surely, was the one that invited the rater to be an oracle and predict for the man: 'Probable highest level to be reached' in General Electric.

In some instances the generalized virtues used on corporate appraisal forms to assess managers seem to be copied from the report cards used to rate children at schools. *The New York Times Magazine* carried a report on methods of appraisal in the late fifties which presented readers an interesting challenge.[2] The analysts offered portions of two report cards to the reader. One was for four-year-olds at a nursery school and the other was used by 'one of the largest corporations in the country for grading its executives.' The reader was challenged to guess which was which. Here they are:

REPORT CARD A

	Very Satisfactory	Satisfactory	Unsatisfactory
Dependability			
Stability			
Imagination			
Originality			
Self-expression			
Health and vitality			
Ability to plan and control			
Cooperation			

REPORT CARD B

	Satisfactory	Improving	Needs Improvement
Can be depended upon			
Contributes to the good work of others			
Accepts and uses criticism			
Thinks critically			
Shows initiative			
Plans work well			
Physical resistance			
Self-expression			
Creative ability			

The report card for executives, incidentally, was Card A. Report Card B was for the four-year-olds.

One executive very near the top of a large company ventured the opinion that the worst weakness of most appraisal systems is that they delude the managers who see the forms. The managers assume that if they can meet all the standards set they will rise to the heights. He added: 'That just isn't true.' Meeting such standards can help a man up to a certain point perhaps, but getting to the top usually involves – at least in addition – elusive or unstated factors that you won't find on any appraisal form: proof of kindredship, skill in politicking, social acceptability, important skills that happen to be in short supply, luck, tenacity, and so on. He added: 'The fact that I'm a Boy Scout doesn't determine that I will get ahead.' He indicated that he felt the usual appraisal systems constitute a built-in disappointment to the individual who is 'following the carrot and finding it doesn't lead anywhere'.

During a round-table discussion of executive potential at the Columbia Graduate School of Business, one executive highly sceptical of the usual formal appraisal systems said he had found an informal method that was much more illuminating concerning a man's worth. He said: 'The test we use is how loud an outfit screams when you want to take the man away.'

When corporations invite psychological-consulting firms in to conduct the appraisal of company managers the assessments are more extensive. They may require the man under assessment to be off the job from one to three days. Richardson, Bellows, Henry & Co. (headquarters New York City) calls such a grand appraisal of a man 'a midcareer review.' Another major psychological consulting firm that does a good deal of appraising – Rohrer, Hibler & Replogle (headquarters Chicago) – uses primarily a clinical interviewing situation that includes some testing.

Some top managements announce an impending psychological appraisal simply by notifying each manager who is to be probed that the appraisal is coming up and advising him of the date reserved for him. Others make a considerable show of soliciting volunteers. One letter requesting volunteers sent out by a top management must have produced uneasy guffaws. It read:

You are invited to join the group which will participate in the survey. We will meet in the — room at 9 A.M. July 15th. . . . We estimate that the complete programme will require approximately three days.[3]

The use of the words *We will meet* . . . not only suggested that every good team player would naturally be there but that the top-management people would also be there, watching to see if their own enthusiasm for the project was shared by the staff.

Earlier in the 'invitation' the management explained that it wished to 'take stock of our resources. . . .' Managers, it seemed, were to be inventoried along with typewriters, lathes, and monkey wrenches.

I had an interesting time with a consulting psychologist in connexion with this 'voluntary' aspect of the large-scale appraising of managers within a company. He was dramatizing for me some of his experiences and offered this description of a typical meeting of managers at which he is being introduced and his assignment in assessment explained:

'My eyes are roaming as I am introduced: I take in every doodle. The men are told of course that they can volunteer and that there is no stigma if they don't. I simply tell them I'll be back next Wednesday. Usually the one holdout is the one guy you want to get. But I know that he will volunteer out of group persuasion. Often the volunteer is not a real volunteer. He is group-pressured. As one controller – a green-eyeshade type – said: "Okay, I'll volunteer, damn it. See if you can find out my abilities!"'

That was a startling statement. When I had a draft of this chapter written I sent the psychologist a copy of his remarks, placed within the context of this discussion of the 'voluntary' aspect of 'invitations' to submit to psychological evaluations. I asked him to check it for accuracy, modify where he felt strongly that modification was needed, or say if he wished not to be identified. In his brief note in response he thanked me for sending him the statement for review and offered me

'Best wishes for your new book'. He had carefully inked out every line of his quoted remarks and neatly hand-printed this replacement over the crossed out lines, with his identification unchanged:

'I try to keep alert to what is happening in the group and insist that the psychological programme be kept on a voluntary basis. It is important that they know there will be no stigma if they don't volunteer. Usually there is one holdout and I am interested in his reasons, for they may be indicative of his problems. Although the programme is kept on a voluntary basis, holdouts usually come around in the long run, if for no other reason than group pressure and a desire to be a part of things.'

No longer are there people doodling and the green-eye-shade type has disappeared; no longer is there a statement that the 'volunteer' is often not a real volunteer. You can take your choice.

Dr McMurry of The McMurry Company uses an indirect approach in his evaluation of executives that at least has the virtue of being less painful. The manager is never asked to talk about himself. He is invited instead to talk about the men who are his line subordinates. Dr McMurry explained:

'We work from the top down in executive assessment (and from the bottom up when we conduct employee opinion polls as a supplement). When both techniques are employed, this affords a triple look at each man below the top and above the bottom: how he is seen by his superior, how he's seen by his subordinates, and what he reveals about himself in assessing his subordinates' qualifications.'

Approximately one third of all the companies that conduct periodic appraisals of their managers use psychological tests, often passed off as mere 'questionnaires' or 'pencil-and-paper forms'. The use of such tests not merely for hiring but also for later career 'reviews' has many enthusiasts (as well as critics) in industry. In early 1961 an official of Telecomputing Corporation was quoted as warning that the executive on the job who shies away from such testing may be slamming the door of promotion in his own face. 'The fellow who dodges the tests often is just "forgotten" after that by the front office.'

One of the tests widely used as a quick rundown on a man's mental ability is the Wonderlic, a twelve-minute, fifty-question test. It was originally constructed to measure the progress of students in school; now fifty-year-old men with yachts, mortgages, and children in college are being told to risk their futures on it. A sample question: ' MINER MINOR – Do these words have (1) similar meaning, (2) contradictory meaning, (3) mean neither the same nor opposite?' You have fifteen seconds to respond and get on to the next question.

The psychological director of one testing-recruiting firm explained:

'These assessments often happen after a merger. We're asked to assess all key personnel. This is one of the major times that they use us, and of course we have been seeing a wave of mergers.'

He added that test results give the top management

'a quick rundown on the talent available. The test is a tool, a technique for getting information about a person that can't be gotten by more direct means. It should be used as an aid for judgement rather than a substitute.'

Executives who are invited to volunteer for psychological probing will at times be assured that the test results will not be used for 'negative purposes', which is usually eyewash. I possess an individual evaluation presented to managements by a leading psychological-consulting firm. The opening page begins with these lines:

Name: *Mr B—P—*
Present Position: *Administrative Manager of Laboratory*
Qualifications for Position: *Average*
Potential for Further Growth: *Poor*

How negative can you get?

An official of a large New York consulting firm that does a great deal of auditing of executives told me: 'We try to give the president a detailed picture of all the top personnel. First a written report, and then we confer. We note both the high-potential people and the low-potential people. We're not God. ... When you are dealing with someone else's potential you shouldn't be final, but you can say this man has a very limited potential or has reached the limit of his development or should be transferred.'

True, as they repeatedly protest, they are not gods – but the clients usually want god-like answers.

A number of the consulting firms summarize the findings of their inventory of all the managers involved by taking the company's organization chart and colouring in the block in which each man dangles. The colour used for each man reveals the consulting firm's verdict concerning his potentiality. These coloured charts are sometimes called 'Go & No-Go Maps'. They give management the big picture at a glance – in colour.

The head of the Klein Institute for Aptitude Testing kindly presented me with a 'Personnel Evaluation Map' drawn up by the institute to illustrate how it presents its recommendations in graphic form. It pictures thirty-six individuals in the marketing department of a corporation. Men are shown in six successive layers on the chart. Under 'Vice-President for Marketing', for example, are three men: Jack Smith, Advertising Manager; John Doe, Sales Manager; and Joe Brown, Marketing Research Manager. Below them hang regional managers. Under the regional managers hang district managers. Under each district manager hang branch managers, and so on.

Each man's block is filled in with one of four colours. The legend at the bottom explains the colours:

> Green – Upgrade
> Blue – Stay Put
> Yellow – Caution
> Red – Downgrade

Of the thirty-six men, twelve have green blocks; thirteen are blue; five show yellow; and six are red.

At each of the first three levels under the Vice-President

there is only one lucky man at each level recommended for upgrading. The lines of succession are set, at least in the minds of the Klein Institute.

Chartists within a company often take into account the possibility that a man marked for upgrading may leave or become otherwise eliminated from the competition. They draft Back-Up Charts to provide for this contingency. These show all the back-up men for each position, sometimes labelling them *B–1*, *B–2*, and *B–3* to indicate priority.

Company managers studying their charts may also worry about 'blocked positions'. If a position is considered a valuable training ground for higher office and the man holding it is good enough to rate 'satisfactory' but not good enough to be rated 'promotable', he is viewed as blocking progress and will somehow have to be removed from that spot.

A large company does not usually drop a man judged non-promotable from the payroll but shifts him to a shelf outside the main channels of promotion – a staff post, perhaps – and may even give him a rise to distract him from awareness of what has really happened to his prospects.

Medium-sized and smaller companies often cannot afford the luxury of maintaining on the payroll a $10,000-to-$50,000 executive who is not performing satisfactorily and will therefore drop him with a minimum of ceremony. The larger company will try to keep him on as long as he does not actively create a problem. And if he *must* go, his dismissal is handled in a manner befitting the dignity of the company and its executives. He is almost never fired. He is encouraged to start looking elsewhere. He may get the hint if he is made vice-president in charge of new projects only to discover that there aren't any. If possible, he must not leave feeling unkindly towards the company. It would hurt the company's image; further, he may know too much about company plans and secrets. The blame for his departure will be shifted, when possible, to a heartless hatchetman from outside, the management consultant who has been studying the company's operations.

Our real concern here, however, is with the man on his way

T—T.P.C.—D

up, the comer who manages to emerge from the evaluations with good ratings and is further deemed promotable because of his particular skills, or because he is in a functional area from which his company tends to draw its top managers, or because he reminds the chairman of the board of himself at that age.

The man labelled 'promotable' is watched and nurtured. If he looks really promising on all the forms, he may get an even more coveted designation: he becomes a fully and officially earmarked man whose promotability clearly extends up into the area near the peak. (The company cynics will call him a crown prince.) Sid Boyden, the search specialist, explains the necessity for earmarking promotable men thus:

'As soon as the appraisal of the top management team has been completed by the president, the next step is to earmark men to succeed his top team in the years ahead. This earmarking process is an important ingredient of any executive planning programme. Middle management executives must be carefully appraised for outstanding, promotable men who appear to possess the potential to move up eventually to top management positions.'

Mr Boyden feels that the earmarked man should know he is earmarked: 'He should, if possible, be able to visualize the route to the top position. This subject should be discussed frankly with him and his progress reviewed periodically.' Furthermore, to keep this earmarked man contented while waiting, 'he should have a sense of belonging. A promotable man should be accepted both businesswise and socially by the men in the executive team immediately above him.'

One way an earmarked man is made to feel he belongs is to invite him to participate in 'management decision games'. In the games – during which the men are again watched carefully – the teams of executive players make believe they are running a company and are competing with other 'companies' to see who can make the most long-term profit.

These games were pioneered by the American Management Association in 1956 as part of its programme in decision-making training. A.M.A. officials had visited the naval War College to learn how military games are simulated from information fed into electronic computers. A manager sent by his company to the A.M.A. games run in New York will spend about two weeks on a team of at least a half-dozen other players. Their 'company' will compete with several other 'company' teams in trying to sell the same product in the same market. The players are given balance sheets and other largely statistical information and told to manage their mythical company for, say, ten years. At the beginning of each quarter of each year they must make decisions about pricing, production, how much to spend for research and development, how much to invest in new plants, and so on.

The games are based on supposedly accurate mathematical models of economic situations. Information is fed into computers, and the player-managers get a quick feedback on the presumed impact of their decisions.

Today many companies have developed their own executive-training games. General Electric has a half-dozen games, with titles such as *Inventrol* and *Uniflo*. *Time* quoted a G.E. official as explaining in 1961: 'The quicker you start to think of a business problem as a thing without human beings, the better you'll do.'

This dehumanizing of make-believe management is perhaps one of the large appeals of the games. It gives the players the sense of precision and of being 'scientific' and of feeling they are dealing with an orderly world that higher-level managers find so reassuring. These games pretend that the crucial pawns in the game – the customers for the product in question – will respond to all the statistical lever-pulling in an orderly manner and, for example, buy more in precise proportion to the amount that prices are lowered or that advertising is poured on. The well-known perversity, whimsicality, and fickleness of consumers, is conveniently overlooked and the inherent value of the product assumed.

Earmarked men are also likely to be sent off for a few weeks, as a part of their grooming, to a special school or institute.

Usually care is taken to see that people of the same approximate rank are thrown together at these schools. The A.M.A. conducts executive-training courses for tens of thousands of executives each year at its classrooms in New York City and at The Grove, Hamilton, New York, home of the Presidents' Professional Association, an affiliate of the A.M.A.

A number of colleges have special programmes for executives. The most attractive geographically is the advanced-management programme at the University of Hawaii. One of the best – at least in the sense of being intellectually challenging – is the Columbia Top Executive Programme. The most famous is Harvard's highly rated Advanced Management Programme. An executive attending Harvard's thirteen-week session is immersed in a programme which seeks to develop in him 'the habit of thinking of problems in company terms in the largest sense'. The six courses of a recent A.M.P. programme were entitled 'Business and the World Society', 'Administrative Practices', 'Cost and Financial Administration', 'Problems in Labour Relations', 'Marketing Administration', and 'Business Policy'.

Some of the larger companies have their own schools for promising executives. The best known is General Electric's Advanced Management Course at its Crotonville, New York, staff college. This nine-week course costs the company a minimum of $2,650 per student and includes 900 executives a year. Heavy emphasis is placed on courses in world affairs and on the 'business environment'.

G.E. officials claim that the course was not intended to groom executives for promotion ('We don't want to crown-prince anybody') but they confess that 'coming to Crotonville is getting to be something of a status symbol'. In 1961 *Business Week* reported that all but one of the company's divisional general managers had been through the Crotonville course.

Some months ago I spent an evening as a guest at a dinner in the Midwest attended by several hundred managers at the local General Electric plant. Most of those who sat near me struck me as rather wooden characters and I had some trouble making conversation. At one point a crisp, beaming, youngish man of about forty strode up to me, welcomed me with a warm hearty handshake, and chatted pleasantly for a few minutes. I gathered he was the programme chairman. When he departed the man next to me cupped his hand and whispered: 'He just got back from Crotonville. He's been tapped.'

PART 3

THE WELL-PACKAGED EXECUTIVE

CHAPTER 8

The Executive Look

Three characteristics of top executives are: slow speech, impressive appearance, and a complete lack of sense of humour.
Johnson O'Connor, founder of the Human Engineering Laboratory and the Johnson O'Connor Research Foundation

The impression one creates by one's physical presence obviously is more crucial to success in some occupations than in others. It is more important to an actor, doctor, or bond salesman than to a forest ranger, nuclear scientist, or meter-reader. The bald-headed fat man will predictably have more difficulty getting a job in a ladies' shoe store than in a men's shoe store.

Does appearance count in executive success? Some vigorously deny that it does and point to men of strikingly different appearance within the same executive suite. It is true there are often noticeable differences. But there are also, over-all, striking appearance patterns among executives. Numerous men who have spent years appraising executives speak freely and often unexpectedly, of the importance of appearance. One gets the impression that physical appearance is becoming increasingly important to executive success and that it becomes especially important for the promising younger executives who are getting up near the peaks of the larger corporate pyramids – and hope to be regarded as having all the ingredients of a 'successful package'.

I was confidentially shown the rating sheet that a management consulting firm uses in appraising *chief* executive officers. One question on the form asks if the man under scrutiny for the job of chief executive officer conveys immediately an image of a leader.

The form used at Mead Johnson to appraise executives

instructs the rater to grade the man (*A* to *E*) on the statement 'Possesses the type of executive bearing that others can profitably copy.'

One also gets a strong impression that the executive recruiting firms find it easier to sell clients on hiring a man who looks like an executive. Some charge that the recruiting firms tend too much to be type-casting bureaux. At any rate, a number of recruiters spoke of the 'threshold effect' – how a man looks when he comes through the door. Does he look like a successful package? Recruiter Bert Antell, who hobnobs in the highest business circles, confided: 'Almost from the minute he walks in you know whether he is someone you would want or not.'

And recruiter Frank Canny, of Hoff, Canny, Bowen & Associates (headquarters New York City), former president of the recruiters' trade association (A.E.R.C.), said: 'Regardless of a man's background he is made or broken the minute he puts his foot through the office door. That initial impression is one that will be lasting. With all the psychological techniques and devices used I still think that how a man presents himself in the first few seconds is of vital importance: it shows a lot about what he is and how he has prepared himself.'

He explained that it is not only how the individual is dressed but also his bearing, speech, and general attitude that help create the over-all initial impression. The recruiter, must, bear in mind, he said, that in making final judgement officials of the client companies will in many cases rely on some superficial devices regarding personality characteristics as well as on knowledge of their own field. The recruiter therefore must know not only all the modern selection techniques, Canny said, but also how his clients are likely to react to the men submitted.

Psychological testers understandably tend to scorn the usefulness of such flashes of intuition. One leading tester burst into obscenity when I cited this viewpoint. Management consultant Robert McMurry, no fan of testing, also is scornful. He begins his seminars for personnel managers by passing out to each manager a sheet showing eight faces. Half are faces of successful industrialists. The other half are of such types as 'East German spy' and 'Translator of Japanese poetry'. Dr McMurry asks his presumed whizzes in personnel selection to identify the successful industrialists. The exercise, he explains, 'provides the personnel executives with a requisite degree of modesty.' They rarely do better than chance. Dr McMurry has of course carefully selected his pictures to drive home his point. Manner and bearing are as important as face in the executive look.

Just how important is appearance to executive effectiveness? We can only guess. Psychological consultant Dr John P. Foley, Jr, of New York City relates that a top executive of a client company confided to him: 'John, a good executive should have big ears.' Dr Foley added that he immediately noticed his informant had 'pretty big ears'. Then Dr Foley went on to make his more serious point:

'In industrial psychology we have recognized for years that when there is a stereotype, however fallacious, you had better consider it if it influences success on the job.'

Dr William C. Menninger, the renowned psychiatrist of the Menninger Foundation, asserts: 'The executive must face up to his role in the organization. He is a symbolic father, whether he likes it or not.' But then Dr Menninger proceeded to spell out how a symbolic father behaves rather than how he looks.

Corporate managements, however, often assume that a man who looks like a leader-father is more likely somehow to be persuasive as one. Consequently there is widespread acceptance of the thesis advanced by two personnel experts who developed training courses for New York Central executives some years ago. These officials advised: 'From the start, you should develop a good executive personality. . . . You should learn to look like an executive, think like an executive, act like an executive.'[1]

How is an executive supposed to look? Gather round, and we will examine the latest folklore on the subject. I say 'latest' because the ideal in executive models has been undergoing some changes.

Is there a current preference in executive physique? Listen to the courtly John Handy, a medium-tall man who has been trafficking in executives for many years: 'The fashion now is for big men. In the old days in some of the companies the tallest executive was five feet five, but now the fashion is for big men even though there are plenty of small men doing a terrific job.' He told of instances where he was asked to submit only candidates who were over six feet tall and surmised that the big man is preferred because 'he has a certain presence'. Mr Handy offered this parallel in suggesting the importance of the gaze-level in dealing with subordinates: 'In the Royal Canadian Mounted Police,' he said, 'a mounted subordinate has to dismount before addressing a superior. If he gallops up and speaks without dismounting he can be punished.'

It might be noted parenthetically that occasionally this same consideration produces a demand for less than tall executives. I heard of a five-foot-ten president who 'hates like hell' to look up to anyone. Recruiters working for him give him men who are five-feet-ten or shorter.

In general, however, the trend is towards towering executives, particularly on the sales side. Repeatedly I was told that in sales jobs the more successful men tend to be those who are more imposing-looking; those who have a striking manner and command instant attention. *Sales Management* reported that four men recently appointed as operating heads of their trade associations in the sales field averaged six feet four inches and speculated that in the future the trade associations might start raiding the National Basketball Association. A certain chemical company, in its screening form for sales personnel, asks: 'Is he physically large and impressive?' And it adds: 'If small, he should make up for it in energy and good health.'

There is less pressure for height among financial executives, but even in this field there is occasionally a specific request for tall men. Ward Howell relates that the head of a large electronics company, asking for a controller, said: 'I want a very tall man for this job, a very impressive guy. He must report to stockholders.'

An official of Hergenrather Associates suggested that although their firm has received specifications calling for a six-footer, most executive candidates have no real problem so long as they are at least five feet eight. He commented that you can get excited about a prospect who sounds tremendous over the telephone; then he walks in 'looking like Mickey Rooney.' He said – from experience with two such shorties – that he might decide the man wouldn't command the proper respect of strong associates in the management team.

A second trend in the physique of the new executive is towards leanness. When I told the vice-president of a billion-dollar financial institution that I was interested in the 'look' of executives, he said: 'I suppose you have already learned that we are all lean.' (He was a lean five feet eleven.) Other informants volunteered similar information suggesting a new interest in leanness.

Not all tall executives, of course, are lean. Some still look like alumni of professional football teams. But these heavy-boned, muscular mesomorphs are generally giving way to tauter, more streamlined models. The fat executive on the J. P. Morgan model is disappearing completely in the large companies. Even plump men are hard to find in the larger executive suites. The managers of these suites appear to be developing what some call a slim-jim complex. Some companies, such as Prudential Insurance and C.I.T. Financial, drive the point home by offering 'calorie-count' menus in their executive dining rooms.

One recruiter offered to pay me five dollars if I could find anyone among the thousands of men in management at International Business Machines under the age of thirty-five who weighed more than two hundred pounds. He said: 'They start out lean, and they stay lean all the way up.' (I've seen a good many I.B.M. men within the past five years and my recollections do not encourage me to hope that I will ever find a plump one. I'll appreciate any tips and will split the reward.)

While visiting the campus of the Harvard Graduate School of Business Administration one June day, I found myself amid several hundred middle-aged men who were back for a reunion. They had name tags on their lapels and were standing outside a vast tent waiting for the speeches to resume. Since the matter of executive physique was then on my mind I began looking among them for a fat man. In several minutes of searching I was unable to find even a robust man. Suddenly before me I saw the back of a bald, bulging, broad-beamed man, the perfect image of the old-style tycoon. I worked my way around to get a better view – and discovered that he was the one man I had surveyed in the entire crowd who didn't have a name tag! He was an outsider who had happened to drop by to chat. Within a few moments he waddled off to the parking lot and disappeared into his car. I suspect he was a grounds supervisor or a custodian chatting with men he had known as students. But I can't prove it.

The prejudice against roundness in executives is not entirely a matter of vogue. Company doctors frown on fat as a health hazard; and management people often wonder whether the fat man can stand the pace of work the company would like to see.

What about the executive's face, posture, and such matters? Among the facts about an executive which Hergenrather Associates believes important enough to file on the man's I.B.M. classification sheet are evaluations of his 'personal appearance: face, dress, eyes' and of his 'poise, bearing, tact.' Here are some of the kinds of thing that could bring a low rating:

Eyes. Are they bloodshot? Do his eyes close or roll too much when he speaks? Does he avoid looking you in the eye? *Bearing.* Does he flop in a chair or hang a leg over an arm of the chair? *Face.* Does he have lots of pimples or physical ugliness? There are managements that just won't hire anyone who is not physically attractive, it seems, even though the person is otherwise fully qualified.

In former years some personnel experts were fascinated

with the idea that they could choose good executives by using the Merton system of face-reading based on 108 check points. *Fortune* gave this good-natured coverage in the early fifties.[2] (According to the Merton analysis, good staff men often have long, angular faces; good line executives often have heavy 'buffers' on the lower side of the face to give a squarish cut to their jib; and weak executives are often characterized by 'harmonious' faces with no conspicuous features.) The Merton system has few adherents today. If there is a preference for faces among younger executives in the larger corporations it is for the clean-cut, young-fellow-next-door face that reflects the corporate image of studious goodwill towards the world.

Although it is almost never stated, many companies controlled by *WASP*s (White Anglo-Saxon Protestants) feel easier about a man if he looks like a *WASP*. One indication of this concern appears in a 'depth' interviewing form prepared for a chemical company. Under 'Appearance, manner, and dress' it asks: 'Does he appear to be the type of man who would be accepted by our customers? Keep the likes and dislikes of our buyers and customers in mind. This item is highly important.'

Five different informants used the word *wholesome* to describe the desirable executive candidate. This nice, modest, wholesome man with the fellow-next-door face of course does not adorn that face with a moustache, which might suggest slickness. Only 4 per cent of the hundred-odd American businessmen at a Harvard course in advanced management had moustaches; none had a beard. This appropriate-looking man doesn't smoke a pipe (which might in the mythology suggest that he was inherently lazy or too egg-heady to be a decision-maker). He doesn't have red hair (because everybody knows that people with red hair are temperamental).

We find, in startling contrast, an endless variety of types in physique, face, and personality when we look at the entrepreneurs who run their own shows, men who build or inherited their own businesses and run them as extensions of their egos. We find the same contrasts among men who run new, fast-growing companies such as Texas Instruments, whose president, an engineer, is apt to greet visitors in a sports shirt.

This contrast between corporation man and entrepreneur struck me forcibly twice within a week in the fall of 1961 when I was invited to be present at two business conventions. One was for executives in the truck-body-building business. Most of the men attending ran their own small businesses (body-building for trucks is still pretty much a custom operation). These entrepreneurs were an outspoken, colourful crowd and came in many shapes and sizes. One very successful man who remains vivid in my mind had an enormous paunch and a shaved, bullet-shaped head. These men roared greetings. One from Washington, D.C., had a passion for bursting into free verse whenever he met a stranger. I was told that this man, who headed a family enterprise, had even lapsed into free verse when giving his last annual report to his board of directors.

But there was another group at this convention: the representatives of the big auto, steel, and chemical companies who were suppliers to the industry. These men ran more consistently to one pattern: they tended to be lean, earnest, handsome, constrained, doggedly friendly.

At the second convention the entrepreneurial ego was even more rampantly apparent. It was a regional convention of the Young Presidents' Organization. To get into the Y.P.O. you must become president, before you are forty, of a company doing at least a million dollars' worth of business a year. Most of the members are supercharged young men who built up their own enterprises or else are running – and expanding – business empires founded by their fathers. The Y.P.O. includes men with full beards, men with shaved heads, and lots of men with crew cuts. At the convention I attended there were downright skinny men and downright tubby men, equally successful. One enormously energetic and idealistic man (who has made millions of dollars) had a spectacular cow-lick. There were men with startlingly innocent, boyish faces who ran multi-million-dollar empires and also a number of men with hard, disagreeable faces – again equally successful.

Quite a few of these men wore alligator shoes. That would be considered ostentatious and probably non-permissible in the executive suites of large U.S. corporations, where the wing-tip shoe is *de rigueur*.

Men in the larger U.S. corporations do not need to be so carefully correct about the specifics of dress as their opposite numbers in Great Britain with the ever-present furled umbrella, waistcoat, narrow-shouldered dark suit, and bowler. And despite stereotypes to the contrary, successful U.S. executives do not – outside the financial districts and the very highest corporate levels – wear homburg hats or waistcoats. The grey flannel suit, though still popular, is only one of a number of appropriate suits for aspiring executives. On the other hand, the corporate man must be careful not to dress in a way that might strike someone as breezy. Bernard Haldane of Bernard Haldane Associates (headquarters New York City), who specializes in what he has called 'career development' for ambitious businessmen, admonishes his individual clients to look like businessmen. He had a client, age thirty-two, working for one of the great chemical companies who was 'not getting anywhere'. One of the young man's major problems, Haldane decided, was that he had been 'best-dressed man in college and had never gotten over it.' He dressed in expensive tweeds and in shirts with wide-spread collars. Haldane admonished him to spend an hour leafing through the better illustrated business magazines to see how executives dressed. The young man first showed deep annoyance but later, as he continued leafing, became humble. Finally he said: 'I guess I had better get a new wardrobe.'

Two qualities esteemed in corporate executive dress, I gather, are neatness and non-conspicuousness, and one can achieve these qualities just about any way one wishes. The 'Man Specification' form for an ideal manager cited earlier specified under 'Appearance and Personal Habits: GOOD – makes a neat and business-like appearance.' Dr McMurry tells of a junior executive who lost his job 'because he wore argyle socks and cleaned his fingernails during executive conferences'.

Recently I boarded an airplane with four junior executives who were evidently from the same company. They were as look-alike in dress as four girls from a clique of thirteen-year-olds. All four wore dark grey suits, white shirts, striped ties, wing-tipped shoes, and brown unpeaked hats. All were about five feet eleven. At the headquarters of a Midwestern railway system a visiting consultant noticed that all the men, including the president, wore single-breasted greys, blues, or blacks. When the consultant kidded the president about this evidence of a 'totem system' at work, the president professed astonishment and promised to drop hints that everyone should dress as he liked (within the bounds of 'good taste'). So the new totem became 'flexibility' and the consultant recalls that when he returned in the fall he observed 'a splendid array of colours'.

As you get into the rarefied atmosphere of executive suites the general rules remain the same, but there are a few differences: the ties become silk, the shirts usually have French cuffs, the suits become more clearly plain dark and custom-tailored, and the socks become long. When Carter Burgess, the tall, genial chairman of American Machine & Foundry, greeted me in his office he came in grinning, with a cigar in his mouth – and saying, 'Lord, what a day.' His dress struck me particularly. He wore a dark blue suit, white shirt, polka-dot blue silk tie, black wing-tip shoes – and long socks. Dr Eugene Jennings of Michigan State's Graduate School of Business Administration, who has had executives under continuous study for many years, told me: 'There is one thing I've noticed about the appearance of all top executives that stands out: they always wear long hose.' Presumably they consider it undignified to permit subordinates to see leg skin when their knees are crossed. Burgess' cigar, however, was no more typical than the fat tycoon who used to smoke them in the cartoons. My observation is that while entrepreneurs frequently are cigar-smokers, the big-company executive usually confines his cigar smoking to the rather ceremonial one with which he tidily indulges himself after a dinner.

Big business values sobriety, respectability, and conservatism – and consequently frowns upon bow ties at the higher level, as well as continental suits, hand-painted ties, bright waistcoats, or any other signs of an exotic taste. The bow tie is considered especially inappropriate in the production end of companies but ·is tolerated at lower levels for men in personnel, public relations, and sales.

The Hat Corporation of America has been saying in its advertisements – to counteract the impression created by the fact that the President of the United States usually appears outdoors bare-headed – that most executives 'prefer to hire men who wear hats.' It advises would-be executives that they can make the 'rough competitive road' to the top a little easier by always wearing a hat. This self-serving claim is apparently a fair statement of fact in a great many corporate environments. Psychologist John Foley relates that a vice-president assessing a candidate for a managerial job whispered: 'Look, John, that man isn't wearing a hat.'

Charles Scribner, vice-president for personnel at Remington Rand, recalled that when he was a thirty-two-year-old corporate staff member in a large motor car manufacturing company in Detroit: 'I had the crew cut that I'd had as a military pilot and had never bothered to change, and I never wore a hat. It wasn't long before I found out that if I was going to represent the company in plants around the country in arbitration it would be a real fine idea if I would let my hair grow out and an even better idea if I decided to wear a hat.' This concept was conveyed to him by his boss over cocktails. He added, 'So I bought a hat and grew some hair. When I left the company I quit wearing the hat.' (He didn't return to the crew cut.)

I.B.M. used to be notorious for its requirements about dress, especially its insistence that managers wear starched collars. Since Thomas J. Watson, Jr, took over the helm from his father the situation has loosened up, but some interesting unwritten rules still apply. These were spelled out to me by two lean I.B.M. men. Salesmen must wear hats (and mechanics must wear ties). It is also still an unwritten rule that you wear a white shirt and a dark business suit (at least at headquarters).

Recently an I.B.M. vice-president called in a man to talk with him about the fact that he had worn a yellow shirt on the premises. Another manager got a pointed up-and-down look from the same vice-president when he came to work in a polo coat. Goatees, moustaches, and beards are not considered acceptable on an I.B.M. man. Further, one informant remembered, 'no one in management has overly long hair. This has to be watched.'

An important ingredient of the executive look – or the threshold effect – is the personal style of the man. Obviously this style, or manner, must be appropriate to the personality of the particular individual involved. A markedly modest man will comport himself in a different way from a markedly haughty man – and both may become outstandingly successful. A candidate for high office in a larger organization today, however, is widely assumed to be helped if in his personal style he conveys these four impressions:

1. The impression of aplomb. A psychiatrist who has worked a great deal with executives calls this impression 'the executive front'. He explains: 'An executive is a very threatened individual. If he shows any kind of weakness at all he is going to be trampled on.' To minimize the danger of being trampled, the careful executive may try to convey an air of success. He exudes self-confidence. If this comes naturally, so much the better. In any case he keeps a close rein on his displays of emotion.

A game that I play to amuse myself while dining alone in a restaurant in a strange city is watching and listening to a group of managers at a near-by table and trying to guess which is the highest-ranking. It usually takes about thirty seconds to reach a tentative conclusion. The top man not only is likely to take command of the discussion but also tends to be the more stately looking and is the one with the quiet, indulgent laugh and the earnest, assured, well-modulated voice.

In London a school for actors, Method International, began conducting in late 1960 a one-week course for middle-echelon executives on how to maintain the aplomb of a good managing director. The executives taking the course were schooled in eye-contact exercise in order to develop a level gaze and were given training in maintaining poise in embarrassing situations. A sample challenge was maintaining aplomb while taking one's shoes off in public.[3]

2. The impression of dignity. A man who hopes to be a symbolic father to thousands of people is presumed to be aided in this endeavour if he projects a suggestion of a Mosaic manner, a certain stand-offishness, an erect bearing, and a slow, solemn manner of speaking which suggests – whether true or not – that every word is chosen with deliberation. Cameron Hawley, the businessman-turned-novelist, relates that when Lincoln Lord, his fictional big executive, was rather desperately unemployed and had moved with his wife into one room, Lord still went to his club almost every day. Although Lord was almost at his wits' end, Hawley writes: 'Moving with the grace of complete composure he walked through the shielded entrance to the washroom.' There in the washroom he hoped to develop a camaraderie with 'some of the biggest men in New York' that could 'never be quite matched in any of the outer rooms'.[4]

Psychiatrist William B. Terhune, medical director of the Silver Hill Foundation, has observed that the executives he has studied over the years had 'become expert in having their status recognized. They made their presence felt at the golf club, at cocktail parties and business conferences. . . .'[5]

3. The impression of naturalness. While executives may enjoy the kudos of high status Dr Terhune mentions, to be successful in today's world they also must be mindful of their role as goodwill ambassadors for the company. They must bear in mind that, if they seem to drift too far from looking like and acting like the common man, radicals may arise as they did in the thirties with cries of 'Down with the Economic Royalists.' Thus the well-packaged executive in the sixties possesses not only dignity but a touch of amateurishness and homeliness. After he talks with you he is likely to tag along with you out to the elevator.

4. *The impression of good breeding.* I hesitate to cite this because I have seen a number of highly successful men who did not convey such an impression. I had dinner one night with the president of a half-billion-dollar company who seemed so crude, so limited in his interests, and so downright loutish that many people I know would feel uneasy about presenting him to mixed company in their homes. I met a top-level official of General Electric who, while obviously brilliant at his job, conveyed strongly an impression of rawness and gracelessness. Still, knowledgeable executives insist there is a strong trend towards favouring younger executives who have achieved 'sophistication'. I've been told of several high-ranking men who were aided in getting jobs by the fact that they were able to confer upon the executive suite of the company hiring them 'a certain social aura'.

The increased use of social settings for discussions of corporate problems probably helps account for the reported demand for sophisticated men who appear at ease in all sorts of social situations. Today business discussions spill over into clubs, breakfast meetings, and conventions. And who knows – nowadays the successful executive may find himself before TV cameras at a congressional hearing. Professor Thomas O'Donovan of the University of Detroit concluded, after making a study of executive traits: 'When they say "He's a good man but he wouldn't fit," that means that he would not fit socially. A man by his whole nature conveys an impression, has an impact, which is right or wrong for particular social positions.'

The head of a consulting company who spends most of his time conferring with executives in many parts of the country has become impressed by the role of the club. He feels that more important than belonging to the right club is ability to behave in the knowing manner once inside. One expectation, he said, is that you wash your hands upon entering the club even if you had just washed before leaving the office. It would be terribly wrong to go into the dining room without first doing this. And at the table, he said, the well-schooled executive is likely to say to his guest, *without looking at the menu,* 'Wouldn't you like some oysters?'

CHAPTER 9

Four Rules of Behaviour for Survival

> *I have come to believe that it is usually easier for you to modify your needs than it is for the company to change its requirements. Companies are funny that way.* From 'Tips to a College Man Going To Work', by banker Robert N. Hilkert in *Personnel Journal*

An ambitious young executive may look every inch the part of a man with a mission and he may show dazzling virtuosity in competition as a ledge-leaper, but he will still need to observe the ground rules if he hopes to get up into the executive stratosphere.

Ground rules are sometimes spelled out, but more often they are unwritten expectations. A top-level executive of a very large metal-processing corporation commented: 'The unwritten things you don't hear about are what may be controlling factors. Business people can't begin to discuss openly the reasons why this guy is chosen and that one is not. The reason he is chosen may well be because he thinks like you do on vital policy questions, or it may be because he more than others has accepted the basic views of the world held by top management.'

In sifting through the many ground rules – written and unwritten – that pyramid climbers frequently encounter, I find these four seem most prevalent and compelling:

RULE ONE – *Be Dedicated*. The vice-president in charge of marketing for one of the nation's largest food processors pointed out to me: 'In our dictionary the word is spelled "dead-icated".'

Top managers share with professional football coaches the conviction that it takes more than salaries to build a winning team. Men are assumed to be in need of pride and a selfless devotion to a greater corporate good if the company is to fulfil the battle cry '*Beat last year!*' That's another phrase the marketing vice-president said he hears many times a year as an exhortation.

A report on the A.M.A.'s survey of the lives of 335 top executives concluded: 'To get to the top, the survey suggests that a man has to put on a pair of blinders to shut out everything except business.'

Perhaps the most eloquent comment yet made on the dedication of executives was that of the young minister in Bloomfield Hills, Michigan, home town of many top-level automotive executives. He was quoted by Seymour Freedgood as saying: 'These men are monks – monks who've traded in their prayer books for a production line. From the way they work, I sometimes think they want to overwhelm God with their cars.'

The pace of work is more frenzied in some industries than in others. Financial companies, for example, tend to assume a more gentlemanly schedule. Pace also varies, oddly, with level of success. The more successful a man becomes with the corporation, the harder he is expected to work! The lower-level paper-pushers may in truth work thirty-five-hour weeks, as some surveys of supervisory personnel show; but the wheelers-and-dealers work sixty, seventy, and eighty-hour weeks, if you count their breakfast meetings, luncheon meetings, dinner meetings, emergency meetings, and homework.

In 1961 the dynamic William P. Lear, chairman of Lear, Inc., maker of aircraft instruments, was quoted in print as admonishing the ambitious young man who wants to get ahead to 'work an extra hour a day.' One of my vivid memories is of an evening I spent in the Lear home outside Santa Monica waiting three hours with Mrs Lear for Mr Lear to come home. He kept calling to say he would be later than he thought. We finally dined (with him) at eleven o'clock. He said that seventy-hour weeks were his normal pattern. (Lear, Inc., has since become Lear-Siegler, Inc.)

RULE TWO – *Be Loyal*. Occasionally this is officially speci-fied. The organizational manual for a major toy company states that one duty common to all executives is 'to under-stand, support loyally, and explain thoroughly the objectives, creeds and policies to subordinates.' At another point the manual explains that the duty of executives is 'in spite of per-sonal feelings to support and willingly enforce decisions rendered by superiors.' And it adds: 'In following channels of contact, keep the superior informed of any matter for which the superior is held responsible.'

In other cases the loyalty is assumed. Three Harvard staff men who made several penetrating case studies of executive attitudes reported of a company they called *Farvell*:

Whatever a man's personal feelings were, membership in the top management group also implied an intense loyalty to the company. A man's behaviour might be judged more than anything else by whether, in countless large and small ways, he reflected this loyalty in his actions.[1]

An even stronger statement of this expectation was made by a high-level official of a multibillion-dollar corporation. He explained that to succeed in a company such as his own the man must 'associate with the right thought. By the time he becomes an executive of importance there is no question of his loyalty. He has lost his capacity to differ. He doesn't see any point in differing. It really comes back to group psychology.'

Loyalty is one facet of a general state of mind that is often loosely and disparagingly referred to as *conformity*. I don't intend to re-argue here the whole issue of conformity in business organizations, which received a thorough airing in the fifties. However, since a number of business journals have recently proclaimed that in the sixties there is a strong swing away from conformity in corporations, we should at least caution the ambitious young man to treat such a procla-mation with extreme wariness.

Consider as evidence an October 1961 report in *Nation's Business*, which is published by the Chamber of Commerce of the United States. It described a survey made at Michigan State University. The article was titled, 'How to Satisfy the Boss'. The M.S.U. study explored the attitudes of sixty-four business leaders in eighteen industries on the qualities they most esteemed in subordinates.

The editors graphically summed up the findings by printing a drawing of a ladder with five sturdy rungs. Each rung was labelled with one of the five qualities found in the survey to be most valued in subordinates. Here are the labels and the headline the editors printed over the ladder:

YOU'LL IMPROVE YOUR CHANCE
OF EXECUTIVE SUCCESS IF YOU:

Rescue the boss

from his own mistakes

Maintain the authority

he has granted you

Be satisfied with your

role as subordinate

Project the image of

the boss he desires

Be properly predictable

in your behaviour.

In every instance the amplifications in the text of the report on the five desired qualities stressed the high value placed by senior executives on loyal support and the risk of actions that might smack too strongly of independent attitude or action. For example, the amplification on Rung Two ('Maintain the authority he has granted you') was devoted almost entirely to the hazards of making any move that might seem to exceed that authority.

In other reports carried by *Nation's Business*, Dr Eugene Jennings, a psychologist, has explored some of the soul-searing complications of comporting oneself as an acceptable subordinate. He describes the dangers of emotional 'over-investment' in straining to gain and hold the approval of power figures. He shows, too, that although the good subordinate is expected always to appear to serve the boss's interests, he must not be 'too open about his loyalty for fear that he will embarrass the boss or will cause him to become suspicious'.

Further, he points out, the subordinate really has two masters to please. One is the 'Company-Mother' and the other is the 'Boss-Father'. The expectations of the two are not always identical. The subordinate must 'conform to the organization's character'. But, Dr Jennings adds, the superior 'has certain needs [from a subordinate] that are separate from those of his organization. . . . Often he wants hard-working, aggressive, personally loyal, perhaps even submissive subordinates who will fulfil certain requirements that he views as important to his career.' The superior may expect 'obedience, respect for superior position and experience, and always, of course, spontaneous work for his crucial interests. These expectations must be fulfilled if the subordinate wishes to succeed.'

To sum up, Dr Jennings concluded that an executive in the average corporation of today can by the nature of things 'mature only by learning how to depend upon figures within the corporate triangle in much the same way that a child learns to depend upon members within the family triangle. We know that if the child learns to submit or rebel too much against these powerful figures, he is not capable of dealing with them in terms of his own interests or needs.'

A subordinate extricates himself from such a triangle, he added, if he successfully serves both power figures, 'gains their acceptance, and eventually finds opportunities to serve them in ways of his own choosing and thereby masters them enough to extend his power and authority over them.' The man who can manage this complex manoeuvre, he said, becomes 'truly free'.

RULE THREE – *Be Adaptable*. While loyalty suggests commitment, adaptability suggests adjustment. James Worthy, former vice-president at Sears, Roebuck and now a management consultant, has commented: 'Organized activity requires a high degree of consensus, and evidence of lack of consensus is disturbing to those in positions of responsibility.'

Industrialists frequently talk wistfully about the need for men who are tigers. What they really want are co-operative tigers, tigers who come quickly to heel and can get along nicely with other tigers. They want tigers who fit in.

The nearest that business spokesmen have come to articulating this desire was again in *Nation's Business* (April 1959), in reporting on a survey the magazine had made among specialists in management development and recruitment to determine what qualities and skills were most in demand. The report was headlined WANTED NOW: THESE EXECUTIVE TRAITS. The opening sentence announced that 'American industry is drawing up new specifications to apply to its key managers.' The first 'new specification' cited – in large type – was:

They're Asking for CREATIVE CONFORMISTS

The report cited search specialist Sid Boyden as observing that 'industry is run by teams today, not individuals'. And it quoted search specialist Frank Canny as pointing out 'The rugged individualist, unless he has the rare quality of being politic, does not last in companies today.' The programme director of the A.M.A.'s four-week executive-development course was cited as saying that *It isn't done* had become 'a mighty important group of words right now. . . . Though companies are looking for executives with more brand-new, creative ideas,' executives are obliged to conform more than ever. The section closed with the sad tale of a promising but unconventional young executive who had to be warned to 'fit in' if he wanted to stay with the company. (A screening form prepared for a certain chemical company instructs the interviewer to appraise a candidate for the sales force on this question: 'Will he fit in with the present men and management?')

Eighteen months later *Nation's Business* ran a series on 'Keys to Executive Success'; in the first article the statement was made that the man who gets ahead 'must adjust readily to the needs and demands of the organization and also make its essential characteristics an integral part of his own personality.'

It is worth emphasizing again that these reports appeared in a publication of the Chamber of Commerce of the United States, and that they appeared several years after the argument about conformity in corporations developed.

Interest in adaptability seems to run particularly high in the hiring and assessing of young men. The head of the recruiting division of Richardson, Bellows, Henry & Co. explained to me that in sizing up older, experienced men you have their accumulated performance from the past as a guide. But with younger men, he said, you have got to project their potential as a team player – as a good member of the team. What is his attitude towards work and towards people?

The most obvious form that adaptability takes is patterning one's behaviour after that of the model provided by the superior. Consulting psychologist Edwin Glasscock tells of finding at one chemical company that almost all of the cigarette smokers on the management team smoked the boss's brand. When the chief executive was replaced, the smokers – to a man – changed to the new boss's brand 'without consciously doing so.'[2]

Although interest in adaptability may be highest at the lower levels, the expectation of conventional behaviour rises with level of responsibility. John K. Hemphill in his study at eleven companies of the 'Dimensions of Executive Positions' found that two thirds of the upper-management executives checked as an important part of their job conduct:

'Even During Most Relaxed Social Occasions Avoid Deviations from Generally Accepted Behaviour.'

In contrast, only a third of the beginners in management were aware of this as a significant expectation. Interestingly, among high-level executives this restraint on behaviour was felt most keenly by men in sales and manufacturing, and less keenly by men in research and development, industrial relations, and general administration.

RULE FOUR – *Be Quietly Deferential*. A survey by *Modern Office Procedures* of friendship patterns in business offices concluded that 'nearly all companies willingly have an office caste system.' Ways of behaviour within a hierarchy, as Mr Worthy points out, 'enforce a certain amount of deference to those in authority.'

This deference often shows up in unwitting pecking-order patterns. Management consultant Alfred Lateiner, who has often had group sessions with management people, told of the way management people typically file into a conference room: 'The top-layer executives will go quite naturally to the centre seats of the front row, and the officials of lesser rank will fan out behind them, with line supervisors discreetly slipping into rear corner seats.'

The best illumination of the niceties of deferential expectations which characteristically exist when superior and subordinate have a chat about a company matter is offered, I believe, in the study of executives in action made by the three Harvard staff men.[3] The senior man was assumed to have the floor. He 'is free to let his thoughts expand and ramble, if he wishes. The junior's defined role . . . is to confine his questions, statements and comments to the openings that are offered him.' Senior has more freedom to vent his aggravations; junior can 'express only those feelings that are clearly sanctioned by the senior's immediate behaviour. The junior's attitude towards the senior's ideas is appropriately one of deference; if critical, he is critical in a deferential way, not a detached one.'

A vice-president of a large company headquartered in New York advised me that, at least at his company, there is a subtlety of deference in the use of the intercom squawk box. He and the president have direct lines to each other. As a matter of actual practice the president interrupts him with direct calls many times a day, but he always channels his calls to the president through the president's secretary. The president might not wish to be interrupted. Furthermore, he pointed out, it is always a good idea to pay this form of respect to the president's secretary. Though officially of low-level status, she has a considerable opportunity to complicate even a vice-president's life.

Of the four rules for behaviour cited – Be Dedicated, Be Loyal, Be Adaptable, Be Quietly Deferential – the first is perhaps reasonable. At least it is relatively harmless to individual integrity. The second is valid so long as in being loyal to the company the executive can also be loyal to himself. (Assuming that he still has a self.) The last two, as commonly implemented, appear to be anachronisms in a modern, enlightened society struggling to learn to live with its giant organizations. The amelioration of these rules seems to represent a substantial challenge for the future.

CHAPTER 10

The Hazard of Mismating Man
and Company

*Some of our best executives have been abject failures who were
fired out of Company A for being no damned good before they
went to Company B where they have been outstanding.* Dr
Frederick J. Gaudet, Director of Psychological Studies,
Stevens Institute of Technology

A man entering a new company can have an impressive reputation behind him, be thoroughly knowledgeable in the new
job, and yet soon find himself beset by the possibility of personal disaster.

He may find himself – knowingly or not – in a company
that is in a sharp economic decline and he may have no bright
ideas for immediately and dramatically changing the situation. Tempers are always shorter in such a company, and newcomers are allowed less time to prove themselves.

But even assuming that the company is prospering, the fully
competent newcomer may face two special hazards. These
were summed up by a high-level official of a textile company
when he told of men he knew who had alternated between
successes and flops: 'A man may find himself in trouble because he has been undermined by opposing forces. Or it may
be that he was mismated on the basis of talent and personality.'

A personnel official of Sohio has reported instances in
which a man was first given a very poor rating and later did
tremendously well in the very same spot after the organization around him had, for some reason unrelated to him, been
revamped.

Although business spokesmen like to glorify the heroic
qualities that make a man a leader, they tend to neglect the

situational factors, which can be decisive. Dr Jerome C. Beam, vice-president of Psychological Services at Clark, Channell, Inc., declares flatly that the corporate environment determines the kind of qualities a man must have to succeed. Some sociologists go even further and contend that leadership does not reside in a person but is a function of the total situation. The choice of leaders thus is dictated by group needs.

Psychological consultants cited instances of having been asked to make reports on an individual being considered by two different client companies. After analysing the environments of the two companies, they said, their recommendations concerning the man are often positive to one company and negative to the other.

Virtually all the experts in executive placement mentioned the importance of first determining the company *environment* before trying to choose a man for an opening. If a man in question doesn't fit the particular environment, his success is out the window.

Environment varies according to industry, company, department within a company, and – in fact – the man with whom your prospect will have to work most closely.

The environmental changes by industry influence the kind of man who can thrive in that industry. An official of one of the great management associations said:

'I can walk into one of our meeting rooms where executives are assembled and after watching and listening for a few minutes can bet which industries many of them are from. The man working for a utility company can be recognized almost as soon as he opens his mouth. He is likely to be a static type. He has everything written out and he talks in a stylized manner. He shows respect for his elders. He has conventional ideas and he goes by the book. Probably he is simply waiting for the guy above him to die. The man with initiative and drive often finds working for a utility pretty deadening.'

In contrast, he said, a man from one of the smaller electronic firms will be bouncy and more at ease than the utility man is with academicians who may be conducting the seminar.

The environments of industries vary in interesting ways. Perhaps the most vivid, in terms of shaping the atmosphere in which a man must seem compatible, is the degree of turbulence in the environment.

Is the environment static, hectic, or something in between?

Industries towards the static end of this scale would be the utilities, banks and insurance companies – and, to a lesser extent, all forms of public ground transportation. Utilities tend to be monopolistic and are subject to government regulation. Changes in services come slowly. As Dr McMurry put it: 'In utilities the executive wonders whether to build a new plant five years from now.' In banking and insurance there is also a good deal of outside regulation, and a great deal of emphasis upon attention to detail. Decision-making is so highly structured by rule book procedures that even the president's job may be almost foolproof. But the new aggressiveness of banks in seeking depositors and overhauling their institutional images may produce a change in requirements.

At the opposite end of the scale are the fluid, fast-changing industries – such as automobile-making and the chemical and cosmetic industries – that require a great many fast decisions on innovations or styling and possible abrupt changes of direction. An official of one recruiting firm described the type of people who can best survive in the retailing field thus: 'They live by their wits and imaginations and frequently see – or experience – sudden death. You will know where you stand a lot quicker in retailing.'

In the static industries, a man's promotion tends to be based on seniority and elevation from within, and there is considerable emphasis on team decisions – which offers some protection against individual incompetence. In more hectic environments there is greater emphasis upon assuming individual responsibility and assigning jobs by merit.

Pay in these hectic industries tends to be substantially higher than in the static industries. Arch Patton of McKinsey

& Company, who is one of the nation's leading authorities on executive compensation, says:

'Over the years, compensation surveys have identified banks, life insurance companies, air transport firms, meat packing concerns, railroads and public utilities as falling in the relatively low-paid category. . . . Surveys list chemicals, department stores, automobiles, steel, textiles and appliances among the top-paid industries.'[1]

All these factors tend to define the kind of man who is likely to thrive in a given industry. Management consultant George Fry said of the type found in banking: 'The banking men are pretty cautious fellows. They never get their feet wet.' (Another leading consultant in Chicago said banking executives tend to run to 'pompous windbags' and added 'I consider them low down on the scale of over-all competence.') Dr Chris Argyris, the brilliant behavioural scientist specializing in industrial administration at Yale, concluded from a study at three banks that the banks tended to seek out the 'right-type' men who were passive, quiet, cautious, obedient, careful persons with a strong desire for security, stability, and predictability in their lives. He felt that active, independent, ambitious types might experience frustration in the banking and brokerage fields. An official of The McMurry Company cites managers of a Chicago bank who decided their management needed rejuvenating and set out to bring in a batch of aggressive young men. He recalls: 'They hired M.B.A.s from Harvard with a lot of enthusiasm and drive and then sat back to watch the kids produce ideas. Soon most of these kids got out. The ones who stayed on really needed structure; they were the passive quiet types who didn't mind not having any decision-making power.'

On the other hand, a fast-moving company taking big risks can't afford to have too many orderly, cautious men around, though of course it needs some – and in important positions.

Another corporate environment is the hard-soft dimension, so named by one recruiter of many years' experience. The hard environments are those concerned with automobiles, trucks, trains, auto supplies, and so on. In such a company men are judged by performance. Their backgrounds tend to be engineering or manufacturing. Personality is of minor importance. In the soft companies – such as food and package-goods companies – one is apt to find nice, attractive guys who sparkle socially and appear to be high-grade types. They get a couple of tries if they make mistakes that are not too serious.

Trouble comes when a hard man strays into a soft company. He can seem to be all elbows. A soft man in a hard company gets torn to pieces. The hard-soft dimension is also influenced by the closeness of the industry to the basic processing of raw materials. Executives in steel plants tend to be strong, tough, decisive characters like their product. In the financial world, remote from smoke-stacks, the requirements more typically are for smoother, more polished types.

The environment prevailing within an individual company will likewise greatly influence a man's chances of success. A free-wheeling Texas oilman may seem like the proverbial bull in a china shop if he is hired by a conservative, tradition-bound, family-run New England enterprise devoted to the distribution of petroleum products. Each company has its personality, and its executive requirements vary on a number of environmental dimensions just as an industry's does. Here are four examples of contrasting company environments:

Conscientious vs *relatively ruthless companies.* A company dominated by a hard-driving man may demand that its executives get results and will not look too closely at how they are achieved so long as the executives stay out of jail and the newspapers. In such a company the managers may get little backing from above and may have to accept being questioned at every turn by their superiors. On the other hand, the management of a conservative, employee-oriented company might be shocked to learn that one of its executives was guilty of kidney-punching to get a competitive edge for the company or of pressing his subordinates too hard.

Volume-minded vs *quality-minded companies*. King Whitney, Jr, told of a sales-minded vice-president who had built a spectacular record working for a consumer-goods company that was fighting to increase its share of the market; but this man found himself in deep trouble when he moved to a company producing a high-quality component sold to industry. To build up volume and profits he began, as he had in the past, to compromise on quality and to use more and more flamboyant marketing techniques. Finally he was dismissed, and now he is back razzle-dazzling consumers and is very happy.

Union vs *non-union companies*. The vice-president of a half-billion-dollar company explained to me that if a company is non-union it needs executives who are skilled at promoting the idea that the company is one big happy family. This is a major consideration. In such a company it is important, for example, that the Grand Old Man make frequent ceremonial appearances at the various plants. My informant said that when a company is unionized – as his now is – the approach to personnel is more matter-of-fact.

Young vs *mature companies*. As companies pass through various stages of growth, they produce environments that favour one type of executive over another. At the young-company stage, the need is more likely to be for enthusiastic, hard-driving men who can wear two hats, share a secretary, and hold conferences in a cubby-hole. As the same company matures and gets a formal table of organization, the same men who were so effective in the early stages may find their toes being lopped off for being out of line or they may become bored for lack of challenge.

Some mature and very large corporations have found it necessary to carry out dramatic shake-ups in order to loosen up the fuddy-duddy patterns that tend to develop over the years and to get fresh thinking. Westinghouse did this quite deliberately when it brought in Mark Cresap. Dr Beam said that he was currently working with a company that had become soft and unaggressive, with a country-club atmosphere, and he was proposing a vice-president who clearly would be an irritant, a foreign body. 'We are proposing him because he will stir the thing up rather than fit in.'

Within a company, different departments may offer congenial or hostile environment to a man – technical skills aside – depending upon his own psychological make-up. This shows quite clearly in the study by Dr Lewis B. Ward of Harvard on traits executives said they favoured in their own subordinates.[2] The executives were invited to check from a variety of clusters of four somewhat related adjectives – covering 112 qualities – those that they would favour in their subordinates. Here, side by side, are the traits favoured by marketing and finance executives:

Marketing	*Finance*
assured	accurate
attractive	ambitious
civilized	careful
energetic	cautious
enterprising	deliberate
entertaining	dignified
jolly	discreet
pleasant	precise
polished	systematic
popular	
sociable	
sympathetic	

It would seem that the marketing men pretty clearly want in their subordinates men with a high degree of energy and social poise, and that the finance men just as clearly want men with a high degree of orderliness and decorum.

Stanford psychologist Thomas W. Harrell has also made an extensive analysis of studies of the common personality patterns found in different functional fields.[3] He found that financial men tend to be more critical by nature and are more likely to be pessimistic than are managers in general. One of their major satisfactions in life is bringing order out of chaos. They tend to be relatively low on imagination and creativity.

Harrell reports that production managers tend to be thing-minded and number-minded and more at ease demonstrating mechanical aptitude than verbal aptitude, in which they are often weak in both comprehension and fluency. They tend to fear failure and to enjoy responsibility. A high percentage are critical and suspicious of other people.

As for sales managers, he confirms their high interest in persuasion and verbal expression (which leads to talkativeness) and their high status-consciousness. They tend to be low in theoretical interest and high in enthusiasm. Their optimism is easily fired. In fact they generally verge on the manic. Most intriguing, perhaps, he reports that the sales managers tend to be more inaccurate, more masculine, and more dominant than managers generally.

How well a man is likely to fit into a given situation comes down finally to 'body chemistry'. This is a nebulous requirement mentioned by several informants. The vice-president of a large company headquartered in New York told of his thorough, objective evaluation of his subordinates while he was looking for a man who would be elevated to a key spot. From his study, one man was the obvious choice. He had a fine record of eighteen years' service with the company. From an objective standpoint he was perfect for the job. My informant told his president of the choice. The president said, 'I'd like to take a look at him.' The prospect was presented to the president. My informant recalls:

'The guy sat down and talked himself right out of a job with the president. I think he talked too much under nervous pressure. And the president just sat there and let him talk. It was an oversell. Under normal circumstances the man wouldn't have done it. Later the president said he thought the job called for a younger man. The real reason was that the man just didn't click with him. Sometimes it seems to come right down to a choice through body chemistry.'

Some of the specialists in placing executives are coming to believe that in corporations – as in marriage – it is wise to match up complementary traits among people who must work closely with one another. (Sociologist Robert Winch of Northwestern University became an advocate of complementary matching in marriage after a depth study of several dozen recently married couples.)

The management consultant who has gone furthest in exploring the possibilities of complementary matching of executives is Dr Jerome C. Beam. The possibilities of this approach are examined in considerable detail in a forthcoming book, *The Organization Approach to Decision and Action*.[4] Dr Beam pointed out to me that while it is true that a company may want a single type of executive in terms of superficial traits – say, only Ivy Leaguers over six feet tall – there should be a complementary matching of men near the top on the basis of certain characteristics important to the company. He explained: 'I just don't believe there are characteristics that make it inevitable that a man will succeed. He is going to have to work in conjunction with other people.'

Dr Beam keeps complementary matching very much in mind when he studies candidates for an important executive opening. He pointed out six kinds of complementary matchings which improve the probability that two top-level executives will work harmoniously and effectively with each other:

1. If one man is strong, it helps if the other is supportive. The strong president tends to like to have around him men who will complement him. If they don't – and seem aggressive – he may well feel threatened or annoyed. On the other hand, if the top man is not strong in terms of self-confidence, he may well want a strong man to lean on – but a man who has enough insight to know how to handle his strength discreetly without flaunting it. Dr Beam said the strongest man will run the show whether he is president, executive vice-president, or second vice-president. He told me of one company division of 5,000 people that was being run – for all practical purposes – by a man two echelons down from the division's president, a man heading technical services. Everyone looked to him for counsel. To be a subordinate leader one must have extraordinary gifts, not least among them being tact.

2. If one executive is a man of action, it helps if the other is a man of thought. Dr Beam cited as an example a client company that had become fascinated with the idea of hiring as a vice-president an aggressive, dynamic doer who had been highly successful as a vice-president in a similar field. Dr Beam noticed in examining the set-up in which this high-powered man had been working that the president was a thoughtful reflective type who liked to be pushed. Beam suspected that the thoughtful president had greatly contributed to the action man's successful record and noticed that in the new situation the dynamic vice-president would be working with a president who was, like him, a very active type. Dr Beam warned that sparks would fly and gears might grind. The man was hired against Dr Beam's recommendation and lasted six months.

3. If one man is skilled in dealing with operations, it helps if the other is skilled in dealing with people. Dr Beam explained that when a person is excellent in making long-range, broad policy and has a sound technical background it is not uncommon for him to be weak on insight into people. He has little grasp of what motivates people and how to instil in them a desire to work towards a common goal. Such a man is greatly aided if his principal associate has these insights.

4. If one man is an excellent idea man, it helps if the other is a practical realist. A yeasty-type president who bubbles with ideas and is always seeking exciting new ventures needs someone nearby to say, 'Look, boy, this sounds great on paper, but let's look it over in detail.' Dr Beam said that if a company has for vice-president an idea man who is up on Cloud Nine, it needs a hard-boiled realist as head of the organization, or vice versa. Financial vice-presidents by nature often serve as the cautious realists. The hazard is that they may become habitual negative thinkers and handicap themselves for advancement because companies usually and ideally prefer in their presidents men who appear imaginative and bold. One problem in combining idea men with realists, Dr Beam added, is that the good idea men are much harder to find than the detail-minded realists who enjoy criticizing the ideas of others.

5. If one man is a risk-taker, it helps if the other is cautious. A capacity for risk-taking is a trait often cited as desirable for the heads of companies. What it really involves, Dr Beam points out, is 'a tolerance for ambiguity'. He contends that someone at the top should be heavy in this tolerance. Such a man is able to function in poorly defined areas and is willing to stick his neck out on the basis of inadequate facts when he knows that if he waits for all desirable data to come in he will be too late. This man with a tolerance for ambiguity can be either the president or the executive vice-president, but he needs a cautious close associate.

6. If one man is a nice guy, it helps if the other is a tough guy. Dr Beam feels that a psychologically soft person is valuable only if he is working with a hard-nosed person who can act as a kind of buffer. In any successful organization there should be someone near the top who is able, without undue squeamishness, to swing an axe and even get his hands bloody when pruning or disciplining is indicated. One might say that there should always be at least one responsible executive who knows how to execute!

Men who have come up the staff route are likely to feel more uncomfortable than the line executive when they must deal with a person in a direct, aggressive way. Strong line executives often really seem to enjoy imposing their will on others.

Some heads of companies don't mind taking this responsibility for firing or reprimanding. When discharged executives have come tumbling out of one cosmetic company (a frequent occurrence) in recent years there has been but little question that it has been the president himself who personally did all the heaving. In other companies, however, the chief executive often does not wish to appear in an unkind posture. He wants to be the father figure. At General Motors, when the amiable, folksy Charles Wilson was president, his chief aide was Mr Roger Kyes, a quiet, dour vice-president who had the reputation of being Mr Wilson's enforcer. When the cheerful, wise-cracking Mr Wilson went to Washington as Secretary of Defence he sensibly took his scowling enforcer with him into the wilds of the Pentagon.

This raises a final question about the mating of man to job: how transferable are executive skills to and from jobs outside the business world? With the growth of giant organizations – business, political, military, educational – it is certainly true that many of the skills required are the same in all four worlds. There are people and computer machines in all four that need to be handled and instructed how to run things.

Mr Wilson, many feel, was less successful on the Washington stage than he was in Detroit, perhaps because at General Motors he had to worry less about voter opinion. On the other hand, at this writing, Robert S. McNamara – who left his brief presidency at Ford to head the Defence Department – is considered one of President Kennedy's more astute appointments. Mr McNamara has said of his changing roles: 'The Ford Motor Company, the United States Government and the Catholic Church are the same in the sense that each is a vast organizational problem.' His critics say that this former controller at Ford is too statistically oriented, but when Mr McNamara was at Ford his critics probably made the same complaint.

An executive who recently made the switch in the opposite direction is retired four-star general Edwin William Rawlings. He bossed the Air Matériel Command before moving to General Mills, where he became president. It should be noted that early in his career the military sent him to the Harvard Graduate School of Business Administration. Rawlings feels 'there is a lot of comparability' in the two situations because in both one is dealing with people, materials, and products. One difference, he adds, is that in business you have to make a profit. Some of the older-style generals who have gone into business have aroused complaints that they are too hidebound about regulations or too careless about profits.

Dr Douglas McGregor of the Massachusetts Institute of Technology believes the difference in worlds is greater than many assume. He says: 'The requirements for successful political leadership are different from those for industrial management or military or education leadership. Failure is as frequent as success in transfers of leaders from one type of social institution to another.'[5] What it boils down to, evidently, is that though many of the skills required are becoming increasingly transferable, one has to work with different value systems. Furthermore, as the president of a Midwestern college pointed out to me, executives in colleges and government, which are not profit-making institutions, cannot issue orders in quite the flat fashion business managers can. They must depend more upon voluntary help and the marshalling of public support.

It becomes abundantly clear that a young man standing at the base of the pyramid contemplating the dizzy ascent must weigh and analyse many complex and often confusing factors – the kind of business, the kind of company, the men he will work with, and his own personality and talents. For a young man this is difficult, often impossible. The breed that succeeds must be able to survive false starts, changes of direction, and bruising tumbles.

CHAPTER 11

The Dilemma of Shifting Personality Requirements

Those people who are better suited for top rather than middle management may display behaviour that is inappropriate for middle management positions when they have to serve in those positions in the course of their advancement. Hence . . . they might well be found deficient. From a report on a survey of self-perception at different levels of management in *Personnel Psychology*[1]

The statement above, if taken seriously, should haunt an aspiring manager. Its authors contend that among those managers who may be judged 'deficient' by middle-management standards of evaluation are 'the very people' one might expect to be 'the ablest future leaders'.

These sombre findings are based on a study of self-perception by two psychologists at the University of California, Dr Lyman W. Porter and Dr Edwin E. Ghiselli. They asked 1,000 top-management people and 170 middle-management people to check from a long list of adjectives those words they believed did and did not apply to them.

The authors focused their attention on 'significant differentials' (more than 5 per cent) in response between the two groups. Here are the contrasting patterns found by the investigators:

Top-management people. They see themselves as capable, determined, industrious, resourceful, sharp-witted, enterprising, sincere, sociable, pleasant, dignified, sympathetic. In comparison with middle management, these top people 'perceive themselves as active, self-reliant and generally willing to take action on the basis of their own faith in themselves. . . . They are willing to take risks when they think they have good original ideas and they possess confidence that their decisions

will lead to success. . . . In their social relations they are candid and straightforward and show confidence here as well. . . .
They see themselves as able to get along well with others
without having to appear to ingratiate themselves.'

Middle-management people. Here are eleven traits that
came out as significantly different in the way the middle
managers see themselves:

> Discreet
> Practical
> Planful
> Deliberate
> Calm
> Steady
> Modest
> Patient
> Civilized
> Intelligent
> Courageous

It should be pointed out that these middle managers indicated by their checking that they did *not* see themselves as
'reckless . . . egotistical . . . disorderly . . . opinionated . . .
aggressive . . . outspoken . . . excitable . . . self-seeking . . .
shallow . . . tense.'

These middle-level people, the investigators concluded in
contrasting them with the top-level people, see themselves as
involved in

careful planning, thoughtful actions and well-controlled behaviour. . . . [They] see themselves as individuals who seldom take
rash actions that are not well thought out beforehand. . . . They
can be counted upon not to make hasty or unfounded decisions.
They seem to place more reliance on operating within the rules
and conditions of the system rather than plunging ahead on their
own ideas when they have not been previously tested. They do not
appear to be willing to take risks or to move ahead when the final
outcome is uncertain. And they do not show the same sort of confidence in their own judgement as do members of top management.

As for their personalities, the authors state of the middle
managers:

They indicate they want to avoid giving the appearance of being controversial personalities and of exhibiting self-centred behaviour. They want to do nothing that might attract unfavourable comment about their behaviour. . . . They seem to describe themselves as stable and dependable individuals who try to avoid making mistakes on the job or elsewhere.

The authors wondered whether two somewhat different kinds of people are needed at the two different levels of our corporations; and if so whether some sort of reorientation or training might not be indicated before trying to induct successful middle managers into top-level jobs. Following this line of thought brashly, one wonders whether it might not benefit the middle manager earmarked for higher things if he was instructed to start saying to himself five hundred times a day, 'I am not a beaver . . . I am a tiger.'

So far we've been talking only about self-perceptions at different management levels. What are the actual facts about a shift in traits considered important to success at the two levels?

I found a substantial body of opinion holding that a shift does occur, and it generally resembles the shift in self-perceptions noted by Porter and Ghiselli.

Everett Smith, senior partner in the nation-wide management-consulting firm of McKinsey & Co., commented: 'Many companies do not want too many mavericks, even though they may need a maverick at the top.'

Dr Chris Argyris made an interesting distinction between the two kinds of maverick in the corporate world. One is ' overwhelmed by anxiety and is fighting the world as an adolescent would. The other kind of maverick is bright and thoughtful, and he does what he does from a deep sense of commitment to the values of openness and risk-taking and experimenting.' Dr Argyris remarked that middle managers are more defensive and submissive than the men at the top, though they talk the loudest about being frustrated.

Dr Lewis B. Ward, the Harvard research professor, noticed that in one clear pattern the executives preferred 'dull', 'apathetic', and 'retiring' subordinates to 'argumentative' or 'intolerant' or 'egotistical' ones.[2] In another pattern the executives seemed to favour 'accurate', 'careful', and 'precise' subordinates to those who are 'courageous', 'tolerant', and 'capable'. Dr Ward concluded that there seemed to be an intense dislike of a possible troublemaker. In noting that there seemed to be a tendency to choose such qualities as 'systematic', 'precise', and 'careful' over such qualities as 'assured', 'capable', and 'considerate', he said the pattern of types wanted as subordinates seemed a far cry from the popular concept of 'a captain of industry'.

Dr Ward asked if a process is at work in organizations whereby they 'may come to tolerate inconspicuous weakness while getting rid of the active dissidents in their ranks'. He also asked whether the qualities sought in those entering the lower ranks of management would not make the men unfit for the top jobs.

Dr Robert McMurry was perhaps the most emphatic of all in pointing to the differences in personality patterns and preferences at different levels. He said flatly that the man who has the attributes of an entrepreneur 'is much too ornery to fit into middle management'. And he added that if you get a risk-taker in middle management his chances of moving up in an organization are very, very poor. He argues that the good president is not just a matured and seasoned version of almost any good middle-management man. The good presidents are 'birds', he claims, of markedly different feather.

Most people in management would not be so drastic as Dr McMurry in delineating the more obvious characteristics of a good middle-management type. He says such a man is 'not a very heroic figure'. The middle manager, he finds, should not be too much of an entrepreneur and should not resent taking orders. He will be sufficiently yielding to avoid conflict with his superior. . . He won't be so ambitious as to be impatient. . . . 'He will be able to tolerate a reasonable degree of regimentation. . . .' And he will accept conventional social standards off the job.

Modern business, Dr McMurry contends, has a tremendous need for people who possess the 'humdrum middle-class virtues', people who work hard, like to follow routines and even appreciate being told what to do.

Fortunately there is usually readily available a large supply of such men within companies to draw upon for middle-management openings. 'Large corporations in particular,' Dr McMurry contends, 'have a very specific attraction to those with an unusual need for security and so come to have a disproportionate share, a super-saturation, of the passive, dependent and submissive.'

On the other hand, Dr McMurry's rare bird who has the potentiality of a good chief executive works hard – but only towards his own goals. He has tremendous energy which is sharply focused. . . . He is a nonconformist, but not just for the sake of nonconformity. . . . He has imagination; he dares to take risks . . . he initiates and innovates, he plans on a large scale.[3]

Consulting psychologist James Farr of James N. Farr Associates (headquarters New York City) made this distinction between the natural-born middle man and the good top man: 'The man who reaches the top is not likely to be sheeplike; instead he asks himself, "How can I use this bunch of conformists to get to the top?"'

If this is true, how does the young man with the traits greatly esteemed in presidents manage to survive the gauntlet of middle management, where quite different traits are likely to be sought? Some take a bleak view of this contradiction. The chief of psychological consulting services for a major consulting firm mentioned that there are many very good men who can function at their best only as bosses. When I asked how such a man would get to the top in a company where men were judged heavily on their team-playing ability, he replied, 'I don't know.' Dr McMurry, as usual, was more direct. When he was asked how the natural-born tiger type gets up through middle management of a large enterprise, he replied, 'He almost never does.'

The situation, however, does not appear hopeless. Companies themselves are becoming aware of the contradiction in requirements, and some are taking steps to make sure that the promising chief executive does not become washed out – or does not become disgusted and quit – at an early stage. There appear to be a half-dozen courses open for the young man whose entrepreneurial spirit and leadership qualities mark him as an excellent top-level prospect to qualify himself if he can survive the preliminaries. He can:

1. Learn to be an actor. Some suggest that the bureaucratic phase be viewed as a role-playing challenge. The head of one psychological testing firm said that the tough entrepreneur type who finds himself in the depths of middle management needs self-discipline to save himself for when he can be permitted to use all his talents. The man who is resourceful and gets to the top, he said, is the same man who five years earlier was a nice guy in middle management, who did all the things they told him to do. This informant even argued that a perceptive firm could identify in middle management the traits such an actor had but was not then using.

How many years such an actor-manager could artificially project himself into an unnatural middle-management role without losing his sense of identity and his integrity is far from clear.

2. The would-be president can make certain that he works under men who are sure enough of themselves to take a chance on an offbeat, innovating type. Management consultant George Fry observed: 'A lot of bold innovators never do get to the top; they retire as assistant sales managers. The best way to get through middle management is to have someone higher up shoving, bringing the young fellow along.' Dr Chris Argyris likewise suggested that one way for the innovating type to succeed is to have an equally bold president, a president with a lot of sense of security, who looks on the man's traits as values.

3. The man of boldness can serve his apprenticeship for a major presidency by building a good record while heading a small company. One large company in seven now goes 'outside' to find its chief executives. Often such managements find that the man who has headed his own smaller company is a better bet than the subordinates in their own larger company

who have never been tested in the fire of full responsibility for operating results.

Dr McMurry believes that the ideal route for a company man who is an entrepreneur at heart is to get out and head his own company until he is invited back to head the big company. The fact that such departing is frequent brings this comment from Clarence B. Randall, perhaps big business' closest thing to an elder statesman: 'The brilliant executive minds and the courageous natural leaders seem to be found more often in the smaller companies than in the large. I am afraid that this is a process of natural selection. Too many men who dare, jump, and eventually a man who didn't have the courage to leave becomes president of the large institutions by seniority, simply because he was there. . . .' Quite possibly the big companies will learn to look more and more to smaller companies for the bold leaders, if their own environments do not encourage boldness in the young executive.

4. He can attract attention by achieving success in a profession valued as a source of chief executives. Dr McMurry believes that the best place to find persons with the all-important qualities of self-reliance and enterprise is in activities which demand them. He emphasizes the professions, particularly law. Other professionals who frequently are brought in for important corporate jobs are tax and finance experts, management consultants (President Mark Cresap was brought into Westinghouse), and members of independent accounting firms (President Lynn Townsend was brought into Chrysler at a high level).

5. He can start his own enterprise on the side while continuing to serve the large company. Naturally he would do this with the large company's full knowledge; and if the management of the large company is on its toes it will watch his experiment in entrepreneuring with close interest.

6. He may be able to run a 'farm' maintained by his big company as a training ground for top managers. At least one large U.S. company has taken note of the fact that many of its best executives were men who had been put in charge of isolated plants where circumstances forced them to run the

show with a minimum of directives and guidance from above. Such discoveries as this and other evidence have inspired a number of imaginative companies to maintain one or more subsidiaries mainly as proving grounds where men of promise can have relatively free rein until it is time for them to be tapped for the top. McKinsey & Company's Marvin Bower tells of one corporate president who deliberately acquires poorly managed smaller companies just to give outstanding younger men something they can chew on.

None of these alternatives for developing or finding bold leaders is a really satisfactory one. And the need for such makeshift alternatives only highlights the problem. A better solution will come only when the large companies start seriously wondering what is wrong with the constricting environment in which they force their young men to compete.

CHAPTER 12

The Search for Ideal Types

The troopers knew a sort of angry joy in belonging to him. Paul Horgan, *The Distant Trumpet*

Businessmen never tire of proclaiming or guessing at the secret characteristics of the really superior executive. A checklist prepared for the American Institute of Management sums up the situation with this statement: 'These three qualities – ABILITY, INTEGRITY, and INDUSTRY – are the essential elements for the business leader.' But two of the questions in its checklist for rating an executive's integrity might puzzle – if not startle – the lay reader. They are: 'Has he respect for the leadership of his superiors?' and 'Do his plans for the future include the company?' Only in the strange world of high-level corporate thinking would the word *integrity* be equated with submissiveness and undying allegiance!

Another list, prepared by a management-consulting firm, stresses these seven qualities as the real trick-turners: 'industriousness, perseverance, loyalty, leadership, self-reliance, stability, ability to get along with others.' This list has the virtue of being shorter than the Boy Scout laws.

Dr Frederick Gaudet has concluded after examining many lists of desirable attributes that the businessmen-authors usually want someone either 'like me' or 'like God, with a few improvements they will suggest later'. Granted that the qualities esteemed in executives vary with companies and by levels within companies, are there 'universal' characteristics that set the real prospect for high office apart from his fellow managers? Do some men, for example, have a special knack for promoting an 'angry joy', a profound awe, a deep respect among business associates – while keeping stockholders reasonably joyful?

In seeking to cut through the romanticizing peculiar to this particular subculture to discover whether there are any personal characteristics that really do produce general superiority in executive performance, we encounter immediately a number of difficulties including a general dearth of reliable knowledge. Are we looking for administrators or entrepreneurs? We'll have to finesse that question by looking for the man who could wear either hat acceptably.

Another bothersome problem is that we may isolate a trait that is clearly important in executive roles only to find that it is also important in fifty-seven other occupations as well (e.g. ambition, honesty, industry, good health). Dr Gaudet, recounting his own search among executives for identifiable characteristics, told me he read a large number of articles on what executives are supposed to have in common and 'the main thing that emerged was that they were men of great energy. The same could be said of iron workers.' (Two Princeton investigators concluded after sifting through a survey of successful executives that their top men seemed to share only these two characteristics: a dread of illness and a tendency to turn to others for help when facing complex problems!)

Another difficulty is that appearances can be deceptive. I consulted G. M. Loeb, the famous broker and investment counsellor, about the way he sizes up the calibre of a company's top management, since this is said to be a matter of great concern to investment men. One difficulty in making such an assessment, he explained, is that a management group that seems to be performing wonders may be enjoying a windfall or be 'going with the tide'. And sometimes, he added, managers who seem to be doing poorly are really putting up a magnificent but unsuccessful fight against impossible odds. He argued that there was no better railroad manager in the country than Alfred E. Perlman of the New York Central, yet the line was losing money at a time when less competent managers of railroads in more favourable territories of the U.S. were making plenty of money.

Consultant Robert McMurry, with pixyish zest, told of an executive who had built a New York manufacturing firm into a concern doing thirty million dollars' worth of business a year. Here, one might exclaim, was a real comer. Dr McMurry happened to discover, however, that the man never made a decision as president 'without getting an astrologer's decision first'. Perhaps it was the astrologer who was the real comer.

Still another difficulty worth mentioning is that a number of supposed authorities on executive behaviour have made contradictory or seemingly conflicting pronouncements on leadership qualities – or have conflicting concepts of the meaning of words used to describe widely cited traits.

One psychologist at a university in Michigan reported that the evidence is 'overwhelming' that 'self-confidence' is a characteristic of leaders of all kinds; another psychologist at the same institution reported that the leaders he studied 'were much less sure of themselves' in several respects (such as getting the job done, getting along with others, and in their own self-evaluations) than were the non-leaders studied.

The contradictions become most bewildering in the pronouncements about the kinds of early background that are most favourable for executive success. A business journal reported that nearly half of the top executives it surveyed were the sons of business executives of one sort or another. Yet the same journal subsequently carried a report on top executives in the auto industry which stated: 'They come almost entirely from poor families.' Since the samples were different, this is not contradictory, but it illustrates the hazards of generalizing in this area.

One psychologist told me that executives tend to come from upper-middle-class families and explained that such people 'have a different conception of society than people of lower status groups who see organizations at a distance as remote, impersonal, and useful only for the services they produce.' A few days later the president of a seven-hundred-million-dollar corporation explained to me that the number one reason for his success was that he was 'born poor', the son of a carpenter. He was raised in a family in which there was a great deal of talk about the need for the children to get ahead. Perhaps he was an exception.

Consider another question about background. Is it favourable or unfavourable to executive success to be raised in an unhappy family? Here again you can take your choice. The psychological director of a large management-consulting firm announced after making a survey 'in depth' of executive backgrounds: 'The emerging executive is a product of a happy home and family life.' But a Yale psychologist cites a number of studies showing that a distinctly unhappy childhood – produced by such feelings as being dominated or rejected by parents or being less favoured than other siblings – is more characteristic of people who develop high aspirations and high mobility drives than of those who do not. Presumably the upward drive can be generated by an intense desire to escape the family influence. A staff man at a famous business school recalls: 'We've seen men who ran away from home when they were twelve years old who have become extremely successful.'

One leading recruiter of executives said he worries when he encounters 'a fresh young guy' who obviously has not been reared by a strong father. Theoretically the strong father would have sat on him when he was fresh. Other experts argue the opposite: that father domination tends to reduce the possibility that a man will develop a real entrepreneurial spirit. (But perhaps a 'strong' father has a different impact than a 'dominant' father does.)

There does seem to be substantial agreement that for most executives it is helpful to have broken one's dependency ties with parents, particularly with one's mother, at a reasonably early age. Also there seems to be a consensus that the would-be manager should as a young man be positively oriented towards his father – or towards father substitutes – so that he can easily relate to father figures above him in the business world.

Perhaps the answer involves deciding what kind of executive you want. Dr McMurry mentioned that in looking for good top-level executives he agrees that a man should be free of dependency so that he can make decisions in the upper echelons. Then he added: 'But for a lot of jobs you want dependent people.'

And now we come to a final puzzle: how much do personal characteristics really count in the effective performance of an executive on the job? Are they more or less important than acquired skills and technical proficiency and an intimate understanding of the intricacies of one's job?

One gains the impression from the immense emphasis placed upon proper technical training by company recruiters sizing up college graduates that knowledge is paramount. If you talk with the heads of small or family-controlled companies you find the same strong emphasis upon technical know-how. They often exhibit feelings of inadequacy or desire for more education in the technological or financial problems that beset them. When the Young Presidents' Organization polled its members on educational needs that greatly concerned them, the compilation of responses indicated an overwhelming desire among this group for more opportunities to gain practical business know-how and technology. The heads of such companies often must wear many hats.

A dramatic shift in emphasis seems to occur, however, among the medium-sized and larger corporations. The higher one goes in such organizations, the more the emphasis is on personal characteristics and people-handling skills and the less on technical know-how. Oil-company executive Albert Nickerson has reported that a survey of seventy-six corporations revealed that lack of specific skills accounted for only a shade over 10 per cent of executive discharges, while character traits accounted for virtually 90 per cent.

When Frederick Gaudet and A. R. Carli asked 177 top executives which was the greater cause of executive failure – personality factors or knowledge lack – the respondents stated that personality factors were the more important by a ratio of eleven to one!

Gaudet and Carli asked these top executives to check from a list of eighteen possibilities the main reasons why some specific executive they had appointed had proved a disappointment.[1] The five most frequently cited reasons were, in order: 'Inability to delegate responsibility. . . . Lack of breadth of knowledge [over-specialization]. . . . Inability to analyse and evaluate. . . . Inability to judge people. . . . Inability to cooperate with others.' Gaudet and Carli correlated the responses with the size of the company from which the responding executives came. They concluded that as the size of the company increased there appeared to be a clear trend away from lack of knowledge and towards mentioning weakness in the personality area.

Two leading recruiters I consulted volunteered the opinion that knowledge was at best only 10 per cent of the executive's job.

A number of convictions about the principal functions of the new high-level executive seem to lie behind such apparently sweeping statements. There is a feeling that many of the toughest problems an executive now has to solve are 'people problems', and that a good executive does not need to understand the mechanics of data processing in order to make use of its results any more than he needs to understand how the automatic transmission of his limousine works in order to enjoy its smooth performance. All he needs to know is how to find and communicate with the best specialist on the technical problems involved. This, of course, tends to leave him without intimate first-hand knowledge of what's going on in his company.

Du Pont's Crawford Greenewalt confesses that even though he came up through chemical engineering he is now so out of touch with that fast-changing field he can't talk on equal terms with many of the young men in his old department.

There is also – and perhaps most important – an often-voiced feeling that a good high-level executive can now take his talents from one industry to another – so that his most useful knowledge is not specific to an industry. This transferral of talent is hardest for a production man. But many marketing men nod knowingly when they read the comment of Granger, a fictional vice-president in J. Harvey Howells' *The Big Company*

Look: 'This is my fourth company. It's all marketing, whether you're pushing drugs, groceries or roofing material.' And many financial men will nod in agreement at the statement of William Wood Prince, the chairman of Armour & Co., that 'business is not beef, tin, or Coca-Cola; it's dollars. . . . The patterns of business are the same whether it's oil, steel, or meat.'[2]

As one comes nearer the top, specialized knowledge is not only less useful but may even label one as 'parochial'. Near the top the management talents required become more and more alike from industry to industry. More important than special knowledge is the felt need today for men who can grasp the whole situation, men who can coordinate, who can seize opportunities, who can get results from other people.

The recent rush of companies to diversify has tended to emphasize the downgrading of special knowledge and the upgrading of pure managerial talent at top management levels. Companies are finding themselves in so many unrelated product fields that no one man is likely to understand the technical aspects involved in the production and distribution of each product or service.

This point came to me with particular force while talking with an administrative vice-president of a multibillion-dollar financial company. I first knew him when he worked for a large management-consulting firm. In the early fifties he left to become a staff vice-president of a consumer-products company. That I could understand. But a few years later he was hired away to become executive vice-president of a producers' goods company. This was puzzling. And my puzzlement became amazement when subsequently he was invited to come to the financial company, whose primary product is money. I invited him to explain how he could function effectively in three such completely unrelated fields. He explained:

'You miss the main point. I moved from a *diversified* consumer-products company to a *diversified* producers' goods company to a *diversified* financial company.'

Presumably his apprenticeship at the management-consulting firm had helped him understand – from contact with many kinds of company – the essentials of good management regardless of the field. In any case, he said, 'The need for specialized knowledge is greatly overrated.'

Some are surmising that in the future an important executive duty will be to manage and take care of decision-making networks, with less emphasis upon decision-making itself.

If personal characteristics and executive skills are believed to be of paramount importance, just what are these characteristics and skills? In recent years many investigators have sought the answer. Several companies such as General Electric, American Telephone and Telegraph, and Standard Oil (N.J.) have been studying the personality characteristics of executives. And a number of behavioural scientists at universities and testing services have tried to understand the anatomy of leadership.

Some investigators have concluded that each specific situation so dominates the requirements that there is little hope of arriving at an unassailable list of 'universals'.

The Personnel Research Board at Ohio State University, after spending nearly a million dollars trying to understand the role of the executive, prefers simply to describe the various types of leader (bureaucrat, autocrat, diplomat, expert, and quarterback) and to dissect the executive function down to the fourteen tasks an executive is likely to need to perform competently. (He plans, evaluates, negotiates, schedules, co-ordinates, interprets, inspects, personnelizes, expertises, publicizes; he maps procedures, he supervises investigations, he supervises technical areas, he offers professional advice.)[3]

There have been, however, a number of noteworthy observations and more specific findings about personal characteristics common to the executives observed. Professor William Gormbley, director of Harvard's Advanced Management Programme, described the executives sent by their companies to that programme by setting down these six impressions of them:

1. They are bright men.
2. They know how to get along well with people.

3. They have all got drive.
4. They are men who have goals.
5. They make the most of what they get.
6. They are not content to sit still.

Researchers for Booz, Allen & Hamilton made an analysis of substantially identical appraisal forms filled out on 1,427 executives to see if there were any 'universal' characteristics that distinguished the men judged 'promotable' from those not recommended for promotion. They felt that they found eight 'executive characteristics' that universally – at all levels of management – seemed to distinguish the promotable from the non-promotable.[4] Those eight, in order of their power to discriminate, were:

1. *Position performance* (How well the man is doing in his present job.)
2. *Drive* (Works with energy. Not easily discouraged. Basic urge to get things done.)
3. *Intellectual ability* (Analysis, judgement, problem-solving, etc.)
4. *Leadership* (Receives loyalty and cooperation from others. Manages and motivates others to full effectiveness.)
5. *Administration* (Organizing work, delegation, follow-up, control.)
6. *Initiative* (A self-starter. Sees new opportunities.)
7. *Motivation* (Realistically ambitious, with well-planned goals.)
8. *Creativeness* (Original ideas, an inquiring mind. Fresh approaches to problems.)

A word of caution: the fact that the traits cited were considered to be significantly present in men judged promotable doesn't necessarily mean that the men were, in fact, the best prospects. Also there may well be a tendency for superiors to attribute high-sounding traits to men they intend to promote anyway.

A number of firms have extra-special checklists for appraising prospective men for the *very top*: the presidents and chairmen. Such lists, I gather, have become much-bootlegged items among would-be presidents, who take them up beside their shaving mirrors. An examination of such a list reveals that certain often-cited characteristics (e.g., judgement, intelligence, ability to communicate), though desirable, are not considered as crucial as certain others. Among qualities singled out for special stress in appraising man for the helm are:

1. Is he a vigorous, vital, enthusiastic person?
2. Can he bide his time patiently?
3. Can he act decisively?
4. Has he shown a good capacity to handle authority relationships, both upward and downward?
5. Is he capable of taking the long view of the company's future?
6. Is he the kind that makes things happen?
7. Does he take a responsible attitude towards the company treasury?

Chris Argyris became suspicious of many of the usual prescriptions for executive success. He found that when he asked presidents to confide their secrets of success he would get back the Boy Scout laws, plus the virtues of hard work. He began going back to the presidents and asking: 'If you were to leave this company, whom would you name to succeed you and why?' Now he began getting quite a different set of abilities cited as important to success. This inspired Dr Argyris to re-examine his notes of talks with executives from many companies. Afterwards he drew up what he felt was a realistic catalogue of some important characteristics of successful executives. Here are the first seven:

1. The successful executive exhibits high tolerance for frustration. He doesn't blow up when provoked.
2. He encourages full participation. He can permit others to discuss and pull apart his decisions without feeling his personal worth is being threatened.

3. He continually questions himself. He is willing to examine himself carefully and ask himself embarrassing questions. At the same time he has a high degree of self-respect.
4. He understands the rules of competitive warfare. (Dr Argyris cites one executive who explained, 'It's not a dog-eat-dog world, but I do get nibbled at.') The good executive is able to play it cool, in the British manner, and he doesn't feel distressed if a colleague shows a little 'fight'.
5. He expresses hostility tactfully. (Dr Argyris explained to me: 'This executive has a real skill for telling the other man to drop dead without batting an eyelash.')
6. He accepts both victories and setbacks with controlled emotions. (Such a man, says Dr Argyris, 'withholds and hides his own feelings of either pleasure or pain. . . .')
7. He can snap out of defeats without feeling personally shattered and can quickly start thinking of the next goal.

Some investigators seeking ways to spot the executive of promise have extended their search back to the time men are appraised as college graduates. They reason that if you could spot at the outset the real comers, a great deal of time and effort could be saved. In view of the lack of agreement on the valuable characteristics that executives already in harness have in common, the difficulty in achieving a reliable 'early identification' of comers becomes manifest.

The American Telephone and Telegraph Company has turned over to a foundation information assembled on a number of college graduates hired, but careful analysis of the data in relationship to the men's subsequent careers will not be available until later in the decade. Social scientists at Standard Oil of New Jersey have spent six years studying the problem of the 'Early Identification of Management Potential' (E.I.M.P.). They gathered information on 443 managers – supervisors to board chairmen – who volunteered with the assurance that the information would not be used 'for administrative purposes'. The investigators are now confident that they have developed tools that can greatly improve the company's chances in identifying men of promise – even though the prospects may vary in personal characteristics – and some of the tools can be used when the man is first hired. Of the many predicting tools tested, the best, they have concluded, are the Individual Background Survey and a specially designed 'Management Judgement Test' which includes problems the company's managers face in their work.

Some may wonder about the reliability of projecting for younger men any analyses of the personality dynamics of mature men who have been through the mill of success. One might suspect that the process of success itself has produced distinguishing characteristics. Tools that simply record objective information about the men's background are another matter.

For approximately a decade, a Selection Study Staff at the Harvard Graduate School of Business Administration has been following the progress of a random sampling of 150 of its graduates in the hope of finding some clues to identify the men of promise. These 150 men were the object, as graduate students, of testing and of psychiatric, sociological, and psychological studies. Dr Ward, Professor of Business Research, reports the study thus far has not been too encouraging to those hoping to make an accurate forecast of a man's future in the business world.

The use of a random sampling of students may have increased the difficulty of finding common denominators of success. The success of a few students will be assured, regardless of capacity, simply because the Old Man controls the company they will join; for a few others failure is likely simply because they would be in some other field if the Old Man wasn't hoping so much that his son would follow in his steps.

At any rate, Dr Ward states: 'My own general conclusions are that opportunities and situations are so important in careers that any attempt to forecast at the upper level who is going to get the furthest is very difficult. On the other hand, we can foresee those who are likely to get into trouble and it really doesn't make too much difference where they go.' He added that many of those destined for trouble are highly intelligent. Their dim prospects stem from the fact that they may have traumatic backgrounds. They have still unresolved personal problems which may inhibit their capacity for growth under stress. The Study Staff noted three broad patterns in the young men under study that seemed to have a bearing on their capacity for growth, and men with the Number III pattern have been found beyond much question to have the poorer prospects. The three patterns:

I. Self-confident, based on well-integrated personal experiences.

II. Confident, but based on accepted codes of behaviour without awareness of one's own feelings or the feelings of others (and work best within accepted codes).

III. Lacking confidence born of either personal experiences or accepted codes. This lack of confidence may come from the fact that they were sheltered too much by others or by themselves from experience; or it may come from the fact that they have withdrawn from experience as a result of scares.

The Study Staff at a midpoint in its investigation developed a concept of man's development that included this statement: 'The development of administrative capacity is impeded by: inadequate available energy; constitutional hyperirritability; poor early habit and attitude development, resulting in feelings of anxiety, insecurity, dependency and inadequacy; rigid emotional conditioning; inadequate intellectual endowment; and inadequate emotional outlets.'

The large testing, consulting, and recruiting firm of Richardson, Bellows, Henry & Co. has taken a different approach in its broad cross-industry study of the challenge of early identification – and has been particularly impressed by six factors which it finds help identify the man of promise.

The R.B.H. investigators have collated information on intelligence, background, and personality factors for approximately 2,000 executives in a number of companies, including Standard Oil of New Jersey (R.B.H. served as a consultant to Standard in its study of 'Early Identification of Management Potential'). The six factors that have most impressed R.B.H.

officials as indicators of future executive success are these:

1. The man matured early. During his teens this man of promise was encouraged by his parents to make his own final decisions about attending religious services and about the courses he would take in school and how he would decorate his room and whether he would drink or smoke or date.

C. P. Sparks, vice-president at R.B.H., explained: 'There is usually all kinds of evidence of independence at a relatively early age. The young man not only does things earlier than his compatriots but he is also nominated and elected by others. On application blanks we see that the man of promise has been captain of his team or an officer of his class.' Mr Sparks emphasized that this early leadership is often not necessarily apparent in formal school activity but the young man may have been an officer of his hot-rod club or secretary of his bowling league.

2. The man of promise rates higher in practical intelligence than most of the people he will ever manage. Practical intelligence is not just I.Q. It also encompasses judgement and breadth of information. R.B.H. found in an analysis of the practical intelligence scores of 2,589 people working for client companies that the managers and executives had an average score (not I.Q.) of 84, the supervisors and foreman averaged 78, and the mechanics and operators averaged 74.

3. He is self-confident but not aggressively so. Such a man is sure he can deliver in the clinch and readily assumes responsibility.

4. He demonstrates fairly early in life that he has broad interests and knowledge and a considerable curiosity about many things going on in the world.

5. He shows fairly early in his experience as a manager that he is developing more than his share of first-rate people. He becomes known as a man-maker, and there is a higher-than-average demand for the men who have been trained by him.

6. He is willing to admit his problems and mistakes. Such a man is not afraid to say 'I don't know.' It is felt that only the emotionally secure person can admit failure.

Most of these factors can be observed by a perceptive

person or can be determined from a background survey of the man's life.

Observers have often speculated about the earliest age at which the natural-born executive can be identified with some confidence. One informant insisted you can spot him in kindergarten – the lad whose hand shoots up first when the teacher asks for volunteers to distribute the milk.

A round-table discussion on spotting executive potential held at Columbia's Graduate School of Business, however, found the experts revealing widely different opinions about the age executive potential can be spotted with any assurance. One panellist thought it could be done by the fifth grade, when it can be noted that other boys seem to hang around one boy and follow his leadership. A psychiatrist on the panel took sharp exception. He said that the onset of adolescence can have a tremendous impact in altering personality in unpredictable ways. Still another panellist insisted that very little predicting could be done with any assurance before a man was twenty-six. Only then, he said, can you surmise whether potential will be translated into action. And a fourth simply offered the observation that little can be surmised about a man until he has been under fire and has proved that he can take it. Reservations were expressed about the practice of singling out a fair-haired group of trainees not only because of the difficulty of identifying the men of high potential but also because it can hurt the morale of others to know that such a group exists.

Some investigators, incidentally, have concluded that early experiences in losing out on something badly wanted can prove a more powerful propellant in pushing a man towards the top in later endeavours than can early success.

CHAPTER 13

Seven Abilities That Seem to Count Greatly

To be a success in industry . . . takes a damn lot of energy. Who is going to put it out? It is the guy who when he isn't striving gets tense or anxious. Dr James N. Farr, psychological consultant to management

Although there is no agreement on the exact personal characteristics that assure success in the modern corporation, there are some areas of consensus in the findings and observations of knowledgeable people.

This chapter will therefore synthesize and explore in some detail what seem to be seven major areas of consensus on the personal characteristics of the effective and successful executive. We must begin by taking for granted that the person in question is reasonably dedicated, loyal, presentable, politically adroit, 'fits in', and is agreeably situated in terms of his ability and personality.

This brief list is obviously not a guaranteed recipe for success. If an ambitious young manager wishes to tuck it under his pillow for a nightly reminder, however, I am sure that it will not do him any harm.

1. *The ability to maintain a high level of thrust.* This is quite probably the number one secret of executive success. It shows up in some form on fifteen of the sixteen knowledgeable lists I analysed and was emphasized repeatedly in discussions. It was mentioned by every single one of six leading executive recruiters who listed for me traits they considered to be especially important in executives.

Most executives of promise have a built-in go-go-go. They have energy to burn. An official of the American Management Association commented of the successful executives he sees: 'They drive, drive, drive all the time.'

The three Harvard staff men studying executives in action observed: 'If any one element is common to all businessmen from the outset of their careers, it is simply "drive" . . .' College recruiters for Procter & Gamble reportedly want to see evidence of energy in men they recommend for hiring. Lyle Spencer, who made a study of the members of the Young Presidents' Organization and who heads Science Research Associates (headquarters Chicago), which has tested many thousands of businessmen, has concluded that high-energy output – or *drive* – is the single most obvious characteristic that most successful businessmen share. He says energy seems to urge from them. Most are on the go mentally or physically during all of their waking hours.

I noticed while attending their convention in Oklahoma that the Y.P.O. men exploded with energy even when at play. They danced vigorously until the early morning hours, and yet all were up by seven-thirty, ready to plunge into the new day.

The men with high drive need not be table pounders. Often they are able to maintain a calm, controlled manner. But the drive is there. Nor do the men with high drive need to be robust. The drive may be largely psychic in origin. Recruiter John Handy recalls that the late Robert Young, the railroad tycoon, was so fragile physically that 'to see him eat a meal you would wonder if he would drop over before he was finished. He had terrific nervous and mental energy. Also he had the combative instinct of the small man who is compensating.'

Dr James Farr was one of a number of consulting psychologists who indicated that they like to see some evidence of underlying anxiety in an executive under appraisal. He explained: 'An organism without need does not act. Motivation springs out of human need. . . . The need to prove something is a driving force. It is driving force – born out of anxiety – that makes a top-notch executive.' He added that 'this is not necessarily an unhealthy anxiety', and that one can be too 'well adjusted' in terms of common concepts of the normal. 'If you were entirely normal,' he said, 'you would really be a cow.'

Whatever their source of energy, consider these random examples of three men with conspicuously high thrust:

Jim Price, who built National Homes up from an operation in a shed to a nation-wide empire, is easy-going and soft-spoken yet I found he was usually throwing himself into some chore even when he was supposedly relaxing at his lakeside retreat. His associates said that during his lean years he seemed to go at a trot eighteen hours a day. And an old neighbour recalled that as a farm boy Jim would be out working even in the rain.

A critic reviewing a biography of Albert D. Lasker, early leader of the advertising industry, commented, 'One is repeatedly struck by the demonic energy of Lasker. . . .'

Non-business executives, too, are often credited with considerable drive. James Reston of *The New York Times* told of a day in the life of President John Kennedy. The President's schedule of handing down momentous decisions, conferring, and making public appearances seemed staggering. Reston observed: 'The man is a calculating machine, with springs. He seems wound up and full of controlled nervous energy.'

How much of this 'drive' of most successful executives is simply impressive to behold and how much is it a significant factor in their success? There seems little doubt that drive contributes importantly. For one thing, they stand out simply because they get more done than the man with low drive. Drive also contributes to dominance, which causes others to accept their authority. And drive contributes to persistence and tenacity, both often cited as important to executives. John Handy suggests that drive consists of three qualities. One is initiative – getting things off the ground. The second is carrying through even though there is a lot of discouragement. The third – and this is the biggest – is wrapping it up. Some people fail at the wrapping-up point.

Professor Edward C. Bursk, editor of the *Harvard Business Review*, suggests that a company president has to have drive 'to give direction and push to an organization.' Drive also makes a man action-oriented, and this apparently is an important attribute for an executive. Dr Harry Levinson, director of the Division of Industrial Mental Health at the Menninger Foundation, pointed out this interesting distinction:

Executives as a group tend more to be people who move towards action. You can't be an executive unless you act on something – move towards it – even if it is a stressful situation. Take the ordinary problems such as a community school board faces. The executive always wants to act on them. A scientist might act on them in his head, and the reporter might find satisfaction in reporting on the problems in an objective way, but the executive has to act on the situations himself.

Finally, 'drive' is considered important because it makes a person restless to change things, to innovate. Whether true or not, managements feel that the only way to run a business is to keep moving. Some industrial psychologists even argue that a well-adjusted man is a bad bet simply because he will not be driven by this restless discontent. The fictional president Lincoln Lord created by Cameron Hawley was described in these words: 'Over the years his mind had been conditioned to the belief that constant change was the demanded measure of accomplishment. He had trained himself into a state of perpetual dissatisfaction. . . .'

At times this restlessness to act for the sake of acting drives executives into action difficult to defend on rational grounds. Dr Sidney Levy, psychological director of Social Research, Inc. (headquarters Chicago), commented that executives exemplify the broad American value of always wanting to surpass some result by such and such a percentage of the gross national product. No one, he said, questions whether or not the quantity is desirable.

2. *The ability to be deft in handling people.* This ability, too, shows up on virtually every list, though under a host of headings. It encompasses some skills that people generally admire, some that people generally deplore (if they recognize them).

This importance of people-handling should not be surprising since top-level executives spend nearly three quarters of their office time talking face to face with people. A manager, it is said, is one who gets things done through people.

Presidents tend to oversimplify definition of this skill by calling it 'getting along with people'. Lyle Spencer found that the young presidents of Y.P.O. listed 'getting along with people' in first position among the personality traits they felt were important to their success. The American Management Association's study of 335 presidents concluded that the young man hoping to become a president should give very high priority to mastering the technique of getting along with others.

'Getting along' *is* important: the good executive is likely to be people-minded, to 'enjoy working with people', and to have a knack for being liked. The executive who is deft in his interpersonal relations, however, is a good deal more than likeable. He is better than average at sizing up people, at inspiring loyalty in subordinates, at delegating work easily without seeming to be unloading it from his own shoulders. He is wise enough not to bawl out a subordinate publicly (unless deliberately). His approach in reprimanding will be to do it quietly and informally with a pat on the back at the end. Thus he has good back-up men below him who can competently fill his job as soon as management begins thinking of him as a possibility for higher responsibility. Without such back-up men pushing him upwards he might be passed over as indispensable where he is.

The executive who is deft in handling people also is likely – on the darker side – to be quick to perceive the psychological needs of subordinates, associates, and superiors, and to satisfy, or play upon, those needs – perhaps by personality manipulation – as his own interests dictate. He keeps rivals off balance, subordinates uncertain, superiors whom he hopes to outflank unwary. He is much too wise to permit feelings of resentment of authority to colour his behaviour.

Nor is our deft people-handler squeamish when he feels he must get rid of a team player. Robert McMurry has admonished executives, 'Be ruthless when necessary.' And Frederick Gaudet in a questionnaire he prepared for executives asked, as one test of how they could perform as executives, if they would be willing to fire a friend if the friend's work was sub-standard. Author-businessman C. Northcote Parkinson suggests (amiably) that the 'surgical touch' is the main thing that distinguishes a good number-one man from a good number-two man in a company.

One of the crucial questions he asks a would-be number-one man is: 'Are you prepared to fire Joe Wittering?' Joe is the well-liked kindly old muddler 'with a popular wife and five children at school.' A really good number one, Mr Parkinson said, will fire Joe not only gently but firmly. He will thereafter 'go home and sleep soundly, not having given the matter another thought.'[1]

At any rate, the deft people-handler strives to keep from becoming emotionally involved with people in his area of influence and tends to keep real friendships on the job to a minimum. He also has some of Franklin D. Roosevelt's famous talent for persuading all squabbling factions that he is their sympathizer. In an intra-office dispute he seeks to blur differences, at least as far as he is concerned. His formula, stated in lighthearted fashion by sales consultant James Mills, president of Home Facts, Inc. (headquarters New Canaan, Connecticut), is likely to be: 'Some of my friends are for this, and some of them are against it. I'm for my friends.'

3. *The ability to marshal a competent mind against the problems peculiar to executives.* Nearly two thirds of all the sixteen lists of characteristics important to executives have an item on mental equipment.

The competent mind I refer to here, I should stress, is not necessarily the very bright mind that rings up a high I.Q. on those twelve-minute pencil-and-paper tests so dear to the psychological testers. Dr McMurry relates that of two of the most amazing scores reported on a famous short-pencil-and-paper test of I.Q. one was made by a man who was unstable and the other by 'a pure nut'. He added: 'Many people are overimpressed by I.Q. as measured by tests. This is a great fallacy. There is no correlation between intelligence and judgement. A man can be awfully smart and be a screwball of the first order. We can go into a mental hospital anywhere and come out with some terrific scores. But these high scorers have to be kept under glass because of their zero judgement.' Judgement is a much more elusive quality than I.Q. to try to measure on a simple test.

Dr Lewis B. Ward of Harvard feels that companies hiring college graduates have been putting too much emphasis on high I.Q.s and high grades. He feels that for most managerial jobs a person should be 'reasonably intelligent'. The *Fortune* survey of 1,700 top executives revealed that though they did somewhat better in college than the average of all male graduates, only one in twenty made the dean's list, graduated *cum laude*, *magna cum laude*, *summa cum laude*, or was valedictorian.

Frederick Gaudet relates that he instructed a staff man at Stevens' Psychological Laboratory to evaluate the intelligence of all managers of a company seeking counsel. The staff man soon came back with the startling information that the president himself had scored 103 in I.Q. (too low to get into most colleges). It turned out the president, though modest in I.Q., was canny about keeping important customers contented and in maintaining a magnificent personal veneer. Further, and probably most important, he had a vice-president with an I.Q. of 165 to backstop him!

Most heads of businesses, according to Lyle Spencer of S.R.A., have an I.Q. of about 120, which is well above average but not a 'leaping mind'. (Top-flight engineers and scientists for example, average around 135.) Psychologist Edwin Ghiselli of the University of California has reported finding relatively little difference in intelligence scores between top and middle management. A number of investigations report that too much mental candle power can complicate the career of an inspiring executive. If he doesn't allow for it he may have difficulty communicating across the mental gap separating himself from his associates, subordinates, and customers.

Dr Jerome Beam believes that average intelligence increases with job level until you reach the level of the department manager but beyond that it begins levelling off, 'so that the average president is not a whole lot smarter than the average department manager.' Others have found that presidents often are less bright in terms of I.Q. than the subordinates who head their research departments.

Some departments within companies tend to attract men with higher I.Q.s than others. Robert F. Moore, senior vice-president of Richardson, Bellows, Henry & Co., reveals that department managers tend to fall within the following top percentages of the total U.S. population on I.Q. tests:

Managers in manufacturing	in top 15%
Managers in personnel	in top 15%
Marketing managers	in top 8%
Finance managers	in top 5%
Research and development managers	in top 2%

Presidents, he said, also tend to fall within the top 2 per cent except in some cases where they inherited the job in a family-controlled business.

With a growth of technological complexity and world-wide markets, however, we may be seeing a growing emphasis on qualities of mind, and it seems certain that in the coming years we will see an intensified need for men who have outstanding minds at the tops of large companies.

What, then, do I mean by saying an executive needs 'the ability to marshal a competent mind against the problems peculiar to executives'?

He needs especially to be able to immerse all his thoughts in an analysis of whatever problem is at hand, to get to the heart of each matter, and to conceptualize alternative solutions. Dr Charles D. Flory of Rohrer, Hibler & Replogle put it this way: 'The good executive doesn't get lost in detail. He is a man of action, not research. He cuts through a mass of detail and comes to the central facts in order to give someone else a sense of direction.'

The good executive also is likely to have an orderly mind. He needs to be able to bring order out of near-chaos, to organize what psychologists call 'unstructured situations.' He needs to have patience for pulling loose ends into place.

Michigan State's Professor Jennings believes that the modern fast-rising executive is likely to be strong in a very special kind of mental ability that he calls 'maze-brightness'. The maze-bright man knows his way in organizational structures. He quickly perceives passages that lead nowhere and learns how to avoid the dead ends. He knows how to adjust quickly to strange terrain, and how to get things done through, and around, channels. In short, he is at home in a multi-layer hierarchy. The growing complexity of modern corporate structures, Dr Jennings feels, is tending to make this a crucial skill for the man who wants to advance. He adds that present intelligence tests do not measure maze-brightness, and he is inclined to doubt that a pencil-and-paper test can ever be devised that will measure it satisfactorily. A man called 'Larson', the fast-rising young manager of a big company described by investigators at Carnegie Tech's Graduate School of Industrial Administration, seemed to possess this maze-brightness to a high degree. The investigators commented: 'One of the striking things about Larson is his continued sensitivity to the organization environment in which he works.'[2]

The aspiring executive is also helped if he has a symphony-conductor's capacity to create what Crawford Greenewalt calls 'a harmonious whole' out of many different skills and functions.

A man who hopes to rise in responsibility needs, above all, *judgement* – and nobody finds it easy to define this word exactly. It appears to mean the application of several of the skills of mind mentioned above – particularly analysis, assessment, and integration – to come up with an answer or mode of behaviour that is right. If you come up with a wrong response your judgement is wrong, no matter how much thought went into it or how appropriate your course of action seemed at the time.

As a matter of actual fact, of course, even the best executives are faulted on judgement too often for comfort. General Dynamics lost hundreds of millions of dollars in the long-range jet-transport field largely because of what was later called 'fantastic underestimating of costs' and 'gross miscalculation of the market'.

The good executive tries to keep his dubious judgements to a reasonable minimum and to be right oftener than not. At the same time, he is helped by an ability to make judgements on the basis of lamentably insufficient hard facts, and to work through people he barely knows. Who could know *for sure* how the public was going to respond to colour television, or jet flying, or electric can openers or dehydrated soup? Every chief executive must often take calculated gambles. The president of an Oklahoma metal products company told me: 'You can't think too long about a problem and still do anything about it.'

This need to be able to proceed with assurance in situations where, often, there are few hard facts raises a provocative question. Is the ability to proceed on a campaign in some ignorance an overlooked but very real asset in executives? John Hite, director of the Institute of Management, Johnson & Johnson, believes it is. He advises: 'No matter how intelligent or able a manager is, one day his responsibility will exceed his knowledge. In fact this is *the* problem of modern management, and it is an emotional one. Most men cannot bear to be responsible for that which they do not know. Yet they cannot take high positions in management unless they can accept such responsibility without paying for it in ulcers or nervous breakdowns.'

Mr Hite made this point to explain why salesmen and merchandising people often make good top executives. He said: 'They are used to being unembarrassed in the face of their own ignorance.' Many accountants, engineers, and scientists, he said, can't stand the thought of proceeding in such a fashion. Mr Hite's line of logic led him to this interesting if indelicate thought for the day: 'One must be a bit half-assed to be a good manager.'

4. *The ability to communicate – and perhaps originate – ideas.* With managers spending more and more of their time in committee meetings, conferences, conventions, and community affairs (as corporate ambassadors), the demand for good

communicators at higher levels has grown. This ability received attention on seven of the lists, including a majority of the lists offered by executive recruiters.

Executives lament that they seem to be selling ideas all day long. A former auto executive told Eric Larrabee what it's like: 'All they do is sell to each other. You never saw such a place for conferences. They spend all morning at it, they go upstairs to lunch together and they are back at it all afternoon, making presentations to each other.' And then, chances are, many of these men will end the day dictating memos – preferably confined to one page – advising their bosses with precision just how things stand.

A number of executive recruiters stressed the fact that the ability to express oneself well – orally and in writing – is tremendously important for the top fellows. Recruiter Ashton Dunn said this ability to express yourself well is so important that he is wary of a candidate who seems unable to explain in clear, interesting fashion what he has been doing at his present job. Dunn said he is always suspicious if it is hard to pull out the man's story. He said he had the most trouble with engineers 'unless they are administrative engineers.'

As corporations increase their number of hierarchic layers the difficulties of communicating with anyone more than two layers away become especially formidable. Written thoughts that go through channels tend to get garbled, both intentionally and unintentionally. A report in *Nation's Business* stated that the higher the executive stands in the organization the more his world is one of words. He is walled off from reality by symbolic representations and abstractions.

Words then become tools of the first importance for the rising executive. And the good executives appear to be well equipped. Johnson O'Connor, whose engineering laboratories across the country have been testing the aptitudes of tens of thousands of people, told me: 'The most important executive characteristic of which we are certain and which we can measure accurately is a large and exact English vocabulary.'

He said that top executives score even higher than college professors and lawyers on word meanings. Further, he has pointed out, the higher up the man, the better his vocabulary is likely to be. In a survey of supervisory personnel in thirty-nine plants presidents and vice-presidents scored 236 (out of a possible 272) on the vocabulary test; managers averaged 168, superintendents 114, floor bosses 86.

Mr O'Connor tells of a study made of a group of college seniors who were about to go into corporations as managerial trainees. He says that every man who scored in the top quarter in vocabulary, while still in college, became an executive within five years. Not one in the bottom quarter on vocabulary became an executive.

Executives rarely use most of the words they know, such as *animadversion* or *adumbration* (unless they are dictating and in a pompous mood). Still, O'Connor says, the words apparently serve in the background as tools of thought and the man who knows these unusual words thinks more correctly at ordinary levels.

The awareness of the importance of communicating accounts for the current fascination among executives with books on lucid writing techniques, courses in public speaking, and visual aids. The quip at Y.P.O. headquarters is that every time two young Y.P.O.ers get together you'll find at least one visual aid.

The feature of the office of Carter Burgess that remains most vivid in my mind is the huge scrap-paper pad standing on a stand by his desk. He explained that whenever he wants to explain something to anyone who comes in to confer he tries to illustrate what he means on the pad. He feels it helps him put across his viewpoint. To illustrate, he began pulling down pages that had in recent days been flipped over the back of the stand. I held my breath because I recalled that some of his company's business was military. Here were Mr Burgess's comments as he pulled down each of seven pictures:

'Here, I was trying to show my young lady how to keep books.'

'This is where I was showing a new idea in handling airline baggage, based on our advice for returning bowling balls.' (Bowling equipment is a major interest of the company.)

'Here I was talking with our chief engineer about a grasping problem on a missile.' (If there were any military secrets in the few scrawled lines, I missed them.)

'Here is a boomerang made out of plastic.'

'Here is the high curve on a business cycle.'

'Here – Oh my! [picture of a crazy-looking house] this was drawn by one of my children. I have five daughters and a new son and it sits better with the family if I bring one along with me when I come into the office Saturday mornings to clean up my work.'

Mr Burgess explained: 'I believe in capturing the eye while I work on the ear. And I try never to say anything I can't illustrate.'

It is frequently stated that another important aspect of the executive's competence as a dealer in ideas is the ability to create them. Management people frequently talk of the importance of creativity in executives – and profess to yearn for more of it. Creativity, in truth, does not appear to be a common characteristic of the executives except in such specialized functions as advertising, where they shamelessly over-use the word. The creativity that is widely prized is more apt to take the form of a generally inquiring mind, a willingness to try fresh approaches (rather than a bubbling-out of original ideas), and an ability to choose, synthesize, and put to use the bright ideas of others.

Mr O'Connor reports that 'executives measure low in ideaphoria,' the outpouring of ideas. Ideaphoria appears to combine creative imagination and loquacity. The person high in ideaphoria is always going in a new direction. 'The executives' job,' Mr O'Connor observed, 'is to put things through to completion and the fact that executives lack ideaphoria helps them to stick to one direction. . . . Their lack of this trait shows up in their slower and very deliberate speech.'

Some executives are good at originating ideas, but ordinarily they are more effective as gatherers and appraisers of ideas. British authors Roy Lewis and Rosemary Stewart observed, in their study of executives: 'To say that all an artist's ideas are those of other men is dispraise; to say that a businessman's ideas are those of other men is merely to describe his function.'[3]

5. *The ability to respond to provocation objectively and effectively.* In some form this was cited in six of the sixteen lists of executive characteristics. Yale's Chris Argyris, you will recall, found many facets of this ability worth stressing: tolerance for frustration, acceptance of signs of 'fight', capacity to bounce back, ability to have one's ideas pulled apart.

People who appraise executives make frequent, admiring use of the word *objective*. The objective executives can keep their personal feelings out of crises and maintain some of the surgeon's approach of emotional detachment. They can be depended upon to be even-handed with subordinates, to be influenced only minimally by their personal likes or dislikes and maximally by what will be best for the organization.

A high-ranking executive must be prepared to close down plants, take actions that alienate many people, and discipline personal acquaintances. Dr Ward said that for some people 'this is very difficult'. Such people, he said, are less likely to be successful as executives than the 'one who is not bothered if he is convinced that he is right'.

The fact that an executive has a good grip on his responses does not mean that he does not speak his mind. Some may emulate the model of the British colonel, maintaining a stiff upper lip in response to pleasure or pain, and think they are being becomingly 'reserved', but the good executive is not distressed by blunt expression of feeling either by himself or by others. Dr Ward put the distinction this way: 'the objective person who has his feelings hurt might say "Damn it, I don't like it!" but he doesn't get perturbed. When a person can express himself appropriately, other people know where they stand. People are distrustful of the person who doesn't show emotion.'

The really good executive, furthermore, tends to thrive on tension arising from provocation or uncertainty. He may be as anxious as the next man, but what is another man's stress is his stimulation.

Provocation creates anxiety in most of us, but we vary

greatly in the way we react to it. Dr Beam distinguished between the 'psychologically tough' and the 'psychologically soft' person. The tough person may feel tense and anxious when he is taking risks or under pressure, but he is *galvanized* by his tensions. He speeds up. A psychologically soft person, on the other hand, is *frozen* by tension. He becomes immobilized. If hostile, destructive tendencies become an important part of the man's response to the stress, then the anxiety is, of course, an unhealthy one.

S. Vincent Wilking, vice-president of the consulting firm of Barrington & Company, told of men freezing under anxiety-producing provocation and developing avoidance reactions. Some, he said, take refuge in being disciplinarians at detail work. He told of the president of a large corporation who was in such an emotional bind that he kept putting off making a tough major decision on whether to authorize a new plant. He spent much of his time instead checking the expense accounts of his associates, and he made quite a splash around the office with his economy wave. Finally mounting pressures forced him to authorize the new plant. During the sixteen months that he had dilly-dallied the estimated cost of the plant rose from six million to eleven million dollars.

6. *The ability to enjoy organizing and running large projects.* The key word is *enjoy*. Many men are straining to attain high executive office because of the status or money that goes with it. They don't really enjoy responsibility or running things. Dr Gaudet happens to be, as a sideline, a director of a number of corporations; but he insists that, though he has had several opportunities, he wouldn't want a high executive post in a major company. He says he wouldn't enjoy the work. The satisfaction of doing a good job at research and teaching offers, for him, a more exciting promise.

The natural executive enjoys making things happen and controlling things, taking on responsibilities and standing accountable for results, making important decisions even if risky. The natural-born executive is a self-starter who likes to make things hum. It thrills him to be able to accept a job with a minimum of briefing, do it in record time, and surprise management by reporting matter-of-factly that the project is all wrapped up. George Fry told me: 'The good executive has the ability to get things done efficiently, quickly and quietly without a lot of fuss and feathers. This is terribly important in the modern corporation.'

7. *The ability to generate confidence.* The successful executive seems to know where he is going and can make others want to go with him. Some variant of this was on six lists.

Dr McMurry advised a president: 'Always give the impression of knowing what you are doing, even when you are not sure at all.' He added, with his usual candour, that this is also the consultant's 'main stock in trade'.

Early in 1962 forty-two-year-old Lynn Townsend became president of Chrysler Corporation. In Detroit he was generally regarded as an ambitious and possibly ruthless young man in a hurry. But a friend told a writer for the *Wall Street Journal*: 'Yes, Lynn is ambitious. But his ambition is to see this company back up where it belongs. I think that as long as he has been associated with Chrysler he's been convinced he could do a better job than anyone else at the top.'

In essence leadership appears to be the art of getting others to want to do something you are convinced should be done. People are more likely to help their leader succeed in a difficult project, in business or elsewhere, if he is convincing on three points:

He must be contagiously enthusiastic about the project himself. A writer may turn out his best work when haunted by doubts, but a business leader must seem to have faith in his own judgement. This need for certitude gives some advantage to the leader who is inherently hypomanic or surgent. He exudes self-confidence and enthusiasm. This may be why people with the characteristics of sales managers – whether or not they ever actually were sales managers – so often end up in the driver's seat. Robert Huttemeyer, a partner in the recruiting firm of Thorndike Deland Associates, was one who placed considerable emphasis upon the importance of enthusiasm. 'Every successful executive I know possesses this quality,' he said.

He must have the integrity to be a source of strength through the worst that may be ahead. The 'angry joy' that the troopers of *The Distant Trumpet* felt in 'belonging to' Lieutenant Hazard was clearly inspired by his most conspicuous traits: utter, single-minded integrity and devotion to honour and duty as he saw them.

He must have a dependable vision of the future. From hindsight and wind-sniffing, he has discerned where the company can be or should be tomorrow. When it comes right down to it, what most managements and subordinates yearn for above all are leaders who seem to know where they are going – and clearly *are* going towards a goal which all would like to achieve.

To sum up, the seven personal characteristics that seem especially useful to an executive are a lot of energy, nervous or otherwise . . . adroitness in handling people . . . a special kind of mental competence which includes a tolerance for ambiguity . . . an ease with words and ideas . . . an ability to respond serenely or energetically to provocation . . . a love for running things . . . and an ability to persuade followers to want to go where you are going. Most of these characteristics are essentially immeasurable by psychological tests. I cannot guarantee that a studious cultivation of these traits will get a man into the president's chair, but the odds are steep that without most of them he won't make it.

CHAPTER 14

The Inner World of the Top-Level Executive

The born executive has a compulsion to be a father-chieftain. . . .
from *Motivations*, published by The Institute for Motivational Research

An aspiring executive needs to understand the mentality of the men near the top who hold his future so largely in their hands. He need not imitate or cultivate their state of mind. That in fact might be dangerous, because the inner world of today's top executives is a part of our social lag and, hopefully, much of it will change by the time the more successful of our aspiring managers start reaching the top a decade or so hence. And hopefully, too, these aspirants will serve as carriers of a different mental outlook. But for the present they need insight into what they are up against.

The top men today don't seem very insightful in explaining how their mental outlook differs from that of other people. Dr Herbert C. Modlin of the Menninger Foundation states: 'Many executives get to the top because they are men of action rather than men of introspection. A difficulty of self-analysis is almost built into them.'

Let us try here to piece together from the fragments of evidence available some of the major features of this top-level mentality. We can ignore the features that are not pertinent – that these men love their country and their wives too (in their own fashion) – and try to focus on those aspects that they may constitute a challenge to an aspirant.

Top executives vary, of course, from tyrannical slobs to delightful, sophisticated, modest men of learning. At best we can only point to what seem predominant patterns. To simplify the problem, let us imagine that we have before us 100 top leaders from heavy industry, often called the bastion of the U.S. economy. We have in this group many exceptional men who rise above any common pattern, such as Clarence Randall, George Romney, and Robert McNamara. But if we focus on our whole imaginary 100 it is possible to arrive at several conclusions about the type of mentality at the top. Any serious candidate for advancement is more than likely to encounter some of the following states of mind among most of those men near the top who will be important to his success.

State of mind 1. This man near the top is likely to be a believer in authoritarianism, with himself the authority to be obeyed. The aspirant should assume, until he has clear evidence to the contrary, that his top managers share this state of mind. And he should take care not to be misled by 'my-door-is-always-open' gestures to the democratic mores of our society.

The pure type of business master currently in power is predisposed to dominate. His natural feelings of ascendancy make it easy for him to ask people to do what he wants. In fact it never occurs to him that his orders, and orders disguised as suggestions, will not be followed. He is the ship's captain. He is the primordial father.

The Institute for Motivational Research, in its study of 'the executive mind',[1] concluded that the born executive sees himself first of all as the father-chieftain advancing the interests of his 'family'. His own strength is what counts most. But he also feels he must be able to demand complete loyalty and have the last word; he must have the authority to discipline, reward, or punish. In this guise the born executive is a biblical figure indeed, at least at the subconscious level, 'proud and jealous, alternately generous and cruel, obsessed by his obligations as well as his rights. . . .'

Top executives like the idea that they are a very select group and they are fond of the trappings of office – such as the chauffeured limousine – that tell the world who they are. Psychiatrist William B. Terhune concluded from his observations of executives that 'they wanted and expected kudos, although they would deny this!'

They also relish the popular idea that of necessity their lives at the pinnacle are terribly lonely and remote. In practice, however, a number of presidents I know go to great pains always to have guests in their houses and on their yachts so that they need rarely be alone.

The Institute's report on the executive mentality offered a fascinating explanation for the profound, implacable hatred most top executives felt for Franklin Delano Roosevelt. On the emotional level, it seems that President Roosevelt insulted and stultified the deepest needs of the executive mind. He became *the* one great father. His was the last word. A later popular idol who was heartily approved by top executives, President Dwight D. Eisenhower, never ceased to speak of the importance to the nation of executive initiative and business enterprise and 'team play'.

State of mind 2. This man near the top is likely to be more than a little self-righteous. He has the primitive chieftain's happy capacity for believing that any project he undertakes is an exalted one. The Institute commented, 'He perceives the prosperity of his wire brush factory or advertising agency as a noble cause worthy of full devotion and great sacrifices.' He hesitates to bend from his stance of certitude even on small particulars because it might endanger his concept of himself as the all-knowing father.

An official of one of the large management associations who frequently sees some of the nation's captains of industry gathered around a conference table told me, as if puzzled: 'While they are struggling to get to the top they usually seem like such nice, decent guys. But once they arrive they begin to pontificate.'

Dr Francis Bradshaw, psychologist and officer of Richardson, Bellows, Henry & Co., suggests that such changes can be explained by 'the Moses complex'. Moses was one of the first leaders on record to lose his original humility as God gave him more power. Top executives find it easy to forget – in their own inner worlds – that they manage to function at all only because of a legion of researchers, consultants, advisers, salesmen, and specialists. Ghost writers have often commented on the alacrity with which corporate presidents accept speeches and statements drafted under their names as their own creations. Dr Bradshaw has concluded as a rule of thumb that the deeper the rug on the floor, the less the humility.

The higher men get in the average large corporation, the more they are protected from any influence that might disturb their self-righteousness. They withdraw from all possibly rude contacts with the outside world. These men at or near the top spend most of their waking hours – whether at the office, where they are protected in depth by secretaries and assistants, or at their very select clubs – in the presence of people who share their view of the world or by definition owe them deference or would hurt their own budding careers by opposing or arguing with the man at the top.

Such a mental state leads many top executives to assume that other people should accept and share their ideas and beliefs in any area.

Central to their own beliefs is a profound 'belief in business' to the exclusion of almost everything else. The survey of executive characteristics conducted by George Fry Associates found this characteristic to be a major one in an executive: 'He identifies himself with his company to the degree that his greatest motivations and satisfactions stem from increased business development.'

State of mind 3. These top men are likely to be dangerously low in sense of humour. Perhaps this is because amiable irreverence cannot be sustained within the human vessel already dedicated to its own sanctification. Also, a lively sense of the preposterous is antipathetic to belief in the modern corporation. This is sad, because humour fosters perspective. A high official of one very large corporation felt there was a great need in big corporations for a court jester.

The three Harvard staff men studying executive action noted that the prestige of top-executive positions precludes much levity. And Dr Sidney Levy, psychological director for Social Research, Inc., commented that in general executives were low on genuine humorousness. He said that there is a lot of joviality but little humour. What humour they exhibit tends to be heavy-handed and often is manifested in the repetition of cruel jokes. Johnson O'Connor, as we saw earlier, commented that executives frequently exhibit 'a complete lack of sense of humour.'

There are notable exceptions. Robert McNamara, formerly president of Ford, reportedly is one, and the executive vice-president of a giant soap company, I'm told, is 'an offbeat guy with a nice sense of humour.' The marketing director of a very large corporation and a director of other corporations – a man who personally loathes stuffiness and calls himself a maverick – told me: 'Most of the top guys today tend to be solemn and stupid. The Bible says you should have some joy in your life. They don't.' Then he added, 'I can laugh because I am old, but if a younger guy did the things I do he'd get fired.'

The solemnity that characterizes the atmosphere of most executive suites not only seeps downwards in the hierarchy but at times influences the outside consultants who evaluate executive candidates. At one large testing firm the president was showing me the profile of a man who seemed to him pretty close to ideal (dynamic mental processes, tact, etc.). However, when he came to the notation 'high in humour' he said, 'This high rating in humour we should take as a caution. He may impress some people as taking things too airily . . . or he may tend to kid a subordinate when he has to criticize. . . .'

State of mind 4. These top men are likely to be at least mildly anti-intellectual and anti-creative, although of course they consider themselves 'creative'. *Business Week* reports a survey by Opinion Research Corporation showing the converse also to be true: people in 'intellectual' pursuits tend to be anti-business. Each group seems wary of the aims and ideals of the other. One testing psychologist showed me Kuder profiles on two men being considered for a 'Vice-president for Sales' job. The graph sheet that had been marked *Poor Candidate* revealed that the man in question was high in 'artistic', 'literary', 'musical' interests. The sheet marked *Good Candidate* revealed that the second man was low – below the median line – on the same three interests. This apparently is no coincidence. The psychologist said there was a feeling that people high in artistic orientation frequently are not 'hard-hitting'. They live 'in a world of feeling' and may be 'hypersensitive and easily upset'.

The massive study made by the National Opinion Research Centre on the kinds of college graduate who aspire to different occupational careers makes some interesting revelations about men planning careers in 'business'.[2] Students entering business proved significantly high in two of the eleven motivating values listed: 'leadership' and 'money'. And they rated significantly low in two: 'help others' and 'original and creative'. The report spoke of 'intellectual values' as an important distinguishing characteristic of career aspirations. It said that in general these intellectual values 'distinguish the more academic careers such as the physical sciences and humanities from non-academic careers such as accounting, business, nursing. . . .'

This difference in values, clear even at the outset of business careers, may help explain the rather virulent suspicion of anything smacking of eggheadism so frequently encountered among people at the tops of corporations, and the frequent lack of more than polite interest in intellectual matters. A highly placed executive of a multi-billion-dollar corporation who is also highly literate complained: 'If you try to talk to these people about politics or music or education or books you quickly find how restricted their world is.'

State of mind 5. The top men here are likely to be strongly in favour of innovating and risk-taking for themselves but take an exceedingly dim view of innovating and risk-taking by others, in or out of business. Many of these leaders are natural gamblers in the sense that they are in their power race for the game, not the money, which they have already made. They will play hard to win – sometimes ferociously hard. Most would agree with President John Atwood of North American Aviation that 'creating change is the key to leadership'.

But changes that may be made by the society around them (as this society tries to keep pace with the technological change the executives have generated) are a source of continual apprehension to these top men. They are profoundly conservative where others are concerned. Politically, of course, most are far to the right (even though they now find it politic to keep a few tame liberals around for liaison work). Perhaps this conservatism represents a nostalgia for better days. Business as symbolized by the modern corporation received its main impetus in the early part of this century when it was in a much stronger position to control society. One consultant made another interesting deduction. The top managers, he said, are fascinated with innovation in their products but not in the way their people do things. They resist any tampering with the company's authoritarian structure.

State of mind 6. These top men are likely to be obsessed with growth. The Young Presidents' Organization organizes hundreds of lectures for its members each year. The most popular subject, year after year, is 'Mergers and Acquisitions'.

The top man verbally flogs his subordinates to beat last year by pushing up all the curves on the charts. One marketing director related: 'There is hell to pay if you don't get your figures up above last year. No consideration is given to the fact that last year may have been a freak year or a bonanza year or that depressing economic forces beyond your control are at work.' Not only must sales rise but the top men want evidence the company is growing faster than any competitors.

This fascination with rising figures can get a top man in trouble if he is not wary. Recruiter John Handy says that sales executives often err in being more volume-minded than profit-minded. He explained: 'They get an emotional thrill when they see the sales go up. Seeing volume increase fills them with ecstasy. They feel that as they get volume up they can decrease cost. This is where they often get in trouble. They should work back from profit.'

The Institute for Motivational Research suggested that some of the drive for growth is motivated by personal rather than business reasons. It found that the executive has a compulsion to lead aggressively onward and upward and to introduce new products, to reorganize, to enter new fields, and devise new competitive steps 'not mainly for business reasons but often to exercise his drive as a warrior.'

State of mind 7. This high-level man is quite likely to have developed a passionate fondness for orderliness. His long years of climbing the pyramid have led him to derive great satisfaction from the well-ordered life his position commands.

This orderliness of the corporate world has its counterpart in – and presumably was inspired by – the officers' way of life in the military organization. The style of life of the corporation has been heavily influenced by the military from the earliest days of the East India Company, when the captains came ashore with their riflemen and ended up running the enterprises. Military organizations tend to be the most orderly – and pyramidal – societies in the world. Status and procedure are detailed for almost every conceivable kind of human response. It is hardly a coincidence that corporate officials take special pleasure in being known as Captains of Industry.

When our captain of industry steps into his building each morning from his assigned parking space the doorman nods and calls him by name, and so does the elevator man who whisks him to a top floor. His secretary smiles sweetly. When he arrives at his desk he finds the top gleaming and bare of any disorderly piles of papers left over from the day before. Pencils have been sharpened and are in place. The carafe has been filled with fresh water. Any memos in the in-basket are written in the prescribed company way. His shoes are shined at the same hour each day by the company shine-boy, who comes around and kneels at his feet. At lunchtime he goes to the prescribed place in the select room, goes to the same table each day, and sits in the same chair. And he arrives and leaves each day in the same seat, whether it is in the private club car of the railroad or in his chauffeur-driven limousine. He usually manages to maintain for himself an orderly environment almost completely under his control.

Quite probably this orderliness, and the control over life it implies, becomes one of the major, deeply felt satisfactions of his life and inner world in an otherwise threatening or misguided society.

PART 4

STRATEGIES AND INCENTIVES

CHAPTER 15

Dead Ends and Favoured Routes

The best route to the top is to own the company. Lewis Bookwalter Ward, Harvard Graduate School of Business Administration

Modern pyramids frequently have at least one upward trail which offers relatively easy and direct passage into the cloud-covered area near the pinnacle. And they have a number of well-beaten paths which, around the second corner, abruptly dwindle as a steep face of rock looms.

The location of the more promising paths varies from pyramid to pyramid. Usually, however, location is influenced by three considerations: what has been the secret of the company's success in the recent past; what people think that secret is; and what is likely to be the key factor influencing the company's prosperity in the future.

Perhaps the first question an aspirant needs to ask, however, is whether there is any route at all that can lead to the top for *him*. In short, is there open competition within the company for the prize?

Many of the most enlightened managements in the nation – as we shall discover – are in family-dominated companies. To the ambitious young manager, a family-dominated pyramid may suggest that second place or a shared leadership is the best he can reasonably hope for. Family domination is most common, of course, in moderate- to small-size companies. Nevertheless, *Fortune* found that in more than half of 175 of the largest corporations close relatives or in-laws were holding management jobs within the same company. The A.M.A. study of 335 company presidents found that one president in seven was heading a company in which there was strong family influence. Among the thousands of young presidents in the Young Presidents' Organization – a majority of whose members are from medium or smallish companies – about half head companies in which there are 'family situations'.

Here are a few of the U.S. corporations where a recently elected president or chairman either succeeded his father or came from a family that has powerful influence in the control of the company: Corning Glass, Borg-Warner, Archer-Daniels-Midland, W. R. Grace & Co., M. A. Hanna Co., Gimbel Bros., Upjohn Co., Weyerhaeuser, Bankers Trust. Three different Grays at the R. J. Reynolds Tobacco Company have held the top job. And young Dwight J. Thomson became chairman of the Champion Paper & Fibre Company, which had been founded by his grandfather and had had his uncle, his father, and his cousin as presidents before he took command.

In some companies a whole troupe of family members can be found in important management positions. This is true at Ford, at Firestone, at Seagram, and at Du Pont, where there are still a dozen Du Ponts in the several dozen top jobs of the company. And then of course there is Crawford Greenewalt, who during his fourth year as an engineer in the company married Margaretta Lammot Du Pont and so in a sense married the boss's daughter – as have many other heads of companies before and since. In August 1962 he moved up to Chairman of the Board and was replaced as President by Lammot du Pont Copeland, a great-great grandson of the company's founder.

Besides family, there are other 'outside' influences that can dictate or influence the composition of a company's top management. One is best summed up in the word *money*, a chronic need for companies. When a business gets into a money-losing situation it is likely to be willing enough to install at the helm men put forward by the specific banks, brokerage houses, or major stockholders that can make or break the company. These interests want someone they can trust to protect their investment. Not long after Ernest Breech went on the board at Trans World Airlines as a representative of the creditors, his friend Charles C. Tillinghast, Jr., was invited into T.W.A. as president.

One informant half-playfully suggested to me that 'the trick today is not to marry the boss's daughter but rather to marry the banker's daughter'. When Safeway Stores found itself in a profit squeeze, one of its directors and aggrieved major stockholders was the late Charles Merrill, head of the giant brokerage firm of Merrill Lynch, Pierce, Fenner & Smith. He induced the long-time president to resign and then nominated his own son-in-law, Robert A. Magowan, a stockbroker, to head the company. Mr Magowan has cheerfully stated: 'I'm not one of these fellows who pulled himself up by his bootstraps. The plain fact is that I married the daughter of a very prominent man.'[1] (He is also credited with being a fine president.)

Another kind of outsider who may come in to take over the top job is the man who is assumed to have contacts and influence and who can get government contracts. Consultant James Mills observes that in today's world of enterprise there are often two umbilical cords leading to a corporation: 'One comes from the banks, the source of money. The other comes from government, the source of business.' Uncle Sam has a nearly fifty-billion-dollar defence establishment without counting non-military aspects of the space effort. He has a highway programme running into tens of billions and a host of other multibillion-dollar programmes. He is the world's biggest customer. Ex-officials from the Pentagon are often offered the presidencies and chairmanships in companies that exist largely on military contracts. General Dynamics has brought in two ex-Pentagon officials in a row to head the company and has dozens of ex-admirals or ex-generals on its staff. Close to 85 per cent of its business comes from military contracts. At least twenty-four major companies make most of their sales to the U.S. Department of Defense.

In most cases, however, management looks first at its own ranks when the office of president or chairman of the board is to be filled. What, then, are the most inviting routes available today for the ambitious younger man who hopes to get that shot at the top?

It used to be considered smart to work one's way to the job as assistant to the president. This was the great dream job, the spot eyed by many business-school graduates-in-a-hurry as a kind of short-cut to the top. The job of assistant to the president does have much to commend itself as a mid-career sort of post: it provides a broad view of company operations and offers a man maximum exposure to the attention of the president. Charles H. Percy, young president of Bell & Howell, found the protégé-assistant route a most expeditious one; Theodore Schlesinger found it very helpful to serve as special assistant to the president of Allied Stores (B. Earl Puckett), but this was twenty-two years before he became president himself.

Carter Burgess recalls that for many years in almost every job he had – in industry, government, and university – the word *assistant* was in his title. He was assistant to the president of T.W.A. before he himself became president. But today as A.M.F. president Burgess has no assistant. He says he prefers to have his good men assigned to specific responsibilities.

George Saum, administrative vice-president of George Fry & Associates, is one who feels that the assistant-to-the-president job has become overrated as a stepping-stone. He explains that 'an assistant to someone doesn't have line authority. He is a staff man and so he has no way of turning in a *measurable* performance. He is not responsible for a profit result. The man who becomes chief has to have a record behind him; he has to have measurable results.'

What are the functional areas in a company (sales, production, research, etc.) most likely to be scanned when a chief executive is being chosen or groomed? A few things can be said with some certainty. The situation varies, of course, with the main challenge in each company. The main challenge of a company selling toothpaste to consumers is likely to be quite different from that of a machine-tool company. The main challenge of a company skirting bankruptcy is likely to be quite different from that of a company struggling to absorb recent acquisitions. And the main challenge of a company in a pioneering industry such as developing a new kind of rocket fuel is likely to differ drastically from that of a 'mature' company trying to think up new ways to sell aspirin at a high mark-up. McKinsey's Arch Patton points out that as the life cycle of a company's major product changes you may get a shift in functional emphasis from research to manufacture to selling to control, in that order.

In general the choice tends to go to the man who seems especially well qualified either to make the company in question a lot of money or to save the company a lot of money. It sometimes happens that a man is chosen for his general outstanding qualities. However, special competence in handling the company's main challenge at the moment is commonly a crucial factor in dictating the final choice of a new president or chairman of the board. This is especially true if the company is going through a difficult phase.

After allowing for these variables, what are the most and least promising functional routes to the top? Let's start with what seem to be the least promising routes.

I found no one who thought the personnel department was now promising, even though it was so considered twenty years ago, when the problem of handling and pacifying employees was causing considerable concern. One industrial-relations director told me: 'The requirements for the personnel administrator have been like those for the Y.M.C.A. secretary – you are supposed to like people.' The more serious handicaps for personnel directors are that it is hard to measure their contribution in dollars and cents and there is a tendency to take them for granted.

Some of them move up to the title of industrial-relations director, which involves broader responsibility over employees. One I.R. director with whom I talked said he was at that moment negotiating eleven contracts with four international unions at seven geographical locations and had nine days to reach agreements since all existing contracts had the same expiration date. A strike could cost millions. Yet he felt that an I.R. director doesn't get the broad exposure to all facets of management that men in such functions as marketing and finance get. He could think of only one I.R. director who had moved directly into a presidency, and that was in an auto-parts concern. Men in personnel and industrial relations often move to different companies to get into a more promising management classification, or make lateral moves within their own company for the same purpose.

Traffic managers, purchasing agents, and directors of community or public relations are also considered outside the main stream that flows towards the top and for many of the same reasons.

Despite the swift advances of technology, there has apparently been a drop-off in the proportion of industrial scientists and engineers who reach the position of chief executive officer. American Cyanamid moved a bacteriologist into the chairmanship and Radio Corporation of America moved an electrical engineer into the presidency. But when such moves occur it is usually because the man is outstanding in his own right or because the company happens to have a particularly pressing technological problem. With R.C.A., perhaps it was the company's rather agonizing preoccupation with getting its colour-TV and computer programme on a better basis that influenced the choice of Elmer Engstrom, a man with a long background in electrical engineering, for the presidency.

In the twenties and to a lesser extent until 1948, the production chief was likely to be a favourite in any presidential contest. He turned out the goods. He was the heart and guts of the business. He was in the main line of command. Today the production man has a relatively slim chance of becoming president. He either has to prove he is a really outstanding all-round man, or else he has to be in a company in which production is still a major preoccupation. In Detroit, the production man still has a fair chance because of the enormous and expensive problems involved in retooling for the annual style change. Thus John Dykstra made it as president of Ford. For many companies, however, the challenge of producing the cement or soap or zinc or electrified toothbrush is not the major one. The make-or-break challenges have shifted else-where.

A number of lawyers have been turning up in presidential chairs, which suggest that the office of legal counsel is a relatively promising spot to occupy at some stage, though some argue it has not been improving as a stepping-stone. While the production chief for a bottle-making concern can, by straining his ingenuity, make some savings for the com-pany, the legal counsel may be able to save millions just by knowing his tax or patent law. Or he may be the only official capable of steering his company through the complexities of a merger. Or perhaps he can rescue the company threatened by an anti-trust suit. Oil executive Thomas Sunderland was offered the presidency of United Fruit although he knew nothing about the fruit business. He was a lawyer with anti-trust experience, and United Fruit had been having anti-trust tangles with the Justice Department.

Possibly another reason for the relatively lively demand for legal men as presidents is that they are likely to have minds well trained to analyse and cope with business problems. Robert F. Moore of Richardson, Bellows, Henry says lawyers get to the top 'not because they are lawyers. . . . I think it is because they have the brain-power to be selected by law schools in the first place. The better schools require that students come from the top tenth of their undergraduate class.' Furthermore, he added, 'there is the broadening ex-perience of conducting a law practice.' The good lawyer is likely to be able to help a company have a breadth of view-point about its place in society that it might not otherwise have.

Marketing has in recent years proved a very promising route to the top, especially in companies selling directly to consumers. Two factors seem responsible: (1) In our eco-nomy of force-fed abundance the big challenge in most in-dustries is not to get the goods produced but rather to get them, somehow, into the consumer's hands, and (2) the marketing executive's contribution to the company's welfare is most easy to prove in dollars and cents. George Saum said he wouldn't be surprised if one reason marketing men are so frequently chosen for the top is that 'they are doing something tangible, measurable. It is easier to put the calipers on what they do.'

Companies that must move vast quantities of their product through supermarkets, drugstores, appliance stores, and filling stations seem especially inclined to put salesmen in the driver's seat. At Procter & Gamble the president, the chairman, and most of the board of directors came up the marketing route. One of its major products, Ivory soap, hasn't changed much over the decades, so that the challenge is not in the factory. The challenge is to persuade the world, over and over again, that Ivory soap should be chosen over the host of rival bars that may be highly comparable. The same marketing route proved the way to the top for recent presidents or chairmen of General Electric, General Foods, Westinghouse Electric, Shell Oil, B. F. Goodrich, Bristol-Meyers, Smith, Kline & French, U.S. Steel, Borden, and Texaco. Marketers are chosen as presidents, however, much more frequently than they are chosen as chairmen of the board. *Printers' Ink* concluded after surveying the top officials at fifty of the largest companies producing goods and services that approximately 29 per cent had some up through marketing.

For companies in general, however, the most inviting of all routes to the top at this writing appears to be through finance. Virtually all of my informants listed this as currently either the best or next-best route. A typical comment is that of recruiter William Clark: 'Back in the twenties we had the age of the production man. Then came sales. Today we are seeing an increasing appreciation of the value of a good financial man.' In 1961 and 1962 a new emphasis upon financial men for top offices was disclosed in a number of reports and surveys.

At General Motors, that widely accepted model of the successful company, a long line of financial men have been chairmen – Donaldson Brown, Albert Bradley, Harlow H.

Curtice, and most recently Frederic G. Donner. At Ford, Ernest Breech, one-time controller at G.M., was followed in the top operating executive spot by Robert S. McNamara, the ex-controller. McNamara had come to Ford in a package deal with a group of ten young Air Force officers who had developed specialities in 'management analysis.' Five of the ex-airmen besides McNamara were still with Ford by the time McNamara reached the presidency. Three were vice-presidents, the fourth was treasurer, and the fifth was in line to be a vice-president!

Within one week in the summer of 1961 two industrial giants named financial men to their presidencies. General Electric leap-frogged its controller over five group vice-presidents, and Chrysler named Lynn Townsend, who had built his career in accounting. Both companies had been shaken by scandals that had been attributed to poor management control.

Until recently financial men – especially treasurers – were considered poor prospects for the driver's seat of a company because they had the reputation of being negative thinkers. They were the watchdogs. Their favourite pronouncement was, 'No, we can't afford it.' They were assumed to lack vision and boldness and willingness to spend money in order to make money. As John Handy put the reservation: 'Brakes are essential, but they won't run a car.'

Today the concept of the chief financial officer's role is being overhauled. He not only raises money; he gets into every corner of the business where money is spent, which means practically everywhere. Backed by his electronic computer, he supervises the construction of statistical models which – it is claimed – can take over and refine decision-making in such areas as inventory control and production scheduling. He has an important hand in working out the details of absorption when another company is bought. If his company has been losing money for several years, he is in an especially strong position because the company's future profits can be vastly influenced by his ability to exploit a multi-million-dollar tax write-off.

In any case, the chief financial officer usually know more about the company – and its over-all objectives – than any of his peers and so is often assumed to be most ready to assume the responsibilities of the presidency. Ambitious youngsters now often vie to get a spot on the central control staff under the controller's jurisdiction.

The value attached to different functions is reflected, perhaps, in surveys made of the income of college graduates a decade or so after graduation. An income survey of graduates of the Harvard Graduate School of Business Administration showed this ranking of income by fields, in descending order:

1. Finance
2. Marketing
3. Production and operations
4. Research and development and other technical functions
5. General administration
6. Accounting
7. Personnel and labour relations

Some observers feel that the new pre-eminence of financial men in corporate affairs is not an altogether happy omen. Often leaders from financial backgrounds unwittingly tend to squeeze the spontaneity, colour, and creativeness out of interpersonal relationships within the hierarchy. The financial man represents order – in fact he embodies order. His rise in influence may help account for the growing primness and blandness of corporate environments. A study of executive personality reported in *Personnel* in 1959 concluded that accounting executives tend to be 'more constricted, less sociable and more withdrawn' than executives generally. One official of a leading management-consulting firm called the trend towards more and more power for financial men in corporate affairs 'the scariest thing in the world'.

What the best routes to the top will be by 1970 or 1980 is anybody's guess. The key factors controlling each individual company's success or failure undoubtedly will continue to change. However, I might offer some predictions as to at least three functions that will be significantly more important

a decade hence in shaping business success or failure:
The growth of automated processes.

The growth in organizational giantism with accompanying growth in need for internal controls and a growth in demand from the outside for legal controls.

The growth in interest in overseas markets as U.S. markets prove increasingly incapable of absorbing all the goods and services the nation's expanding and automated industries can provide.

All this suggests that in the near future companies will have a special need for the bright people who can help a company maintain a comfortable relationship with automated equipment, with government bodies, and with the outside world.

CHAPTER 16

The Manoeuvres of the Power Players

> BRUTUS . . . *'Tis a common proof,*
> *That lowliness is young ambition's ladder*
> *Whereto the climber-upward turns his face;*
> *But when he once attains the upmost round,*
> *He then unto the ladder turns his back*
> *Looks in the clouds, scorning the base degrees*
> *By which he did ascend.*
> *– Julius Caesar*, Act II, scene 1

It was a helpful management-association official who first suggested to me the pertinence in today's corporate world of Brutus's words. His job puts him in frequent contact with many of the nation's top corporate officials. He and many others pointed out that in most companies it is still impossible for a man to rise solely on the basis of job proficiency. The man must also be recognized and be tapped by someone higher in the power hierarchy. To win the tap in many companies one must supplement proved talent with personal manoeuvring and playing the power game.

In business there is a pretty firm taboo against even discussing the possibility that personal strategy – or politics – may be a factor in promotion. Such discussion is contrary to the U.S. business creed. Anyone who depended upon the textbooks and most of the business journals for his insights would believe that merit alone prevails when candidates for an opening are considered.

One elder statesman who has been candid about the taboo is Chester I. Barnard, former head of New Jersey Bell. He said: 'The fact that a junior executive in business is completely dependent on the goodwill of a few of his superiors for promotion is not recognized in the ideology. . . .'[1]

One vice-president of a Midwestern corporation told me that in the two medium-sized companies for which he had worked he had never seen a single instance of 'politics' or power-playing or of a man being advanced on any basis but merit. I mentioned this conversation to Robert McMurry, who shrugged and said: 'He doesn't want to see politics. All you were getting was an expression of the value system: nice people don't play politics.'

For several decades Dr McMurry and his associates have been getting a close look at the behaviour of thousands of the 'nice people' in corporate hierarchies. When they are making an analysis of the functioning of a company they request permission to talk with five people in each department who really know the department's problems. The talks are confidential. The McMurry people start at the bottom of the corporation and work all the way up to the top. Dr McMurry commented that when you get five people talking confidentially you learn who the natural leaders are and you learn who is undermining whom, politically. He concluded: 'Rival camps in the executive suites are one of the facts of life. The president is Papa, and Papa picks successors. In nearly every organization, there is continuous rivalry for favour with the top. . . . Segmentation, rivalries, backbiting, lack of cooperation, proliferation, factionalism, and empire-building are *typical* phenomena within larger business organizations. . . .'

Dr McMurry doesn't find this surprising, because any aggregation of people banded together for business or for any purpose is in fact a *political* organization. Furthermore most supervisors select their subordinates, and nearly everyone selects his subordinates in his own image.

Another industrial psychologist who has devoted a great deal of study to power playing in corporate suites is Dr Jennings. He reports a study conducted by Michigan State researchers of the confidential views of 162 executives at all levels. The surveyors found that though few executives would state specifically how they themselves played the power game, almost all the top executives showed awareness of its existence and one in three admitted that his own success was based partially on playing that game. Further, most of these executives showed a strong interest in knowing more about how the game is played.

Dr Jennings concluded that subtlety in playing the power game well in all lines of executive endeavour is more important in determining who gets where than knowing the techniques of administrators. In fact, he commented flatly that you've got to have a strategy for moving ahead. 'A guy doesn't move ahead accidentally.'

The widespread interest in understanding the ramifications of office politics – for either offensive or defensive purposes – has inspired some of the executive counsellors, 'career consultants', or executive coaches to offer to try to help their clients map step-by-step strategies for getting into that big corner office at the end of Mahogany Row. Their services, needless to say, are a source of controversy among management consultants. Executive Job Counsellors, for instance, helps its executive clients develop a twelve-step programme for getting ahead – which includes mapping the political terrain. Reed, Cuff & Associates, which specializes in 'executive development', also occasionally finds itself giving a client insight into the internal politics of his organization. Dr Jennings is in a category by himself, so far as I know. He began counselling high-level executives on techniques for advancement some years ago as a sideline, to deepen his insight into executive life. He confines his 'practice' to the people high enough to 'want to throw their hats in the ring'. The aim is to help a vice-president become a president. He told of four high-level clients he had recently counselled. Three have made it to the presidency. The fourth, a personnel director, didn't make it and, Dr Jennings has concluded, probably never will; but he sighs and says that at least he was able to give the man 'shelf-insight'. In at least half of his cases, Dr Jennings says, he helps the client set up a political strategy useful for counteracting the strategies of a rival. He finds that just one man can force all the others to play the political game for self-protection. The candidate who has the indispensable quality of maze-brightness is usually also one who is not afraid to admit to himself that he is politicking. This candour with self, it seems, enables him to direct all his energy to the task at hand.

The amount of office politics a candidate is likely to encounter varies greatly from company to company. One leading recruiter reported that the roughest political infighting he had encountered was in the major oil and food companies; he singled out General Foods and Pillsbury as notable cases in point. At one large consumer-product company a former state governor – who presumably should have been able to hold his own in political infighting – was brought in partly to improve the company's public image. A management consultant told me the man was now 'being cut to pieces' by high-level operators within the company's management.

Politicking is likely to be especially intensive when contacts are considered particularly important in establishing one's standing; when a great deal of emphasis is placed on extra-curricular socializing (wives get into the act); when much of the important news flows by grapevine; and when there is a general lack of candour in superior-subordinate relationships. Politicking appears to be notably light in new, rapidly growing companies; in companies whose executives are drawn in large numbers from scientists and engineers in research and development; and in banking, insurance, and utility companies, in which the managers are not so highly motivated to advance as in corporations in general and in which many promotions are known to depend largely or entirely upon seniority.

What follows is a description – without offering any value judgements at this point – how the game of manoeuvring for position is often played in the conventionally run company.

Strategies for attaining 'visibility'. Dr Frederick Gaudet commented that if a man is going to go up the ladder he must be visible to the people above. 'Increased personal visibility' has become central to the strategy planning of many of the knowledgeable young men in the large organizations. Committee meetings and staff conferences may be largely a waste of time, as one study already cited showed, but to the ambitious junior they spell opportunity to make himself visible to many different people of superior rank.

Professor William Dill of Carnegie Tech has spent a great deal of time following the careers of a few young men who are obviously corporate comers. One is the man he calls Larson, a cool, highly competent big-company climber who is much preoccupied with maintaining visibility. He made a special point of introducing himself widely in the company and of gaining assurances that he would always be moved to a new assignment within two years. He gladly took on what had in the past been considered a routine job of organizing the vice-president's file of reports and devoted great thought and energy to making the file more valuable to the vice-president. He saw in the job the possibility of improving his visibility. The vice-president was properly pleased by his diligence.

Bernard Haldane, founder of Executive Job Counsellors, advises his clients never to ignore the formal line of command but still to watch for permissible tangential moves that will improve individual visibility. He tells clients that when they write reports to their immediate superiors they might mention: 'I think Mr Johnson would be interested in the information on page five.' Mr Johnson, of course, is the man whose attention is being sought. Or the young executive may mention to his boss, 'Say, maybe I should talk with Mr Johnson about this.' Haldane tells of a man who discovered – from a study of the organization chart and job-description tables – that the assistant to the president happened as one of his chores to be in charge of a special library on executive development. Haldane's man thereupon became a student at the library and became friendly with the man who had the president's ear.

Such exposure may, if successful, generate favourable comments about the aspiring executive in the executive dining room or bring calls for his services or his part-time assistance. All this notice, it is assumed, may pay off at evaluation time.

Since visibility is deemed so important, the man stuck in a branch office far from headquarters may understandably feel handicapped. Such isolates may develop neurotic feelings of exploitation or neglect. The outlying people may see the people at the New York or Cincinnati headquarters as an all-powerful, menacing, controlling, to-be-feared 'they' force. The cool climbers, on the other hand, will become extra-ardent report writers to reduce the distance factor. They will find reasons to visit headquarters. And they will be extra-helpful when teams of inspectors from the home office come visiting.

The visibility-conscious junior will, at whatever office, plunge into extracurricular activity as a way of attracting notice. This may be volunteer work for the trade association, helping to raise money for a new community building, organizing the company's annual outing, or writing for the trade journal. At the most crass level it may involve joining the boss's country club.

Perhaps the best way to attain visibility is to receive a seemingly unsolicited offer of a good job from another company, preferably in a related field. Our man of course makes it clear that he does not consider the offer seriously. To take it seriously might raise questions about his loyalty. But the offer does give him an opportunity to mention lightly the fact of the bid to his superiors and to inquire what his 'future' is with the company.

Dr McMurry has constructed a hypothetical case history ('the Rake's Progress') of a man, age forty-two, who rose to the presidency at an unprecedentedly rapid rate and later tried to determine the main reasons why he, rather than his highly competent competitors, got the job. In addition to his dedication as a worker, the man gave major credit to two factors. The first was his election to the presidency of his industry's dominant trade association, with its business and government contacts. The second factor, an out-growth of his trade-association work, was the offer he had received to head his firm's principal competitor. Dr McMurry remarked that it was this offer which had made him 'an indispensable member of his management's team.'

Strategies for looking good. Dr McMurry's hypothetical

new young president also surmised that a key to his meteoric success was his early recognition of the paramount importance of personal compatibility with one's superiors. Dr McMurry, explaining how a good operator works, says that if a man has not made himself compatible with his boss he can have every conceivable positive attribute and still not make a good showing at evaluation time if the superior really doesn't like or trust him. He said this is true even though few superiors wilfully show favouritism.

How does one assure compatibility? Listen to Dr McMurry: 'If you are a real hypocrite you endear yourself to the boss's value system. Does he want obsequity or can he tolerate a pretty agressive guy? The smart junior attunes himself to the boss's expectations.'

James Cuff, partner at Reed, Cuff, told of a vice-president who had built a fabulous reputation in sales and yet had been notified by his president that he would lose his job in the coming merger. In reconstructing the man's career Reed, Cuff found that the man had unwittingly been sticking his tongue out at the president by demonstrations of independence. He had avoided taking the boss on trips, he had refused to play golf with the president's group, he had failed to consult the president to make him feel he was contributing to the great success of the vice-president's division. Under Reed, Cuff's guidance our endangered vice-president, in a respectful mood, had a long talk with the president. He began joining the president's golf foursome and he took the president with him on a tour of his division's offices. The upshot, Cuff states, is that the man did not lose his job in the merger. Instead, it wasn't long before he was executive vice-president and his salary had been increased from $30,000 to $75,000.

John Handy says there is no better way to make friends than to ask advice, even of the president. Others made the same point. Bernard Haldane pointed out an often-overlooked benefit of advice-taking: 'If you take the man's advice he becomes obligated to help you fulfil the results which the advice should have made easier to attain.'

The smart junior often tries to hitch his wagon to a star in the company who is going places, not one who is topping out. A boss on the move is likely when promoted, if only for self-protection, to take with him his most useful and loyal subordinates, even though they may be less competent than other men available who are not so well known to him. This is known variously as having a sponsor, an advocate, or a good shirt-tail.

Having two sponsors or shirt-tails is even better, of course, since one may fall from power, leave, or die. I met in the South a haggard-looking divisional vice-president. His hand had a tremor. One of his friends confided to me 'John's sponsor died. Everything John did that pleased the old president, whom he grew up with, annoys the hell out of the new president.'

Dr Jennings points out that most bosses have one key subordinate, occasionally two, but rarely three. How do you become a key subordinate? Dr Jennings says you don't do it by getting high scores on psychological tests, because the qualities that make a man a key subordinate cannot be tested; furthermore, even if they could, the shrewd boss does not permit a crucial promotion to be made on any basis beyond his control. The key subordinate knows how to heighten the boss's effectiveness and sense of well-being. He must be a man who can be trusted without limitation and will not usurp authority.

Usually the operator has thought through the problems involved in gaining maximum credit and minimum blame for himself. In his reports on the work of his own subordinates the good results come from a we-effort and the bad results from a they-effort. He seeks the right to sign his own letters – instead of letting his department head do it – but when he finally becomes the department head himself he may find it wise, as the British authors of *The Managers* pointed out, to introduce a rule requiring that he sign all letters and reports, or at least that all such be written under his letterhead. As he gets near the top he may be able to afford the luxury of being what sociologist C. Wright Mills called the Maybeman: 'Speak like the quiet competent man of affairs and never personally say No. Hire the No-man as well as the Yes-man.'

Coping with the boxed-in feeling. Edmund Burke is reputed to have observed, 'There are critical moments . . . when they who are too weak to contribute to your prosperity may be strong enough to complete your ruin.'

In varying degrees most ambitious managers probably feel boxed in at some point in their careers. Perhaps they have a superior who doesn't like signs of strength below him and makes sure that his subordinates have little opportunity to come in contact with top officials. One informant mentioned that inability to tolerate strength is not usual in supermarket chains, where the boss is often a former greengrocer and tends to view his subordinates as capable but dependent outsized clerks. Furthermore, and of greater significance in my informant's view, too great strength in a store manager is highly undesirable because this will tend to make him insufficiently docile and submissive to accept the rigid and sometimes mindless regimentation to which the chain may subject him.

The situation may be even more oppressive if the superior exhibits neurotic symptoms and seeks to keep subordinates in line by harassing tactics and by bearing down heavily on the observance of rules and regulations. Or the problem may be a wily superior who seeks to encourage rivalry or ill feeling among subordinates in order, he hopes, to keep them all more firmly allied to him and dependent on his favours.

The boxed-in feeling may also come to the ambitious young manager who finds himself assigned to a man who has obviously gone just about as high as he can in the company. This senior man has 'plateaued out,' to use a phrase favoured by consultants. As Mr Handy put it, 'Every man has his ceiling. One of the hardest things a man has to handle is a boss who has hit a ceiling when Junior hasn't. This can be rough. You have to go through, over or around.' Or you get out. Perhaps the most galling situation of all is to work under a competent, well-meaning man who – when asked from above for candidates for advancement – does not mention the name of his brightest young subordinate simply because the subordinate is doing such a marvellous job.

How does the ambitious manager who feels boxed in manoeuvre himself out of such situations? Here are some possible moves that were mentioned to me:

He can frankly seek to clarify his future with the company by tactful talks with his own superior and more candid (but still careful) interviews with higher-ranking officials who may be glad to offer fatherly advice – the kind who like to boast that 'the door is always open'. Perhaps he can extract a promise that he will not be expected to stay where he is for more than two years.

He can move sideways into other areas of the company not so well staffed.

He can take on added responsibilities that will find him reporting to more than one boss. As Clarence Randall once noted acidly: 'To be connected with only one boss on the organization chart . . . would be an announcement of inferior status. The men who have really arrived will be spider-webbed off in several directions by mysterious cross-hatching.'

He can work on improving his visibility.

He can create pressures that will thrust him upward – and make sure he is not locked in because of being 'indispensable' in his job – by training excellent subordinates who obviously need advancement.

He can leave. This is the soundest solution if he is working under a jealous superior. Life is too short to spend one's years seething. William Lear, who made a fortune in aircraft-guidance equipment, summed up the problem of departing in this advice to young men: 'As soon as you've learned how to do your job as well as it can be done, ask for more responsibility in your company – or a different job. If you don't get it, get the hell out.' And get out, he might have added, before you get so much equity built up that you are locked in by the fear of losing retirement benefits, stock-purchase benefits, and so on.

Coping with rivals and dangerous subordinates. In companies in which feuding for position is common, executives near the top take their 'vacations' a few days at a time. They feel they must be on guard against a squeeze play. In such a company the executives usually keep on the immediate staffs subordinates who are weaker or less aggressive than themselves. The hazard to the company here of course, as Dr McMurry points out, is that the law of diminishing competence comes into play. 'When this selection of weaker subordinates has been repeated several times . . . the low man in the hierarchy is often weak indeed.'

There is also a tendency in such companies to have a fairly open formation of defensive alliances near the top. Some of these alliances may include the president himself and some board members. The office politician may build a number of limited alliances not only to protect himself but to multiply the power of his eyes and ears so that he can know what his rivals are up to. Usually he will try to stay out of an alliance with any man who has a more dominating personality than he has. As a good politician he will also make every effort to help his allies attain their goals (so long as they don't conflict with his own).

Occasionally, when rivalries become intense, an outright operator will back-date memos to prove to the president that he was right and his rival wrong on a project that failed. Or he may resort to a strategy which the *Wall Street Journal* found had been used by the vice-president of a corporation in the East. He kept a rival from attending an important meeting by plugging the carburetter of his automobile.

The most vivid report I received on rumbles in the executive suite was from a talkative, outspoken management consultant for one of the smaller consulting firms. I first met him by chance on a plane coming into New York on a Friday night. He looked beat. He said he had travelled 4,200 miles that week to see clients who, I gathered, were mostly the smaller and more speculative, new-product companies. He began talking about the tribulations of the presidents he worked with. They were lucky indeed, he said, to hold their jobs for six years, the par for presidents. At this point we had not introduced ourselves, though I later visited his mid-Manhattan office. Here are the highlights of his comments as we – two strangers – chatted on a plane:

'The average president I see is in a terrible spot these days. He doesn't own control, he doesn't have much stock, and he is at the mercy of his board of directors. For many it is a terrible strain, and hits them in the heart or in the mind.

'I just had one of these. He had called us in almost too late. His enemies in the company really had him back on his heels. He was exhausted, punchy. He was taking his work home nights, weekends. He wasn't delegating responsibility because he didn't know whom he could trust. He didn't know who was working against him. We were able to tell him, by going back over the reports that had been made to him over the past two years. Then he really went to work on his enemies in the company. We even had detectives digging into their background. Now he has them on the run.

'One of our functions as consultants is that we are drawn into counter-intelligence work. You've got to understand that in these companies the only way a vice-president can become president before the president is due to retire is to grease the skids for him, throw some banana peels in his path. Often the president can't trust the advice that one or more of his vice-presidents is giving him. This is where we come in. Sometimes we work under cover in the sense that the rest of the officials don't know we are advising the president. He can get us on the payroll in a dozen ways without their knowing it. He can put us on the payroll of a subsidiary or on the legal staff. He passes along to us the reports of his department managers. We study them and prime him on how to respond and how to chew their tail with embarrassing questions at the next staff conference. That convinces them that the Old Man is really way ahead of them and so they don't give him trouble.'

My informant offered the novel opinion that if he were a young man starting out he would, among other skills, learn dancing and charm because many of the smaller companies are now dominated by widows. 'On your way up,' he said, 'you must dance with these old gals.' Many companies in Manhattan, he stated, are controlled – sometimes through foundations – by widows who stay at such hotels as the Gotham and St Regis and in some ways run the companies from the hotel lounges. 'By threatening to sell or buy ten per cent of their stock they can rattle hell out of a corporation,' he said.

The 'real good operator' in office politics is likely to take a contemptuous attitude towards the recent talk in corporate circles about the need for more communication. As a politician he knows the power that comes from having access to 'classified' information and timing its release to others (or perhaps letting the others have carefully distorted versions). He also believes that his power can be enhanced by a careful use of both flattery and fear. He avoids close friendships at the company in order to maintain 'flexibility'. And he understands how to control people through detail. Chris Argyris has frequently seen this technique in action in companies operating on the basis of traditional superior–subordinate relationships. A defensive president, he said, will ask his immediate subordinate, the executive vice-president, 'a ninth-level question' – one that should be known by someone nine levels down in the hierarchy – like 'what's the price of sandwiches in the cafeteria?' He said that in one company he found subordinates spending hundreds of hours developing *J.I.C.* files. (Just in Case the President asks.)

Planning the moves. The number of coaching services available to executives is small but apparently growing. The coaches range from those oriented to the Dale Carnegie approach of making people like you to those offering campaigns drawn to some extent from the insights of the behavioural sciences.

Executive Job Counsellors reports success in helping buyers become divisional merchandising managers within a year and in helping account executives become vice-presidents. It helps its ambitious clients make a 'success-factor analysis' of themselves and offers them, among other things, instructions on how to be on the march upwards.

One of the most intriguing coaching jobs I've encountered was done by Michigan State's Dr Jennings, author of several recent studies of executive behaviour.² The executive in question was in his fifties and was vice-president in a utility company somewhere between the Alleghenies and the Rockies. Dr Jennings had approximately fifteen sessions with the man. Here are the highlights of his ninety-minute narration of the case:

'My client knew that the presidency would be open in less than eighteen months because the president was approaching compulsory retirement age. There were three other vice-presidents but my man considered only one of them a real competitor. It was believed that the president would pretty much pick his successor. In many situations the president doesn't have that much control and can only block.

'When my man first discussed his aspiration with me he was worried because he felt a cooling-off period had started between himself and the president. He was wondering if he should go to the president and ask frankly if he had done something to offend or disappoint him. I told him this would be a tragic move. It would have revealed that he was concerned about his future, which would indicate insecurity. I urged him not to show his concern.

'My client's shortcomings were several. He couldn't articulate well. He was crude: he tended to holler on the telephone. He was an anal character: tight, retentive, sticky. He was tight on money, tight on love, tight on affection. He was aloof, austere and very prestige-conscious. Finally he was rather lazy and hadn't done much real thinking about the future. He hadn't tried to see ten years ahead. In short, he was low on vision; and my theory is that if you're going to get to the top you ought to be something of a visionary.

'I set up a strategy that mainly involved – in addition to improving his performance – making him into a more plausible presidential prospect. First of all I urged him to talk to as many informed people as he could and start coming up with a vision of the future of his particular utility in his particular area. He did his best to comply.

'Also I worked on his political skills and advised him to quit picking on his principal opponent. My man was a classic obstructionist – always cracking jokes that were cutting in the presence of his colleague. I suggested that he cut it out, that he was being transparent and furthermore was simply creating bad feeling. I suggested he follow the pattern of John Kennedy and Richard Nixon in the 1960 presidential campaign. They publicly credited each other with being sincere.

'This man used humour only to obstruct. Basically he was tight and couldn't laugh. I tried to get him to relax if he was going to be humorous, and to laugh more. My main problem was to get him to relax, to get him to feel secure in his attitude towards his career. I felt he had to impress these people that he was relaxed. In America we still don't like the insecure guy at the top. My man worked so hard at relaxing that he kept slipping away from me.

'His overaggressive attitude towards his opponent showed up in the way he chose a seat each noon at the "King's Table" reserved for the president and vice-presidents. He always sat opposite the enemy. The president was likely to sit anywhere. I asked him why he always sat opposite his opponent and he said: "I just haven't thought about it." I suggested that next time he sit next to him. He did and this helped break up the conflict relationship at least at the visible level. And it helped to demonstrate his ability to reduce conflicting relations with other people. This is an important skill for a president to have. I felt that if he could show that he could reduce conflicts he had a better chance for the presidency; also he was safeguarding the future in case the colleague made it and he didn't, because the colleague would never let him sit near the throne if he was an enemy.

'I even worked on his telephone manner. He would bark, "Hell, no," over the phone and was even loud with his secretary. I had him go through his telephone routine many times and he began getting the point.

'One of his disadvantages was that while his opponent could think on his feet my man was a plodder. So one major strategy was to minimize this disadvantage by arming our man before important board meetings with information on problems that would come up. For example we had his secretary regularly get from the secretary of the Board the agenda so that he could be more intelligent in answering questions put to him.

'Finally, I had him work to shake up the president a little to get the president more fluid. The president had been taking my man too much for granted. You shake up a superior by varying your tempo. In this case the president had always kept him on the defensive with such comments as "What's this I hear?"

'One day at my suggestion my man said to the president, "Say, who was responsible for that television programme of ours last night?" The president, startled, said, "Why . . . I was. . . . Why?" My man then said, "Nothing. It was a damned good programme." And so he was able to shake up the boss and get a little control of him. You shake up a person by starting out with a statement that seems critical and then when you get him off dead centre change to something friendly.

'About a month before the decision was due on the president's successor, my man was invited to a cocktail party held at the chairman of the board's house. He came away disappointed. He said, "I still don't know a thing." I had to restrain myself from calling him a damned fool. I assured him that he obviously had won. This was the final size-up and the crucial fact was that his opponent wasn't there.

'And so he got the job of being president at $40,000 a year and his opponent was encouraged to keep his job.'

As we indicated earlier, utility executives in general tend to be well down the scale in competence. In this case we can only hope that the company got the best of a not very impressive lot in its new president. At least his own competence for leadership improved.

On the gaudier side of coaching, here are seven steps one Manhattan coaching firm with thick rugs and a handsome suite of offices recommends to its ambitious clients:

1. Write up sketches on index cards of all the important people in your company who are on your level or above.

2. Keep a file on all the important people you meet and ask your wife to keep it in order.

3. Keep an idea file.

4. Examine your daily performances on the job in order to make regular reports to your boss. Performance may be taken for granted unless you take the initiative in communicating your projects.

5. Communicate outwards – try to write for publications, trade journals that are hungry for new material.

6. Communicate upwards – a realistic person accepts politics as part of the job. . . . Sometimes this may edge out into social spheres. Entertain fellow employees. Follow your immediate vice-president into your favourite bar and have a drink with him.

7. Take your job specifications sheet to your boss and encourage him to discuss it with you. Try to get him to make some notations on it if and when it needs adjusting. After six months take some of the best examples of your achievements and talk to your boss again with your original and your present job specifications. Let him know how you have grown and how the job has grown.

It may indeed be possible to help an ambitious young man get ahead with such coaching. But it is reasonable to surmise that if he faithfully keeps this card file on all 'important' people and dutifully follows his immediate vice-president into a favourite bar, the coaches will have succeeded in producing a real grade-A corporate creep.

CHAPTER 17

The Problem of Being the Right Age

If the man is forty-five and has not yet had a responsible job he should, sad as it may seem, be shunted aside. . . . The world is full of people who haven't moved along very fast. We are dealing with a pyramid. Comment by an official of one of the nation's leading executive-recruiting firms

The people who size up candidates for executive openings are likely to say the candidate should be a 'good age', and let it go at that. Some state laws make it illegal to discriminate on the basis of age (i.e. being 'too old'). In actual practice the managements of a great many companies – and their recruiting consultants – take age very much into consideration in filling openings and weighing a man's future.

Management people talk about 'age-position relationships', 'back-up policies', and 'successor-planning policies', all with age factors in mind.

They also agree ruefully that, so far as age is concerned, the pickings tend to be relatively thin today in the age bracket where they normally prefer to look for candidates for top-level jobs: the group now between forty-five and fifty-five years old. Relatively few young trainees were getting management training during the Depression and World War II years when this group was at the trainee age. Not enough were being trained in view of the explosive growth of industry and the growth in ratio of managers to workers.

Dr Gaudet drew for me a U-shaped curve to depict how, over the years, the number of candidates coming into management-training programmes has varied. Our present prime prospects for presidencies in the forty-five- to fifty-five-year-old group came into management at the bottom of the U. This is particularly likely to be true if they are in an older company. Younger companies tend to have younger top executives. (And all kinds of companies have filled out their management pools by recruiting men who really got their basic management training while working for the wartime government. Robert McNamara is a good case in point.)

In general, however, it can be said that the prime prospects for top jobs in this age group are in a wonderful seller's market for their talent. To turn the coin over, it might also be suggested that the survival-of-the-fittest law has not worked too rigorously with this group. Quite a few of them are sad excuses for executives by any standard. Today's young men, especially those under thirty-five, face a much tighter competitive situation. In some ways this is a hopeful development – or could be in a situation where the criteria for success are ethically and socially sound ones that challenge the young men to become outstanding leaders and not just to win on the basis of blandness, adaptability, and political skill.

Most of the serious candidates for corporate presidencies in the U.S. today are in their early fifties. They will, on the average, be tapped by the age of fifty-five. In Great Britain they are tapped somewhat earlier.

U.S. corporate leaders may conceivably be influenced to name more younger men as presidents by the example of a man in his early forties taking over the presidency of the U.S., although some corporate elders view the ensuing developments in Washington as good reason for their wariness of upstarts in high office.

Patterns vary drastically by companies, of course. The executive suites of a number of successful companies – usually fairly new electronics or prefabricated-home companies – are manned almost entirely by men under forty. An ambitious, talented man may hesitate to join such a company because, barring upheavals and premature deaths, he might have to wait at least two decades to get a shot at the top. On the other hand, in many other companies, particularly in the utility field, the executive suites are occupied almost entirely by men over sixty who are apt to feel strongly that a man is incapable of assuming serious responsibility unless he is near their age. In one utility company in the West all but two of the company's top sixteen men are in their sixties or late fifties.

In any company a man at any level may well conclude that his future progress is likely to be slower if men his own age move into the important positions immediately above him. Such a man, who feels he is blocked or has been by-passed because of age factors, is 'movable'. The executive recruiters, as suggested earlier, are constantly searching for 'movable' – or secretly discontented – men (and women). They can often look at the age pattern of the top six or eight men in a company and then say, 'Here is your movable man.'

A good example of a movable man was Cramer W. La Pierre, who grew up at General Electric and at the age of forty-three found himself in a spot where the layers directly above him were filled by men from his own age group. He was then reportedly making between $10,000 and $15,000. So he decided to accept a vice-presidency at the much smaller American Machine & Foundry (at more than double his G.E. salary) where he filled the position with distinction. Three years later the G.E. management, looking over its outstanding alumni for a possible vice-president, hired him back. In 1961 he was given a newly created job of executive vice-president at a total compensation that may well exceed $150,000. Recruiter John Handy feels that quite probably he would not have got past all those layers if he had not got out and made the end run.

The president of a half-billion-dollar Midwestern company modestly attributed his achievement in attaining such high office by the age of forty to 'poor succession planning'. The founder of the company, he said, had 'expected to live forever' and had given little thought to providing for the development of a strong line of succession.

Few major corporations today are guilty of such neglect. Sid Boyden, the search-firm leader, told a presidents' forum of the American Management Association in 1960 that proper *timing* belongs in every executive development programme. He was referring to the effect of age and its relationship to the problem of executive retention. A second-level team often finds itself behind a top team which still has years to go before retirement. This second team often contains outstanding men who are fully developed and ready but, because of bad timing, are frustrated and stymied and consequently receptive to offers from other companies.

In some instances the larger, older companies reportedly slow down the progress of a highly promotable young man simply because they fear that the spectacle of such a young man skyrocketing up through the ranks might create more anxiety among other managers in the hierarchy than his services at the top would be worth at that point. Similarly, I came across instructions in an appraisal manual which specified that a man over fifty should not be considered for the job of manager of field sales – regardless of his qualifications – because this post should be reserved for a younger 'back-up man' who could ultimately replace the general sales manager. It was felt that a man over fifty could never make it to the general sales managership, and so shouldn't be moved into the back-up position.

John Handy suggests that 'the appraisal of a man's growth potential cannot be determined by simply plotting an extension of his earlier progress. Every man has a ceiling to which he progresses easily and without serious check, but when he reaches this he commences going sideways. . . .'

The younger a man is when he reaches any point in a hierarchy the better he is likely to look on the form charts. He should never get into a position where he is competing with younger men, because everyone would rather have younger than older. If a man is fifty-two and hopes to be a department head it is possible that he is being compared with men who are department heads at the age of forty-five. Up in general management, however, he can be sixty and not be considered too old.

Career counsellor B. Vernon Reed of Reed, Cuff explained the hazard in these words: 'If the man is at the same spot at forty that another man is at by the age of thirty-five he is not going to get the same consideration. Other things being equal, they will look for the younger man because of the desire for continuity of management. They prefer a man of fifteen years' potential rather than one of ten.'

A man who falls significantly behind his age group faces the danger of being classified – formally or informally – as a competitor who has topped out. One of the questions that interviewers of candidates for a certain chemical company's sales force are expected to answer is: 'Is he past his peak?' Some suggest that there is a need in corporations today for more approved and honoured ways that men who are not ambitious to reach high levels can win recognition at their present levels.

It should be noted that impressive recoveries have been made by men presumed to be over age. Arch Patton relates: 'Executives who have fallen behind those in their age group on the organizational ladder frequently do outstanding work when given encouraging leadership. For example, a man who had been a divisional plant superintendent for ten years, suddenly, at the age of fifty-two, started a meteoric rise that lifted him to the executive vice-presidency of the company at fifty-nine.'[1] It seems that the man, by nature uncompetitive, belatedly realized that his contemporaries were moving ahead of him and he opened up with a brilliant burst of effort that made him stand out.

Similarly there are many occasions when a seemingly over-age man is sought for an important job. George Saum of George Fry & Associates reported that his organization was looking for a man approaching sixty for an executive vice-president's job that would pay $125,000 a year. The very promising younger men coming along were not ready and the company did not want to block their way by bringing in someone of their own age. This company, he said, had not reasonably phased out its development of leaders. He cited another instance of a company that hoped to find a good man approximately sixty-two years of age who could serve as financial vice-president of a hundred-million-dollar company for about three years until a young man the company was bringing up was ready.

A good deal of thought has been given to assessing what Mr Handy calls the 'Age–Position Relationship' as one variable factor in establishing a man's potential. Where should the man be on the success scale at each age level and what should he be doing about his career?

On Handy's scale, for example, anyone over thirty-three should be making more than $15,000. Or as he put it to me: 'Any man thirty-three years old and making $15,000 a year I would like to see. On the other hand if you have a man of forty making only $18,000 a year you wonder if perhaps he has started going sideways.' To put the relationship in terms of job title, he said that it looks fine if a man is a chief industrial engineer at the age of thirty-four but if he is a chief industrial engineer at the age of forty-four one wonders how much more potential he has.

A Boston recruiter, Martin Flesher, had drawn up an 'Age to Earnings Ratio' that involves five checkpoints.[2] To separate the doers from the 'dreamers' he has posed these minimum earnings:

By 25	$5–6,000
By 30	$10,000
By 33–35	$15,000
By 40	$25,000
By 45	$25–35,000

Hergenrather Associates, which functions nationally but mostly on the West Coast, advises me it has arrived at a slightly different age–earnings relationship for 'top drawer' men:

Age 27–30	$9–12,000
Age 30–35	$12–18,000
Age 36–40	$18–25,000
Age 40–45	$20–30,000
Age 46–50	$23–35,000
Over 50	$28–50,000

(The Hergenrather people believe that particularly at the over-fifty age level West Coast salaries tend to be depressed by the fact that many high level executives with an eye on retirement are anxious to get located out there.) Some other recruiters questioned whether any age–salary table could have much meaning nationally because of all the variables.

How should a man of high ambition comport himself at each level? Ideally, in the years between twenty-five and thirty-five the ambitious man should be running hard to get himself out in front of the herd. Executive counsellor Reed suggests that 'a man should be pretty well up into middle management by thirty-five. If he is not well advanced by thirty-five he won't develop enough momentum in the next seven or eight years to carry him into a top spot.' Mr Handy offers the thought that 'it is a blessing if he does not meet the right girl until he is twenty-eight, because he should hold himself free to move from one company or industry to another, and to any area of the country, where his best opportunity for experience and growth lies. He should try to avoid during these years finding himself in a spot where he must consider any other factor in the selection of a job than the prospect that it will develop him, and presents a logical advancement in his career as planned.' Mr Handy considers it wise for the man under thirty-five to broaden his experience by taking three or four different jobs – provided that he stays at least two years on each and confines his jobs to the same industry or line of work.

By the age of thirty-six, however, 'your gambling years are over,' Mr Handy states sternly. By then the man should have a pretty good and realistic concept of his potential and his goals.

It is in this next period – thirty-five to forty-five – that many aspiring managers become profoundly restless. One survey found that more than half of all executives in the thirty-five to forty-five group wanted to move. Some suggest this restlessness is due to 'career menopause'. Perhaps another explanation is that many men who in their early years have had a number of easy and fairly rapid advances find themselves bumping up against ceilings.

When a man reaches thirty-eight, Mr Handy contends, he

should figure on settling down, watch carefully his percentage of successes, try to get into organizations that are well managed, and work towards a position in general management.

The youth among the men who have passed beyond functional responsibilities up into the area of general management is forty to forty-five, he says. 'Companies are looking for the fellow age forty-two who has a proven record of success and has proved while on management committees that he has good judgement. One of the biggest steps in growth is to go from being a department head into general management. The head of the sales department, for example, may well know more about the department than anyone under him. But if he gets into general management he will have people under him who know their jobs better than he knows their jobs.'

The major companies do little hiring of new men who are over forty-five. The Hoff, Canny, Bowen survey found that only about one executive in ten who changes jobs is above the age of fifty. Mr Handy suggests that the years from forty-five to sixty-five should be viewed as the 'years of realization'. The man should continue to improve his effectiveness and realize that though he may continue to progress it may well be that the price of the further progress will be stiffer and stiffer in terms of risk and sacrifice.

The executive past forty who is eased out of work is a man who indeed deserves our compassion, especially if he loses out because of a reorganization following a merger (as often happens) rather than because of simple incompetence or offensiveness. He must maintain his dignity and his expensive style of life under trying circumstances. Relocating may take six months to a year or longer. Forty-Plus clubs help thousands of out of work older executives keep up their morale by giving them an office to go to until they can relocate. The members are required to devote two days each week to duty on the mimeograph machine, the typewriters, or the telephone, or going out to make a presentation, on behalf of the club, to company officials who might have a spot for some member. The New York club at 15 Park Row gets out a monthly 'Executive Manpower Directory' with information on members – usually about eighty – who include ex-presidents and range in salary desired from $8,000 to $35,000.

One reason that the larger companies are more reluctant than smaller companies to hire the older out-of-work executive, regardless of his competence, is that all their lock-in devices such as pensions – which are devised to keep managers loyal – unintentionally serve to lock out older newcomers. Some out-of-work executives talk their way around this obstacle by going onto the payroll as 'consultants', which leaves them outside the pension system.

Another way to view the stages of executive life is the psycho-dynamic one. Dr William E. Henry, social behaviourist now at Michigan State University, studied the personalities of three groups of executives that had mean ages of thirty, forty, and fifty. He subjected them to projective tests in which they were invited to make up stories about pictures. Dr Henry was particularly interested in how they resolved any conflict between organizational goals and their need for personal identity and found considerable differences at the three different age levels:

The thirty-year-olds. For them life seems 'amazingly simple'. They see the world in which they work as demanding achievement and are convinced that 'assertively following the leads provided them by that world will result in success. This younger group is thus oriented to the organization, to what they understand to be the expectations of others.'[3]

The 'sense of identity' for men in this group is highly similar to the formal goals of business organizations. In short we seem to have here, in purest form, the kind of organization men in grey-flannel suits so well and so often described.

The forty-year-olds. These executives, in contrast, are starting to see the world as far more complicated. 'They are by no means as certain that the objectives of the organization are inevitably correct, and they begin to wonder if wholehearted devotion to achievement and accomplishment in the business world is indeed the one true life,' Dr Henry noted. Along with a more questioning attitude these men are also beginning 'to re-examine their own inner lives and personal desires. This frequently takes the form of wondering if they should not have chosen some other occupation, one they propose as more attuned to human values, to the rewards of interpersonal relations.' Although more questioning, they hold to their earlier goals in business but see the goals in broader perspective.

The fifty-year-olds. The concerns over conflict of values continue, yet tend to be resolved on more internal and personal terms. More than either of the younger groups, the fifty-year-olds become 'contemplative and philosophic'. Their concern is more with 'integrative schemes than with the earlier direct action'. They seek to derive a *rationale* and a meaning from their previous experience as guide-lines for the future. Some, Dr Henry pointed out, work out sound, analytic *rationales*; others simply fall into patterns of 'nostalgic reconstruction of their successes' and seem like repetitious windbags to the juniors who must work under them.

Dr Henry's finding of an increasing interest in personal identity and individualistic values as executives get into their forties and fifties raises a most interesting point. William Whyte had noticed that some of the older top executives he examined were privately sceptical of the organization-man creed and qualified their fealty but Whyte appeared to assume this was because they were relics of an earlier, more inner-directed way of life in America. If indeed advancing maturity – and not just old-fashioned ideas – helps breed scepticism of organizational goals, there would appear to be more hope for individualism.

CHAPTER 18

The Six-Figure Incomes
and Other Lures at the Top

If people in business were more clearly identified by the luxury of their offices, those of lower status, if properly indoctrinated, would strive harder to do a better job and reach the higher positions. Steel magazine, reporting advice given to a personnel conference of the American Management Association on the effective use of incentives[1]

Non-business leaders at times wonder why on earth, in this era of abundance and opportunity, grown men willingly submit to the indignities, perils, and obligation to sacrifice that are common experiences on the pyramids.

There are a number of explanations. For some of the climbers, the mere exhilaration of reaching the top is reason enough for the climb, just as it is for many men who risk their lives to climb the Himalayas. Others seek the joy of running things, the sense of authority, and the power to dish it out to others. And some climb to try to escape the harassments and humiliations of low office in the corporation.

But of all motivations none is so powerful for most aspirants as the prospect of financial gain. To a red-blooded executive the phrase 'a shot at the top' means first of all a chance at the best pay-cheque in the company. In one company out of five the top pay (and power) goes to the chairman of the board (General Motors and U.S. Steel are examples). But in most companies the top pay goes to the president.

Nation's Business concluded from a survey that in 1962 approximately 100,000 executives were stepping into the $15,000–$20,000 job category, another 50,000 were moving into the $25,000–$50,000 range, about 20,000 were moving into the leather swivel-chair class ($50,000–$100,000), and at least 400 were getting up into the swivel-with-headrest group ($100,000–$500,000). Cornell economist Ernest Dale notes that in recent years executives have been voting themselves salary increases entirely out of proportion to corporate earning trends.

The size of that top pay-cheque varies, naturally, with the size of the company. Average pay for 335 corporate presidents studied by the American Management Association in 1957 proved to be $68,000; but in 1961 the total pay of the chairman of that giant of giants, General Motors, was more than ten times that figure. G.M.'s Frederic Donner took home $696,000. That year nine other General Motors executives were paid more than $400,000. Robert McNamara left the presidency of Ford, a job paying $410,000 a year to become U.S. Secretary of Defence – the world's biggest business – which pays less than one fifteenth the Ford figure.

Perhaps the best peek at the pay of the top officers of the nation's larger corporations can be seen each spring in *Business Week*'s tabulations of executive pay drawn from proxy statements. The average compensation of the best-paid men in 113 major corporations reported for the year 1960 or 1961 is a figure slightly under $200,000. That is quite a bit more than the pay of the President of the United States. And this figure covers only salary and other direct compensations. Companies have developed, in addition, a host of plans to offer their executives shelter from the United States income tax laws, which can swallow most of any six-figure salary. These take such forms as deferred payment plans, contributions to pension funds, very generous expense allowances, and chances at stock options (which lost much of their power to enchant in mid-1962 when a sharp decline in stock prices began). A whole line of business has grown up to help top executives hang on to a larger share of their compensation. An executive recruiter once told me of shifting a man from a $75,000-a-year job to a $60,000-a-year job because of the latter's 'vastly superior tax shelter and deferred income plan'.

Executives insist that after 'a certain point' getting more

money is not a prime incentive, since most of any increase will go to the U.S. Treasury. Still, they concede, it is important that their money 'label' be right. If they are to hold their heads high while consorting with their peers they want the proxy statements to show them wearing a nice label. The nicest label is a six-figure income.

Below the number one, the pay for key men falls off on a carefully devised pattern that is pegged to the top man's pay. Thus if you know the salary of any one man near the top you can often make an educated guess about the salary of anyone else in the top line-up. The usual pattern of pay is designed to provide a maximum of status enhancement for the top men and a maximum incentive to hustle for those below. Dean Rosensteel of the A.M.A. is probably the nation's leading authority on executive compensation scales. His conclusion, after studying the executive pay scales in thousands of companies, is that most commonly the number-two man gets 70 per cent as much pay as the number-one man. If number one is president, then the number-two man in many cases will be the executive vice-president.

Below number two, he explains, you see a dropping off in 10-per-cent steps. The number-three man (frequently the top marketing man) gets 60 per cent the president's pay. The number-four man (often the financial vice-president though sometimes the marketing man) gets 50 per cent as much as the president, and so on down to the lower end of the key jobs.

In a hundred-million-dollar company, Rosensteel indicated, you might have a pattern of pay like this:

President	$100,000
Executive Vice-President	$70,000
Marketing Vice-President	$60,000
Financial Vice-President	$50,000
Manufacturing Vice-President	$40,000

From there the fall-off would become increasingly gradual as you dropped down through the treasurer, controller, industrial relations, or personnel director until you got to the purchasing agent, the chief engineering executive, the research and development director, and the public relations director. These last are likely to be $25,000 jobs, at best.

In many giant business organizations – unlike the federal government – total compensation drops off rather precipitously as one gets below the top layers of the hierarchy. This can be seen in the case of a General Electric official who was caught up in the price-fixing conspiracy. He was a department head four levels down from the top. As a twenty-first-level man his annual pay – including incentive compensation – was about $80,000 a year. But when he was demoted to being a seventeenth-level man (before being pushed into resigning) his pay dropped to $27,600.

Some presidents have found it necessary to arrange a hefty increase in their own salaries for the high-minded purpose of permitting the company to raise the salary ceilings of restless subordinates.

Because increases in pay lose some of their meaning after that 'certain point', companies have sought increasingly in recent years to promise those who reach the pinnacles a lushness of surroundings and another reward such as a private dining room with chef.

The patterns of lushness vary, but it is not uncommon for the successful competitors to be offered not only outer offices with a half-dozen windows but also swivel chairs with headrests, original $10,000–$50,000 paintings for their office walls, and leather-bound folders with their names printed in gold for taking conference notes.

At the New York headquarters of a company making alcoholic beverages, the chairman has in his inner sanctum a water closet of carved marble. Another corporation near-by has a Picasso on display in the men's room of its executive suite. At the world headquarters of an oil company in Dallas, the thick wall-to-wall carpeting of the executive suite on the top floor runs right into the men's washroom.

When Hollywood producers set out to make a movie that called for an executive-office setting (*North by Northwest*, starring Cary Grant) they borrowed the new executive suite of a financial corporation on Madison Avenue, New York.

It is more dramatically sumptuous than anything Hollywood designers could imagine or afford. The company was interested in creating an image of 'solid modernity' for itself. A few hundred thousand dollars quite probably went into art work alone. The walls glow with original Légers and Afros. At least one picture, a Léger, is valued at $18,000.

The company's vice-president in charge of administration happily showed me about his spacious inner office. He is a modest, studious man in his mid-forties who had just come to the company from another company in the Midwest. His office is a symphony of colours keyed to the tan Chinese grass paper on the walls. He said he had been permitted to go on a shopping expedition for art and, after consultations with the company's decorator, to buy two matched abstracts ($4,000) for his walls. A thoughtful feature of his office that startled him most pleasantly when he arrived was the compartment for telephone books by his desk. He found two telephone books in the compartment. One was for Manhattan, the other for his home town in the Midwest.

Many companies see to it that their higher executives are also assured a sumptuous existence while on duty away from their office. The *Harvard Business Review* concluded, after polling 2,800 executives, that 'Most executives believe that high officials should "be more comfortable" than lesser officials while away from home.' Many top officials reported they now take their wives on business trips at company expense. (The wife of a division manager winked at me when she said she often serves on 'the entertainment committee' as an 'official hostess'.) Top-level conferences increasingly are held in such comfortable and rejuvenating spots as Hawaii, Las Vegas, Miami Beach, and White Sulphur Springs.

The plush public rooms of San Francisco's Fairmont – perhaps the nation's most elegant hotel – are considered more appropriate settings than college classrooms for executive seminars. An official of an Ohio university which was holding seminars for local high-level executives said one of his problems was adding such features to the regular classrooms as lounge chairs and white-jacketed waiters to serve coffee so that the executives might feel more at home. He said, 'These-guys are used to pretty fancy surroundings.'

When the executives travel to Washington they will probably stay in the company's special suite for top officers. One company suite, which is pretty much reserved for the occasional visit by the chairman, has such thoughtful appointments as a phone in the bathroom, bathrobes and a stock of liquor.

The top executive of a major company is likely to travel to Washington and elsewhere by private plane or by chauffeured limousine. One wife of an executive of a very large corporation said that the way her husband and his associates habitually travel is a disgrace which Congress should investigate. Her husband's company is one that no longer prints the company name on its executive planes. Such labelling is not considered a good advertisement, especially to stockholders who may happen to be waiting at the airport for a scheduled commercial flight.

For long trips, the use of the company plane to transport an executive can cost twenty times as much as a first-class ticket on a commercial airline. Several thousand companies now provide company planes for their executives and a number of companies maintain fleets of more than a dozen planes. One cannot help being impressed by the compassion that companies show for their executives if one visits an airport in the Cape Cod area on a Friday night in the summertime. Company planes, with crews of two to four, come skimming in to deliver weary executives to their vacationing wives.

Companies in both the U.S.A. and Western Europe are showing more and more thoughtfulness in helping the men who reach the heights to enjoy a proper style of life off the job at company expense. Such fringe benefits take the form of supplying country-club memberships, keys to hidden lodges, use of company yachts as well as chauffeured cars, permission for wives to ride on company planes and accompany their husbands to spas for free medical check-ups, and in a few cases even company-owned, rent-free homes. In Europe these are called the *perks* (perquisites).

The *Steel* article quoted at the beginning of the chapter listed proposals made to the A.M.A. conference for improving the incentives offered to potential executives. Two points were of particular interest:

MORE CLUBS FOR THE UPPER CRUST. Club memberships of ascending importance for the various ranks would serve to spell out who is who and to what level he belongs.

COMPANY FINANCING OF UPPER CRUST HOUSING. Companies could sponsor financial backing for various levels of housing, retaining the most expensive architects for upper level executives and some of the lesser ones for lower ranks.

There has been a tendency, too, in recent years for companies to become more open-handed in bestowing lustrous titles on the people who get near the top. This upgrading of titles is non-cost incentives and has been stimulated to some extent by the great growth of companies through merging and diversifying. If a large-sized company swallows a middle-sized company, what title is now assigned to the man who has been president of the swallowed company? Properly he should become a division manager. Many companies, however, let him also keep the title of president. In a recent count, Borg-Warner Corporation had forty presidents or chairmen: I.B.M. had seven presidents; Firestone Tire & Rubber had a dozen presidents. In such situations it is not uncommon for the presidents of subsidiaries to work under the direction of a boss at headquarters who has the title of vice-president.

Status inflation has become so flagrant in the handing out of vice-presidential titles in the financial and advertising businesses that it is not difficult for the office boy to visualize that someday he may at least become a vice-president – in title if not authority. Foote, Cone & Belding, the advertising agency, in one count, proved to have sixty-nine vice-presidents; and New York's Bankers Trust Company had one hundred and eleven vice-presidents.

Such openhandedness with titles in banking and advertising not only serves as a non-cost reward to the titleholder but flatters outside clients who must deal with an official of the company. It is always nicer to know you are dealing with a vice-president, not just some flunkey. In some advertising companies there is one vice-president for every twenty-five employees. In old-line manufacturing, by way of contrast, you are likely to find there are still several thousand employees per vice-president.

All these very considerable and increasingly sophisticated rewards of title, salary, deferred compensation, perks, and lush trappings of office are felt to be necessary – in addition to high salaries – in order to make high office in the modern corporation seem irresistibly alluring to a great many talented climbers. On this the system, as constituted, absolutely depends: the executives, no matter what the hazards, must continue to want to climb.

PART 5

HAZARDS AND HARASSMENTS

CHAPTER 19

The Worst Kinds of Places

Of the eight vice-presidents in office when Mr Bendetsen became president [of Champion Papers, Inc., two years ago] only two remain. The Wall Street Journal

As any minister's wife knows, some jobs make more personal demands upon a jobholder than others. There are often unwritten expectations about behaviour.

The Educational Testing service, for example, found that within a cross-section of major companies some executive positions made stringent demands on the personal behaviour of the incumbent, requiring that he show 'an unusually high concern with the propriety of his behaviour, especially in his interactions with superiors. . . . He senses obligation to conduct himself according to the stereotype of the conservative businessman.' Positions found to be notably high in such personal demands were vice-president for manufacturing, director of purchases, budget administrator, manager of accounting, division works manager, controller.

The personal demands vary most importantly in the harassment – often downright anguish – likely to go with the job. In a stress-producing spot the executive may feel he is working in a sweat tank. The most upsetting strains, for an aspirant to high corporate office, are likely to be associated with three kinds of job situation:

Working under a corporate autocrat. The autocrat can be a plant manager or he can be a president. A few U.S. companies have the reputation for being notably democratic. American Motors, General Foods, American Cyanamid, and Continental Can are examples. In general, however, American managements are authoritarian (though less consistently so than French management). Frequently it is the structure that is authoritarian, but in some instances whole-hearted autocrats are in charge of the structure. They see the corporation as their private preserve, their job as an extension of their magnificent personality, and their subordinates as expendable pawns. If they have a model from the recent past it may be the late Sewell Avery of Montgomery Ward who, though past the normal retirement age, relentlessly broke up any management team at Ward that became strong enough to question his indispensability. One alumnus of this period at Ward recalls that Mr Avery got rid of sixty-seven vice-presidents, a lot of them outstanding men.

Probably among the most colourful of the modern-day autocrats are Lewis Rosenstiel of Schenley Industries, Howard Hughes (who has long controlled Trans World Airlines), and the Chairman of a cosmetic company.

Of the temperamental Mr Rosenstiel it is related that when one executive reported to work on a Monday morning after he had displeased the great man he found his door was locked. Colleagues gathered around. Someone finally found a janitor who opened the door. The office was bare.

Of the erratic Mr Hughes (who has conducted important negotiations by flashlight on a municipal dump, who has disappeared for months at a time, and who prefers nocturnal business meetings in cars) dozens of startling stories have been told about his autocratic treatment of subordinates, including his presidents. He has had five presidents in fourteen years. One of them, Carter Burgess, told me he had been president of T.W.A. for six months before he ever saw Mr Hughes.

An aide to the cosmetic king reports that he has held on to his job by 'avoiding all contact' with his chief. The tycoon, a taut-faced perfectionist who had a row of pill bottles near his desk the only time I saw him, reportedly has fired as many as five men out of a single position within a year. Two of his relatives are among those who have departed from the company. In one year executive turnover is said to have been 130 per cent. An alumnus of this firm's management gave voice to one theory about his chairman's psychodynamics when he told an investigator for *Sales Management* that his chief, 'having had only limited formal education, seeks to prove his superiority by hiring – firing – college graduates.' Some say that recently he seems to be mellowing slightly.

A thoroughgoing autocrat is likely to insist that any important communication within the company or to the outside world cross his desk. He is likely to subdue and harass his managers by keeping them busy memorizing dozens of manuals of operating rules. He may further intensify their chronic anxiety by keeping as a ready-reference item near his desk a record of who supported and opposed each major action.

An official of Richardson, Bellows, Henry recalls how one presidential autocrat of a chemical-processing company 'had his entire executive staff so cowed that they would not say anything he didn't like to hear. They would try to guess instead what he would like to hear. The whole bunch had so lost their self-confidence that not one was effective when a new president finally was brought in, after the old one retired. The new man found a beaten-down group and had to bring in quite a few new men. He was able to salvage some but many were too broken in spirit to be effective. Some sought only routine responsibilities that did not expose them to any risks at all.' As I listened, it sounded to me like the description of experimental rats after they had been overexposed to electric shock whenever they tried to reach the cheese.

Working where there is a high degree of individual insecurity because of the nature or state of the enterprise. Companies struggling to survive not only are prone to fire or reassign executives who may conceivably be contributing to the company's trouble but are also more vulnerable to outside raiders or acquisition hunters. A successful invasion – even though it may solve the insolvent company's financial difficulties – brings suspense to the individual executive. He must wonder which unprofitable aspects of the company operation the raiders will scuttle in order to make the company's stock jump nicely for them. In an ordinary merger the executive can't be sure whether in the reshuffling he will come out better or worse. And he must wonder how he will mesh with new superiors and associates.

When a company finds itself in a messy situation it is also prone to turn over its direction to a strong-willed man who doesn't mind playing rough if it helps the company's cause.

Some lines of executive work are inherently more turbulent – and insecure – than others. In most companies there are certain jobs that are vulnerable to abrupt turnover. Sales and marketing executives are usually more exposed to the hazards of sudden dismissal than any other kinds of executive in a company. Cadillac Associates, Inc., the executive-placement firm in Chicago, finds that companies dealing in consumer products are likely to have a faster turnover of executives than companies specializing in industrial products.

Advertising executives – especially those working for agencies whose fate depends upon keeping a few major clients satisfied – are among the most insecure of all working executives. The Life Extension Foundation, which checks the health of thousands of executives each year, finds that 21 per cent of all advertising men examined suffer from 'constant tension'. This rate is three times as high as it is for men at the other end of the spectrum, doing research work. (The Foundation also reports finding 'constant tension' at unusually high levels among executives who dislike someone with whom they must work, or who suspect they aren't getting fair credit, or who are afraid to express themselves.)

The strains common to advertising-agency men erupted in the letters-to-the-editor column of *Advertising Age* when the wife of an out-of-work advertising executive voiced her wrath at the industry's seemingly cruel system of handling people. Her husband had been wooed out of a job as a corporate advertising manager to work for a large agency with a big new account requiring a man with his talents. The account soon was lost and later two others. An 'axe date' for her husband was announced. 'You have never seen so many men – earning from $15,000 to $30,000 a year – so utterly petrified in all your life,' she wrote. 'Not only account executives but people . . . right down to secretaries. . . . Men who had been there nine and ten years were thrown out with hardly a word – men with homes and children and huge expenses. Men who had played the game of beautiful clothes, expensive restaurants and showy fronts. . . .'

Another letter-writer echoed her lament. 'The adman's wife soon learns to have a pitcher of martinis waiting. If he doesn't turn up she'll take care of it herself. Each evening she wonders whether he is going to make it and when she is to begin typing up résumés.'

The median age of death of advertising men is around sixty-one, or a half-dozen years earlier than for executives in allied fields. Men working for brokerage houses also experience an abnormally high amount of strain. One study by two doctors found that the curve on a chart of heart attacks among stockbrokers appeared to follow the stock-market curve. The head of a branch office of a major brokerage house complained to me that he had lost five account executives in their forties and early fifties within the past ten years because of heart attacks and bleeding ulcers.

Working in an environment in which plaguing ethical questions frequently arise. Commenting on the behaviour of officials involved in price fixing in the electrical industry, a writer for *Fortune* commented that 'it is getting increasingly hard to know what's right or wrong about a lot of business practices.' Many of the agonizing ethical questions that confront a good many executives are not simple temptations to feather personal nests – though these exist – but rather involve ways of responding to the expectations of higher officials. The order comes down to 'beat last year' or 'increase our share of the market by 10 per cent.' Perhaps the superior unwittingly sets impossible goals. Or perhaps he is a hell-for-leather operator who wants results and is indifferent to the human cost. The sales manager of a very large corporation questioned in a survey on business ethics by the *Harvard Business Review* commented: 'The constant everyday pressure from top management to obtain profitable business, unwritten but well understood, is the phrase "at any cost".

He added that to do the expected sometimes required 'every conceivable dirty trick'.

Another kind of response to such demands is to become dishonest with the company. Norman Jaspan, who heads a large organization of business investigators and consultants and is sometimes called 'the J. Edgar Hoover of business', relates: 'When we impose upon people impossible tasks, unrealistic quotas or budgets, something usually snaps. The juggling of figures can be traced to a whole host of pressures. . . . Many feel forced to resort to manipulations not so much to line their own pockets as to "get off the spot and look good". It is only a short step from manipulating records in order to avoid pressures to manipulating for personal profit.' In one recent year 60 per cent of all the $60,000,000 of losses uncovered by his Investigations, Inc., was attributable to employees at executive or supervisory levels.

I do not wish to overstress such ethical conflicts as a part of executive life – or to suggest that other occupational groups don't have comparable ethical problems – but still the evidence suggests that a good many aspiring executives do face disagreeable problems that must be resolved at the conscience level. The *Harvard Business Review* survey reported that 'four out of five executives giving an opinion affirm the presence in their industry of *practices which are generally accepted and are also unethical*!' And *Modern Office Procedures* reported a survey finding that most of the managers questioned felt that in the course of moving up through the ranks a man was likely to be expected at some point to take part in activities not usually considered honest or decent.

The kinds of ethical question that a rising executive may have to face are numerous. If he is in charge of soliciting business for a large trucking or shipping company he may discover that some of the traffic managers he must deal with in order to get transportation business expect $1,000 or more a month kickback. He may be expected to install illegal wiretraps if necessary in order to find out what product the main competitor is about to release. He may be expected to arrange call-girl entertainment for important male customers at a convention (or gigolos for women executives). He may have to cooperate with labour racketeers, or help modify the company's records for tax-evasion purposes. If he is an engineer he may be expected to modify a reliability report. And if he is in marketing he may find he is mapping advertising strategies that involve half-lies or an exploitation of the consumer's hypochondria, dread of age, or fear of sexual inadequacy.

And then of course there is the agonizing, and recently sensational problem of price fixing. This may range from the hard-to-prosecute practice of 'following the leader' of the industry in setting prices or bids to outright collusion. Evidences of price fixing have been all too clear in segments of many industries, but nowhere have they been more publicized than in the field of electrical equipment, which produced an indictment of forty-eight executives and thirty-two corporations, touching virtually every major producer in the industry. Federal District Judge J. Cullen Ganey, who heard the case in Philadelphia, called it 'a shocking indictment of a vast section of our economy, for what is really at stake here is the survival of the kind of economy under which this country has grown great, the free enterprise system.' Most of the men before him had been torn 'between conscience and approved corporate policy'. All too many of these men were the kind of conformist who 'goes along with his superiors and finds balm for his conscience in additional comforts and the security of his place in the corporate set-up.'

Our concern here is only with the kinds of personal dilemmas the executives involved had encountered. The conspirators met in resorts, homes, and hotels to set prices, rig bids and split up markets. Their meetings were called 'choir practice', the companies had code numbers, and bids were often rigged in an ingenious system called 'phase of the moon' which enabled each company representative to know when it was his turn to bid low.

Some of the executives at General Electric, who were required to sign a company policy directive (20.5) promising obedience to anti-trust laws, testified that they were verbally instructed by superiors to forget the written pledge and attend price-fixing meetings. In some instances, the testimony indicated that stern verbal orders against attending meetings were followed by a broad wink. In one case, a puzzled sales manager said to his superior, 'I didn't see you wink.' The superior said he hadn't winked. But the same manager continued to meet with competitors to fix prices, ultimately became a $135,000 vice-president and was being discussed as presidential material before he was jailed.

A number of the G.E. executives indicated that it was painfully plain to them that if they wanted to get ahead in the company they would have to cooperate in the price fixing. It was called 'a way of life'. The marketing manager of the switchgear division, a man named Walter F. Rauber, was replaced after he refused to violate the 20.5 directive he had signed. The man who was brought in to replace him testified at the Senate hearings that he was told that Rauber was not 'broad enough' for the job. This replacement soon felt he was under orders to fix prices. At some stage he resisted the pressure, but ultimately went along with the price rigging. Richard Austin Smith of *Fortune* reported a colleague of this man as saying that all the pressures produced profound changes in him: 'He used to be a hail fellow well met . . . until he was put under that great pressure for profits. Then he simply shrank into himself; everything got to be cold turkey with him – without any warmth at all.'

It is the built-in harassments of many executive jobs that make the $50,000-and-up salaries that go with them seem less solidly gratifying. An eminent British scientist, the late Lord Rutherford, was once chided about the fact that he made less money a year than many dismally unsuccessful business managers. He is said to have replied brightly:

'Yes, but it is only fair: look at the nasty work they do.'

CHAPTER 20

Private Strains: The Executive as Lover, Father, Neighbour

As a man climbs the ladder of success he becomes . . . unwilling to engage in the kind of sex experiences that he did in his early life, looking upon them as . . . out of line with the dignity which he must maintain even with his wife. Lester Dearborn, director of the Counselling Service, Boston, and former president of the American Association of Marriage Counsellors

It is perhaps unfortunate that the rising executive does not punch a time clock. That would remind him that when he leaves the premises of the company he is returning to private life. As it is – especially with so much of his work and semiwork carried on after hours in clubs, conventions, at home, and even town-hall meetings – his sense of being an individual apart from his job is often negligible. He is like the thespian who forgets he is in his own bedroom.

His company is likely to approve of this forgetfulness. Here are two comments that reflect a common corporate attitude. A writer for *Nation's Business* admonished: 'The manager must be flexible . . . able to mould himself to his organization's pattern even in his manner of living off the job.' And an advertising executive in Akron (a former 'corporate man') commented approvingly in *Advertising Age* in late 1960: 'When you join the corporate way of life, it is taken for granted that you will live up to your income and travel in circles "befitting your rank".'

Perhaps the first thing to be noted about the rising executive's private life is that he is a man in motion. His motion upwards in the company's hierarchy usually causes him – whether he likes it or not – to leave old houses, old neighbourhoods, and old friends behind.

Our man is also often in motion geographically. He is away from home a great deal on trips. *Business Week* estimates that the average corporate official spends 'at least one third of his time on the move – mostly by air.' The magazine explained: 'Not too long ago you put a good superintendent in charge of a distant contract and let him run the show. Today the business has got too big, too complex, too competitive. It takes constant shuttling by the specialists – safety men, labour-relations experts, purchasing agents, tax experts, attorneys, technicians – to keep things going.'

This geographic motion is also likely to involve a great deal of job reassignment. This means packing one's furniture and family off to a new part of the country every couple of years. Some recruiters in evaluating a man rate him on his 'geographical flexibility'. Long-distance movers report that the managerial group provides them more business than any other. One report on inter-state moves shows that nearly two thirds of all customers are from this group. Allied Van Lines has concluded that the average executive changes localities five times. The other day I met an old high school classmate who had married a man now serving as a sales executive for Philco. She said they had moved fifteen times since they had been married.

Companies have gone to great pains to ease the financial burden of moving, by paying all direct and many indirect moving costs. Some will even take the executive's old house off his hands if it is impossible to sell the old house quickly except at a big loss.

The recent 'slow' market for homes in many areas has forced companies to acknowledge that the man they wish to transfer may have a new reason for dreading the uprooting. Until recently the value of houses was going up, up, up. But with a glut in housing in many areas, the executive who moves faces the strong possibility of losing a few thousand dollars. *The Wall Street Journal* cited one company's housing executive as estimating that three out of four men being transferred by that company were taking a loss on the sale of their house. The loss comes not only from the possible sag in value of the house but also from the realtor's fee for selling – often running $1,000 to $3,000 – and legal fees for closing the sale. A company seeking to ease the executive's moving pains may offer to buy the house or make a loan to the executive based on the average of two appraisers' estimates of the real current value of the house. In mid-1962 Westinghouse reportedly had 300 unsold houses on its hands.

The companies usually stress that the aspiring manager can turn down any proposed move that does not appeal to him and his family. But the unstated alternative, one president of a shoe manufacturing company told me, is 'the company cemetery'. If the manager has a good excuse he may get another chance. But in general, a part of playing the role of a good manager is to go where higher authorities feel your talents can for the present be best put to the advantage of the company.

A woman realtor who has spent several years selling many dozens of homes to executives in Westchester County, New York, briefed me at length on the problems of executive mobility. Her Briarcliff-Tarrytown area offers an excellent observation point for executive mobility because large numbers of executives and semi-executives of I.B.M., General Electric, General Foods, Union Carbide, Shell, and Addressograph, which have nearby offices, try to nest there. She said, 'There's something terrible about all this corporate moving.' In one town in this area one fourth of the entire population leaves every year. She told of one executive and his wife who refused to move. 'The wife put her foot down and said, "I've had it." The husband knew of course that he was now dead-ended with his company so he soon arranged to take a job with another company in the area. Six months after he took the job this new company moved him out to the Midwest!' (I met one executive who was moved, with his family, from Fairfield County, Connecticut, to Los Angeles, only to find his job abolished within eight months. He has moved back to Connecticut, at his own expense.)

The big companies in this realtor's area keep files of all houses for sale or rent. To assist incoming people, some have books which cover every detail of financing and buying houses. One of these books is called a 'relocation manual'. I.B.M., she said, maintains two sets of books. One is for research people, the other for the managerial types. She had the very definite feeling that some of the companies tried to steer incoming executives into areas appropriate for their particular level in the company hierarchy.

One aspect of the I.B.M. way of life stirs her compassion. 'They come down from Endicott or Poughkeepsie [other I.B.M. strongholds] where they have been living in a palace that cost them $18,000 and find that they can't find anything here that is as good for $30,000.'

She believes that the mobility of their lives is having a very definite effect on the kinds of homes the executives coming into Westchester want. She said these younger executives want very conventional new houses. They don't want any troubles. They like the developments, they love them. They want an entirely saleable house. She added: 'So we're starting to get nothing but ranch houses and split levels. I think this trend is going to change the landscape of America. Most builders in this area are most reluctant to build anything unusual. It is only the really top executives who are individualistic in their preferences.'

Wall-to-wall carpeting is considered to be a sign of high status in America, but in this area the executive types don't want it. Wall-to-wall carpeting is a headache if you have to move a good deal. You've got to get your money out. Only the older executives who know they aren't going to move any more are attracted today to wall-to-wall.

I talked with this realtor in her own home, a sort of split-level house but somewhat original in design. 'This house would not be acceptable to the corporation man,' she said. 'The lay-out is not typical of this area, and it has the built-in bookcases. Those are the real drawback. Most of the young executives don't own books. You never see more than a few in their homes, and they are apt to be old textbooks.'

The effect of all the moving on the individual is far from clear. If there is strong family solidarity, it is now felt that such movement does not seem to produce too much stress. Youngsters who are raised as 'corporate brats' become adept at making quick, easy adjustments. Some might say this ease of adjustment should in itself be a cause of parental concern. One executive's wife who has moved many times said her children seem to meet the new situations well. It is exciting. But she said they all missed the fact that they have no roots anywhere, no family homestead. One top executive of a large company told me he resolved to stop accepting promotions that involved moving after his teen-age son complained: 'Gosh, Dad, I'd like to live just once in a house for four or five years!' Dr Lewis B. Ward of Harvard tells of an executive who advised his company; 'I'll move anywhere you want now, but when my children are adolescent and get into high school, I'll quit rather than move.'

There is general agreement that, in terms of emotional stress at least, the executive himself is affected less than other members of his family by all the moving. He still has his ties to his company, which remain a constant in all the change. The man's job seems to be the one stability in the lives of the families who must move frequently. But as Dr Harry Levinson of the Menninger Foundation points out, this fact becomes an emotional hazard if the tie to the company is threatened. If anything happens to the business, this dependence makes it pretty rough for him.

Psychologists point out that during the Second World War the U.S. Army learned that individual morale remained higher when replacements were sent into strange new situations in units rather than individually. When buddies were moved in a group, the men still had their stabilizing ties to other members of the platoon even when all of them found themselves in a strange territory. Perhaps this suggests that if in the future executive mobility continues to increase it might be helpful to send the executives, as far as is feasible, into new areas in platoons.

The most serious effect of the frequent moving on the executives is apparently not emotional stress but rather a philosophic feeling they often get of a shallowness in their lives as citizens of their communities. This was mentioned to me by several executives and they attributed it to their company's insistence that in spite of all the moves they be 'corporate citizens' in their communities and make a great demonstration of being community leaders. When *Dun's Review and Modern Industry* asked its panel of presidents if it was true that they expected their subordinates to be active in community affairs, 86 per cent of the presidents did 'expect company executives to extend their leadership outside the company.' The report added: 'Private clubs and public charity are not considered so important to the company as are civic and community affairs, where altruism and responsibility, along with more practical motives, are cited.' Others report that for the men sent into a town from outside to manage chain supermarts or chain hotels or motels, their ability to be ardent community leaders often ranks as more important than their skills in management.

Management Record reported in mid-1960 that 'companies seem to be growing steadily more community-conscious. An increasing number of them encourage their employees to join various civic groups like Rotary and Kiwanis clubs, the Lions, the Elks, Chamber of Commerce, etc.' It added that some companies spell out this 'encouragement' in policy statements and cited this statement as an example: 'All employees are encouraged to take part in civic activities as individual time and inclination dictates. Individuals who assume civic responsibility increase their list of friends and develop leadership, which reflects creditably upon the company's place in the community.'

Executives say that it is when you superimpose this growing insistence that executives engage in community activity upon the ever-increasing mobility of the executive population that you get the rub, the feeling of shallowness. A top financial officer of a very large corporation which has offices in many cities complained to me: 'The moving and lack of a permanent home is the big problem. You are not a full citizen in your community. Frequently it is a forced citizenship. The executive is moved about and is expected to play a stereotyped part in community life, the Chamber of Commerce, and so forth. He is not doing this as a citizen but rather as a company representative – which is a much different thing. It is totally wrong to assume the executives are participating in their own right. Sure, I participate here in my town, but there is no question that a part of my acceptance in the community is that I am thought of in terms of the company, not as a person. We executives lead a nomadic life. We are gypsies. We are not making notable contributions towards the advance of a stable civilization.'

One observer described the adaptive technique developed by many an executive in these terms: the company wants its manager to get involved in his community but wants him to stay ready to move. So he learns to look involved without being involved. If he *really* became involved in his community, he wouldn't want to move.

The expectation that the executive will be active in community affairs extends to politics. Presidents on the *Dun's Review* panel agreed that 'political activity among executives is becoming increasingly important. Some believe this is necessary to counteract labour's political activity.' When the hat is passed down Mahogany Row for political contributions – as it frequently is – it is almost always a Republican-owned, right-wing hat. Recruiter William Hertan observed that in most of the older-line companies, 'if the top men are Republican, everyone is Republican.' A manager on the fringes of top management told me: 'I'm as high up here in my company as a Democrat can go.' The common expectation that any aspirant to high corporate office will be an out-and-out political conservative represents one of the most severe infringements by the corporation on the citizenship rights of its people. An aeronautics executive in the Southwest revealed he had been specifically admonished by his president to 'get straightened out' on his politics, which meant backing Goldwater-type conservatism. He was shocked.

Perrin Stryker, who has a wide following among executives, explored company attitudes towards political loyalty in his

The Men from the Boys when he drew up an imaginary correspondence between a puzzled junior executive and a retired elder statesman of the company.[1] Junior, in his troubled inquiry, asked the older man if he – Junior – should feel obligated, as a matter of company loyalty, to 'defend the company and all its policies no matter how much he might personally disagree with them.' He said this point came up because of a company request in a recent political campaign that employees such as Junior 'express ourselves clearly in public on current issues including high taxes, government-in-business and labour monopolies. Frankly this policy is not setting too well with me and several of the other fellows in our executive-development programme. . . .' 'The funny thing,' he added, 'is that all of us who disagree with the company's new policy are Republicans. . . .'

Senior replied that of course Junior shouldn't be just an unthinking company stooge. Then he added: 'But if you've really thought through your political convictions, then loyalty to the company could mean accepting the new policy and going out and supporting those convictions the company publicly supports.' He added that if Junior disagreed with the company's positions he should of course keep still in public, but not necessarily privately. As a parenthetical thought Senior added, 'I need scarcely say that a manager who publicly espoused political views his co-managers did not share would not be likely to get to the top echelons.'

Some of the more broadminded companies do urge their people to participate in politics without the usual assumption that the participation will be on behalf of political conservatism. I.B.M. is one such company. In fact Thomas Watson, Jr, supported the Democratic candidate for the Presidency in 1960.

In one large company headed by Republicans a young executive just below the top was active in Democratic politics. He seemed to consider this a plus factor. 'Someday someone is going to need a Democrat on the top floor here, and 5,000 cards in the computer are going to be processed and my card will be the only one that will pop out.' Others suggested he is over-optimistic, and that the farthest 'left' an ambitious executive usually dares to be is 'independent'.

Whether he is Democratic or Republican, real political activity has one very important value to the corporation-bred young man. One executive who dined with me before going on to a political meeting explained: 'You can't work in politics at the local level without developing certain concepts about human relations. For example, if I want to get something done now I think first of whose toes are going to be stepped on. You never learn that in the management-training courses, which tend to be superficial and mechanical.'

The executive's frequent identity as a company representative first and an individual second tends to make him preoccupied with status symbols. Whether he likes it or not he may feel impelled to present an image of success by sending his children to private schools, owning a sailboat and a place in the country, having the right club memberships, having three cars in the country or, if he lives in a larger city, a limousine and driver or a self-driven Cadillac convertible. A city-dwelling executive may get by with a part-time driver obtained from a chauffeurs-for-hire service. One of the major can-producing companies subsidizes its more promising younger executives so that they can buy homes in a Fairfield County, Connecticut, town that is regarded by the company as a good address.

A Shell Oil executive and his wife who adored one specific house in Westchester County finally decided it was out of the question. He felt he couldn't possibly buy it because four doors away in a comparable house was another Shell man who was his junior in status.

The company will often be concerned too that its executives join the 'good' clubs. William Hertan has concluded that the question of whether a man belongs to the right club increases in importance as he gets into the upper echelons and in the smaller-city areas. The question is of less importance at middle-management levels, especially in large cities. He added that another problem in terms of social acceptability is 'watching that you do not join clubs that are in disfavour.'

The vice-president of a large company in the Detroit area quit his job and took a job working as an administrator for a small rural college at half his salary when he found he was expected to join a fashionable Grosse Pointe country club that cost $1,800 initiation fee and about $100 a month to maintain membership.

On the other hand, a young corporate vice-president who moved to a Fairfield County, Connecticut, town was so desperately anxious to get into the one 'right' country club of the area that he had every single member of the membership committee as guest of honour at dinner parties in his home. He also offered one older non-golfing resident $300 if he would drop out of the club and let him take over his membership. It was explained to him that this just wasn't done.

A survey made by the National Industrial Conference Board of the practices of forty companies revealed that twenty-five of them were actually paying for memberships in country, athletic, and downtown dining clubs for selected executive employees.

The company's expectations about the aspiring executive's private life also extend to his – and his wife's – preferences for social companions. This is particularly true in so-called company towns.

The forthright, folksy wife of a vice-president of a middle-sized company in a mid-Ohio city confided to me that she has a special problem because she has for decades been a close friend of the wife of the founder-chairman of the city's largest enterprise. The problem is that the wife of her husband's president is not particularly esteemed by this grande dame of the city; so my informant and the grande dame, by agreement, keep their socializing on an intimate, secretive basis.

A manager who is rising in the company hierarchy is often expected to break clean all his socializing contacts with families he has left behind. The most explicit statement of this expectation – at least for lower-level managers – appeared in an article entitled 'The Office Caste System' which was first printed in *Modern Office Procedures* and was reprinted in the American Management Association's *Manage-*

ment Review (July 1960). One question centred on what a supervisor should do about his old friendships when promoted to a level above his old friends. The article reports: 'His question gets a brief, sharp answer from the personnel director of a large company: "Cut 'em off. If a man cherishes his old friendships, he'd better not take the promotion." Most companies agree it's best to amputate.'

At a later point the article conceded that such amputation was harder on the wife than on the supervisor. It quoted one supervisor who confessed he had had a fight with his wife because he suggested she had better drop out of her bridge club with seven wives of men from her husband's former level in the hierarchy. The article commented: 'Unfortunately, companies don't agree with her. One executive speaks for many companies when he says, "The wife has no choice. She can be downright dangerous if she insists on keeping close friendships with the wives of her husband's subordinates".' The article indicated that children also are affected by an unstated need to avoid children of people their father has surpassed.

As a gesture towards offering a constructive ending, the article suggested that a manager withdrawing from old socializing patterns should do it 'gradually', find 'logical excuses', and added: 'He can accept invitations at first to subordinates' homes, but should reciprocate only with group invitations – then not accept at all.'

Such attitudes have induced most company wives – according to a survey by John A. Patton, Inc. – to remain as aloof as they can from corporate socializing and make their close friends outside the company.

All the demands and expectations that are made on the executive and his family often colour the marriage relationship which began with such high hopes and personal warmth. Many couples allow for the pressures and by their resolve and love build fine, satisfying, enduring relationships. Others falter. In general, the executive's way of life is not conducive to good family life. That at least is the flat assertion that has been made by Dana L. Farnsworth, M.D., of the University Health Services, Harvard. From the wife's standpoint, there are three special sources of strain, beyond the demands on the husband's time and expectations of mobility:

She often feels unemployed, isolated, because the company demands so much commitment from her husband. For most aspiring, hard-driving executives, the job comes first. One study on alcoholism revealed that the wives of executives showed the largest increase of alcoholism of any of the categories studied. Furthermore, many wives who feel they are losing their husbands to the company try to turn their sons against the fathers with admonitions not to 'be like him'.

She is often made to feel inadequate because she does not maintain as orderly an environment at home as her husband has become accustomed to in the precisely ordered corporate environment. His long exposure to the corporation has usually given him an acquired taste for orderliness. He may come to see it as a supreme virtue. But when he gets home he may find himself coping with the normal chaos of everyday living. His son is late meeting the train. His daughter is flunking a crucial course. His wife has forgotten to mail a cheque (his secretary would never forget). He finds there is no ice in the trays. And so he explodes with Goddamnits. Home may loom to him not as the widely assumed quiet retreat where he can recharge his psychic battery but rather as a source of disruption and confusion in his otherwise orderly world. So he works later and later, and on weekends retreats to his golf club where everything is well ordered and his status is confirmed at every turn. A good many anxious wives take their cues from such behaviour and compulsively seek to establish a hushed, pin-neat environment of order at home that rivals that at the office.

She often feels her husband-executive forgets he is in a different obedience system at home and is not dealing with subordinates when he deals with her and the children. Dr William Menninger says: 'There is a tendency I've seen too often on the part of executives who think they can run their family like they can run a business. We have a certain amount of authority in our organizations with which . . . we can issue edicts and pronouncements . . . and there isn't any argument. The fellow who tries to run his family that way doesn't get along, or at least the family doesn't get along.'[2]

Finally, the love relationship itself is often affected. Or, perhaps more accurately, often neglected. The aspiring executive is frequently such a busy, restless man that even sexual activity plays a lesser role for him than it does for most men. Sociologists W. Lloyd Warner and James C. Abegglen in their survey of 8,300 executives concluced that the men, as a group, had no great interest in sexual activity.

Executives and their consultants tend to react with visible indignation to suggestions that executives may be sexually inadequate. One management consultant exclaimed: 'Why, some of the most virile men I know are businessmen!' Their virility is not in question, but the amount of thoughtful attention the executives give to the romantic and affectional aspect of their lives.

Psychiatrist William B. Terhune, who has worked with a good many executives, has stated of one group of men he assessed: 'Contrary to popular opinion, they had only moderate sex drive. Sex, women, and home actually meant little to them. . . .' In another connexion he stated flatly: 'It is found that most executives truly know very little about one of the most important things in life – the true meaning of love in its broadest sense.' Tenderness may not come easily to such men. The executive may be immersed in the contents of his briefcase all evening. When he becomes aware that it is midnight, he stamps out his last cigarette, restuffs his briefcase and goes up to a new area of concentration, his wife. But by then she is either asleep or cold to his businesslike advances. The edition of a business journal who thought it unfair to call executives poor lovers explained matter-of-factly: 'It has to be quick because they have less time.'

An official of a leading management-consulting firm, who described the typical executive as 'a hell of a poor lover', suggested that the executive's taste for orderliness acquired at the corporation again complicates his relationship with his marriage partner. Even in bed it is hard for him to get it through his head that his partner is within her rights in not being in the mood to do what he wants to do. Chaos looms. The official suggested that many executives take the orderly way out by establishing themselves in separate bedrooms and taking much of their sex drive out on their work.

I took up the controversial matter of executives as lovers with Lester Dearborn, director of the Counselling Service of Boston and one of the nation's most respected marriage counsellors. Over the decades he had heard an earful, especially from the wives of executives.

Many a wife has confided to him that when she first married her executive husband he was a very good lover and she thrilled to her introduction into sex life. But as the man advanced up the executive ladder he became so enamoured of his work that he was less conscious of his role as a marital lover. When he did approach her for such a relationship, Mr Dearborn continued, 'it was rather hastily arrived at and without all those preliminaries that mean so much to a woman.'

Mr Dearborn said this negligence on the part of the executive husband is not universal. 'We do have a few executives,' he said, 'who take time out for the purpose of making love. They will take their wives away on a week-end trip, take them to a hotel. They want to do something to get away from the strain of the business world and from the demands of their friends.' Many of those who do not find ways to have such interludes with their wives 'seem to feel that the only way they can have sex under relaxed conditions is in the arms of a mistress. A wife whose emotional needs are not being met becomes a frustrated and irritating person to live with, and this certainly doesn't enhance the frequency of wanting to share intimate experiences.'

Another problem is that matter of dignity many executives feel they must maintain. Mr Dearborn said that the problem of maintaining dignity can lead the husband executive to a call-girl. 'The executive can go to a convention and get away from where he is known and take time off to associate with a call-girl. By doing this he can take off his dignity with his clothes and be just a devilish playboy. I think he actually has a need to do this.' But with proper insight, he added, the rising executive 'could do it at home or take his marital partner with him to the convention and act the same way.'

All his years of conferring with executives and their wives have led him to this irreverent conclusion: 'Executives may be at the top of the ladder vocationally but they are at the foot when it comes to making love.'

CHAPTER 21

When Stress Becomes Distress

A well-adjusted executive is one whose intake of pep pills over-balances his consumption of tranquillizers just enough to leave him sufficient energy for the weekly visit to his psychiatrist. Attributed to Arthur 'Red' Motley, former chairman of the U.S. Chamber of Commerce

U.S. business executives should be among the world's healthiest specimens. They eat well, they play golf and paddle tennis, they sail more than most, they are chosen for fitness in the first place, they take more vacations, and they are subjected to periodic assessments of their health by outstanding doctors. One gets the impression from reading business journals, however, that executives have killing jobs, that tension among them is increasing at an alarming rate. KEEPING THE BOSS ALIVE is a sample headline.

Much of this certainly springs from the executive's prone-ness to hypochondria and self-pity. Executives come out approximately average – despite their great advantages – in both mortality and rate of mental illness (except, as noted, in such lines of work as advertising). Even a statistically average amount of emotional distress in executives has serious implications, however, because the subordinates of such a distressed person are likely to absorb some of the distress. And of course the higher up the distressed person is in a hierarchy the more emotional havoc he is likely to create down through the ranks.

Some interesting patterns in ailments afflicting executives emerge. A Chicago executive health clinic found, after making what the American Medical Association called 'one of the most exhaustive surveys of executive health ever completed', that men and women in high-level jobs suffer less from deficiency diseases than Americans generally, but tend to suffer much more from metabolic disorders. These include high cholesterol and low rate of thyroid secretion.

The executive pattern also seems to vary so far as tension is concerned. Parke, Davis & Co., in its booklet *Patterns of Disease*, reported an interesting variation. Executives are 47 per cent more likely to suffer from 'anxiety states' than workers. *Dun's Review* reports: 'Studies have shown anxiety, worry and brooding to be far more common among highly placed businessmen than among the public at large.'

There is some evidence that executives are better skilled than average at keeping their anxieties from being conspicuously apparent to others. Psychiatrist William B. Terhune, medical director of the Silver Hill Foundation in New Canaan, Connecticut, states:

'Executives are subject to the same psychiatric disorders as other people, but it is a fact that they have fewer severe nervous breakdowns. They know that if they break it usually means liquidation. They keep the lid on their emotions until their emotional life becomes an arid desert, and life loses meaning and value ... they hold their jobs in spite of a deteriorating emotional state – until they explode, some of them into an emotional illness which is frequently catastrophic.'[1]

Susceptibility to the kinds of tension that produce physical or mental ailments seems to vary significantly with a person's position in the hierarchy. There seems to be a medical basis for the often-cited executive boast: 'I don't get ulcers – I give them!'

It is not at the top of corporations that you find most of the ailment-producing tensions. It is among the people lower down, the strainers and the ageing 'junior' executives who feel frustrated because they were ambitious and fear they have topped out or feel they are caught up in a giant organization that is so big that it does not permit them to maintain a personal identity. Such people often seethe. In the process, if the seething is prolonged, something in the mind or heart may give.

Dr Paul Dudley White, the eminent heart specialist, is one who has noted that it is not the senior executive who is the most likely candidate for coronary thrombosis. Rather, he says, the candidate is 'a junior executive, probably striving for the top, or a white-collar worker surrounded by frustrations. He's short, stocky, muscular, large-boned . . . often an athlete. His personality is vigorous, ambitious, aggressive.' A study of executives and subordinates at Standard Oil of New Jersey reached much the same conclusion about the incidence of high blood pressure and ailments of the arteries. And psychologist James N. Farr suggests that the highest proportion of neurotics is not at the top but rather 'down at the next lower level – this is where you get the neurotic striving, the frozen perfectionists.'

The aspiring executive, as we have seen, has many grounds for feeling a heavy load of stress. Most executives can handle the stress or at least keep it from becoming seriously disruptive, if they aren't too neurotic to start with. Earlier in this book I have quoted psychologists to the effect that a certain amount of neurotic tension often serves as a propellant in thrusting an ambitious young man up through the executive layers. But along the way the neurosis can start making trouble for him. Feelings of stress can be magnified and made severe by a number of factors that add oppressively to the usual stresses of executive life. For example, there are:

The stress of working for a prolonged period under a superior who seems erratic and non-rational as well as critical.

The stress of maintaining what Dr Terhune calls 'the executive front' – the serene, friendly, flexible façade – when the going gets rough. A great many executives make a fetish of never showing emotion (including irritation) or seeming to be ruffled. They are overintegrated types. This can be dangerous. Du Pont's chief psychiatrist, Dr Gerald Gordon, put it this way: 'Emotions are an internal flowing of vital energy, not unlike an electric current. This energy can build up to a high potential if you try to bottle it up. Ultimately it will find an outlet.'[2]

The stress that accompanies success and the rising through

not only hierarchical layers at the company but also simultaneously rising through several layers of the nation's social structure. Psychiatrists have reported that such highly upward-mobile individuals are more than normally susceptible to psychosomatic disorders.

The stress of the highly aggressive individual who feels blocked, and of the inherently passive, dependent type of man who finds he is expected to show more aggressiveness.

The stress that comes seemingly at the peak of achievement – 'Promotion Neurosis' – when, for example, a man who has won promotion because of his skills as a specialist is thrust into a situation in which he must employ general executive skills in areas where he knows less about details than his subordinates. Similar stress also may afflict the young man who is promoted beyond his depth too early and can't cope with his job.

The stress of the older man who finds himself fighting off bright younger men.

The stress of prolonged compulsive overwork and straining by the person who is so stress-blind that he fails to recognize that emotional exhaustion is approaching.

Dr Robert Felix, director of the National Institute of Mental Health, has suggested that there are three ways in which businessmen react unhealthily to stress: by disorders of bodily functions, by disorders of thought, and by disorders of behaviour.[3]

The beginnings of these disorders can often be observed by perceptive associates and subordinates.

Among the *disorders of bodily functions* commonly observed in stress-ridden executives are the psychosomatic ones of hypertension, coronary-artery disease, ulcers, colitis, and arthritis. Seymour Freedgood in his study of the home lives of high-level auto executives living in Bloomfield Hills, Michigan, cited a report that many of these men's wives 'live in constant dread of a phone call telling them their husbands have had heart attacks.'[4]

The man with the 'ulcer personality' is commonly characterized as the hard-driving, overintegrated type who is unable to give vent to his aggravation. A man who is over his head in harassing or unusual work and who is a poor administrator may be afflicted with attacks of diarrhoea or indigestion, or – more seriously – come down with colitis.

Psychologist Robert McMurry suggests that many of the bodily disorders resulting from stress take the form of 'flight reaction', a suppression of anxiety feelings which results in a conversion neurosis comparable to battle fatigue in soldiers. The commonest manifestations of this sort of reaction are upsets of the gastro-intestinal tract, hypertension, and allergic reactions.

Disorders of thought in executives commonly take the form of indecision, apprehension, anxiety, chronic worrying that leads to insomnia, distaste for responsibility, obsession with details, and the more serious disorders: hallucinations, delusions, including an insistence upon personal infallibility. Psychologists report that the neurotic executive who finds himself unable to make decisions can be most ingenious in procrastinating by using such flight mechanisms as escaping into detail, ordering research studies, or denying that any problem exists.

The more common *disorders of behaviour* seen in distressed executives are flights into rage, taking out hostile feelings on one's family or subordinates, jitteriness, hitting the bottle. Mrs Marty Mann, executive director of the National Council on Alcoholism, believes that the same characteristics which may help propel a man towards executive success may also propel him towards heavy drinking when his load of stress becomes oppressive.

More dangerous symptoms of behavioural distress are a growing rigidity of behaviour or radical changes in behaviour, as when a once-quiet person starts being noisy and quarrelsome. Several psychiatrists who have worked with executives comment that the aspect of executive stress which has most impressed them is the emotional disturbance that spreads to the wives and children. One psychiatrist told me that neurosis is rarely confined to one person in a family. 'It breeds difficulties and you find that where there is one neurotic you soon have a nest of neurotics.' (Others – especially industrial psychiatrists – blame the stress on the executive more on the home situation than the job.)

A number of U.S. corporations now provide opportunities for all managers to have regular or frequent chats with company-paid psychiatrists or psychologists to gain insight into their stresses and anxieties. At least eight companies – including Eastman Kodak, U.S. Steel, I.B.M., and Du Pont – have full-time psychiatrists, and a couple of hundred companies provide the part-time services of psychiatrists.

Many executives who realize they are seriously troubled are reluctant – perhaps understandably – to confide their emotional problems to a company-paid psychiatrist or psychologist, despite assurances that the relationship would be confidential. Many seek help outside the company. The psychiatric department of the Montreal General Hospital has established a Night Centre which permits executives, among others, to work by day and be tested for their emotional troubles at night. At least three New York hospitals – Gracie Square, Mt Sinai, and Montefiore – have experimented in recent years with similar after-work services. At Montreal the executive checks in after work for the night as he would at a hotel, receives individual counselling as well as periodic group therapy.

Some executives go – on their own or at the urging of the company doctor – to a secluded sanatorium which caters in particular to 'exhausted' executives. Such a non-profit retreat for the diagnosis and treatment of nervous disorders is the Silver Hill Foundation in New Canaan, Connecticut. Dr Terhune, its medical director, has observed that 'most people in business over forty are beset by conflicts and frustrations and anxieties and angry projections not always recognized by themselves, but often embarrassingly evident to their associates.'

To encourage executives to catch any emotional difficulties early, his organization offers a six-day 'emotional check-up' for executives. It is hoped by the Foundation that executives will come to recognize the need for such a periodic check-up

– whatever their emotional state – as readily as they recognize the need for a periodic physical check-up. The six-day check-up – in a pastoral setting – involves taking a psychiatric life history, making an analysis of the man's characteristic emotional responses, an analysis of his intellectual equipment, a thorough psychological examination, a personality study, and a complete physical check-up.

Dr William Menninger also advocates a regular 'emotional check-up' for executives. If he were making the check-up of an executive's emotional health, he states, here are five things he would particularly want to know:

1. What is the constancy of the executive's personal relationships? All of us have occasional 'bad' days and difficulties in getting along with some people, but how often does this man have bad days and quarrels?

2. Can this man accept a good deal of frustration and is he patient enough to work and wait for what he wants, or does he insist on having what he wants when he wants it?

3. Does he get much of his satisfaction from a constructive giving of himself, or does he always want to be on the receiving end?

4. Is he reasonably free of anxieties and tensions – and can he find release from those he has by his patterns of relaxation off the job? Dr Menninger adds, 'If one is chronically tense and anxious, and is unable to relieve his distress, he is emotionally sick.'

5. Can he listen to counsel and seek help as well as he can give out advice and admonition? Dr Menninger believes there are times when it is important that the executive be 'a good listener'.

Getting a hard-driving, authoritarian, self-righteous high-level executive accustomed to deference to become a 'good listener' is quite a trick, even if he is nearly immobilized by anxiety. Dr Menninger's five questions suggest the potential seriousness of the executive neurosis.

PART 6

IMPLICATIONS AND POSSIBLE HAPPIER COURSES

CHAPTER 22

The Bland New Leaders

Conspicuous personality is a requirement of great leadership.
Dr Eugene E. Jennings[1]

The results of the success process that we've been exploring
presumably can be seen in the kinds of younger men who get
selected for the top, much as the pudding's proof is in the
eating.

All kinds of men, of course, get selected. And some are old-
fashioned rough-cut colourful types. Sherwood Egbert, the
quick man with a haymaker, became president of Studebaker-
Packard. But, come to think of it, perhaps this was exceptional. Studebaker-Packard was desperate, and it did go
outside to a smaller company to find him.

Let's concentrate for a moment on the younger men who
have risen up through the ranks of large companies (1)
which have a wide dispersion of stock ownership and (2)
which operate pretty much on the basis of the traditional
pyramid of authority.

A pattern in personality emerges. Few show signs of resembling such of their memorable professional forebears as
Andrew Carnegie, Owen D. Young, Sewell Avery, William
Randolph Hearst, J. P. Morgan, Charles F. Kettering,
Charles Steinmetz, Henry Ford. Instead, the tendency is for
them to be polished, cool, handsome, adaptable, highly
energized, soft-spoken, overintegrated, non-oddball power
players. Often they also have demonstrated during their rise
a conspicuous ability to keep their heads down and their
noses clean. The common image of blandness is reinforced by
the fact that many of today's captains are generalists operating by remote control with only modest knowledge of the
thousands of functions of their business.

A suggestion of some of the above traits appear in print. After Charles H. Sommer, Jr, was promoted to become president and chief executive officer of Monsanto Chemical at the age of forty-nine, *Fortune* reported: 'His manner is quiet and unfailingly courteous. A Monsanto associate of many years describes him as one of the new breed of "highly efficient, smoothly professional business managers – skilled, intelligent, precise".' When Albert L. Nickerson became chief executive at Socony-Mobil at forty-seven, the magazine reported: 'He was spotted at an early age by management, carefully rotated up the line. [He] is an amiable man with a high gloss, equally at ease with junior executives and his board of directors.'

Once executives reach the top they are expected, in the mythology at least, to be bold innovators, strong leaders, and to become known as industrial statesmen of vision and widely respected wisdom.

But even if the new men have the potential for such a role the chances are increasingly unlikely that they can play it. In the first place they lack any assurance that they will be around long enough or that they will have the backing necessary for bold innovations beyond what backing they can muster with their own persuasiveness and alliances when the chips are down. If they manage to entrench themselves to the point where they can control nominations to the board, then perhaps they can swing it on a team basis. On their own they rarely control even ·5 per cent of their company's stock. More and more the majority of their boards of directors are people from outside the company's management and so beyond their effective control unless their group has become sufficiently self-perpetuating to control the nominations. The trend is away from management majorities on the board.

For this and other reasons (such as enforced retirement at sixty-five) the average tenure of presidents is becoming shorter and shorter. Executives may well be approaching sixty before they get the job, and certainly in most cases will be well up in their fifties. German companies, in contrast, try to place at the helm men of great promise who still are

young enough to serve for many years if they perform well.
Thirty years ago the average U.S. corporate president served
fourteen years. Today six years is better than par, and many
companies have several presidents within a six-year period.
Business Week commented that 'some companies are whip-
ping through chief executives so fast there's hardly time to get
their portraits hung in the board room.'

A man does not become nationally known as a great industrial leader until he has been in command long enough to
become firmly entrenched. Alfred P. Sloan, Jr, served as
president of General Motors for twenty-three years. Arch
Patton points out that if Sloan had served for only four or
five years it is highly doubtful he would have projected such
a strong and permanent shadow on his company and on the
national scene.

Some suggest we are moving towards a system of corporate
leadership comparable to the football platoon system. Add
to the short term at the top the now firmly held conviction
among captains of business that the well-bred executive shuns
the public limelight, except as it may benefit the corporation,
and the extent of the trend towards anonymity begins to
emerge.

The result is that most of the nation's leading presidents,
bland or not, are relative nonentities on the national scene.
They are considerably less well known to the public than, say,
the senators from Arkansas (J. W. Fulbright and John L.
McClellan) and in years gone by this was definitely not the
case. Try running down a list of the presidents of the twenty
mightiest industrial giants with annual sales in the billions of
dollars. Virtually all receive at least four times as much pay
as senators – and also considerably more pay than the President of the U.S. Here are fourteen of the names: F. W. Jenks,
J. H. Wetenhall, Porter M. Jarvis, J. F. Gordon, G. L.
Phillippe, Herbert Willetts, J. W. Foley, E. D. Brockett, J. E.
Swearingen, E. D. Johnson, M. E. Spaght, E. W. Wilson,
H. I. Romnes, E. F. Martin.

Most of the rest of the twenty (M. J. Rathbone, John
Dykstra, L. B. Worthington, L. A. Townsend, Lammot du

Pont Copeland, M. W. Cresap) have either already been
mentioned in this book or received publicity during the
electrical price-fixing scandal and the ill-fated steel crisis of
April 1962. Undoubtedly all twenty men are well known in
their localities and their industries. But it is also almost certainly true that if a national identity poll on them were to be
conducted, fewer than 1 per cent of the Americans questioned would recognize more than two or three of the twenty.
When the *Saturday Review* asked its readers some years ago
to name a man who was a leader great enough to help solve
the world crisis, not one businessman was named.

Du Pont's Crawford Greenewalt, in his book *The Uncommon Man*, sought to develop an admirable rationale for
the general obscurity of modern corporate chiefs.

The more effective an executive, the more his own identity and
personality blend into the background of his organization. Here
is a queer paradox. The more able the man, the less he stands out,
the greater his own immediate circle.

Queer it certainly is. Some observers feel distinctly uneasy
over the blurring of responsibility that comes with team and
committee leadership exercised by professional managers on
behalf of stockholders so dispersed that ownership in any
active or responsible sense is largely mythical. A number of
the larger corporations are now making strenuous efforts to
find ways to be accountable to stockholders – through such
devices as regional luncheons and random telephoning – but
by and large the separation of managements from the main
body of their stockholders is almost complete.

A high-level executive of one major corporation in fact expressed private dismay at the lack of personal commitment,
involvement, and responsibility that has come with the growth
of these mechanistic empires. He used the word *danger* and
cited the fact that many German industrial and political
leaders were caught up in Hitler's disastrous power drive by
such an attitude of non-involvement and non-responsibility.
(Today West Germany's leaders place considerable emphasis
upon individual responsibility.)

One of my major personal surprises during this investigation was my development of a new and very considerable respect for the family-dominated business empire as an institution. Once I had shared the widespread scorn for the despotism and nepotism commonly associated in the public's mind with family-dominated companies.

There is certainly nepotism and there may be despotism, but what is more interesting, I believe, is that many of the most impressive, colourful, thoughtful, and dedicated business leaders I encountered were family heirs. They were broadly educated men and had the confidence and assured backing to act on their convictions.

The senior executive of one large company was reminding me that industry today was indeed producing a number of men who were true men of breadth and statesmanship. To amplify he listed six men as outstanding examples. What struck me was that five of the six were from within families that had long had controlling voices in their companies – Henry Ford II, of Ford; Thomas J. Watson, Jr, of I.B.M.; David Rockefeller of Chase Manhattan Bank; General Robert W. Johnson of Johnson & Johnson; and Crawford Greenewalt, of Du Pont. The one non-family man mentioned was John T. Connor, forty-eight, of Merck, who before entering industry served as general counsel for the Office of Scientific Research and Development in Washington.

Three other impressive 'family' men who might well have been mentioned in the same breath are Richard K. Mellon, the Pittsburgh banker who led the battle to rejuvenate downtown Pittsburgh in a spectacular way; Joseph L. Block of Inland Steel, the first major steelman to refuse to go along with Big Steel's price increase in April 1962; and Roger Sonnabend, the young, articulate, and bold president of the Hotel Corporation of America and of the Young Presidents' Organization.

The case of Henry Ford II is interesting because several of the outstanding executives of the past decade, by any standard, have worked with him at Ford. William Hertan gave full credit to Mr Ford and the Ford family for developing or hiring a number of extremely able executives rather than mediocre conformists. He explained that in creating an environment in which such outstanding men can emerge and function at their best 'the man at the top has got to be sure of himself.'

An official of the American Jewish Committee made a remark which also points to the relative boldness of family-connected chief executives. He was talking about those few large industrial companies in which Jewish executives are able to advance to high positions even though the management is largely gentile. Two that he singled out for special admiring mention were I.B.M., whose chairman, Thomas J. Watson, Jr, represents the Watson family, and Reynolds Metals, whose president R. J. Reynolds, Jr, represents the Reynolds family.

If the publicly owned, pyramidal-type corporate power structures are producing more and more blandness at the top, what is happening to the managers who are still lower down? Many evidences of manipulation, dehumanizing and deindividualizing suggest that the pressures towards blandness are even stronger below than they are at the top. And there are additional pressures towards passiveness. Dr Chris Argyris believes that 'the pyramid itself creates dependence and submissiveness. This is increasingly so as you go down the line.'

One of the strongest statements of warning about present trends came from General Robert E. Wood before he retired as chairman of Sears, Roebuck. He said: 'In our striving for efficiency we have created more or less of a totalitarian system in industry.'

The pressures are to relate to the system. It is often explained that business today is too complicated to be run by a bunch of rugged individualists. One forthright effort to put a happy face on the submersion of the individual appeared several years ago in a book called *Climbing the Executive Ladder* by two men who had prepared an executive-training programme in human relations for the New York Central System.[2] They cautioned their executive-type readers that 'there is no room for grandstanders. . . . You must think of the team and the company first, and yourself second. Here in general, is the proposition you must get across to your employees. The company's basic goals and those of its employees are identical. . . .'

It has become fashionable to suggest that everybody is opposed to conformity of thinking but that conformity in behaviour is simply good manners. Others note, correctly, that all kinds of large, well-structured organizations – and not just business ones – tend to promote conformity of behaviour on the part of their human participants.

But how long in terms of years can a man act a role and mind his manners without his total personality becoming involved? How long can independence of mind withstand such muffling? It does not seem reasonable to assume that any profound spirit of independence can persist in such situations over decades. Dr Argyris suggests that there are 'some basic incongruities between the growth trends of a healthy personality and the requirements of the formal organization.' The conditions prevailing in the typical pyramidal structure of authority are seen as leading to conflict, frustration, and psychological failure.

Perhaps the strongest statement about the effect of conformist pressure found in corporations comes from Lawrence Stessin, writing in *Forbes*. He said it goes far deeper than mere interactions between superior and subordinate. Many executives who get caught up in a don't-rock-the-boat outlook 'apply this stultifying concept in their relations to those outside the industry milieu, turning themselves into men of no positive stands or opinions. Ask such an executive what he thinks of his company's new price policy, and like as not he'll hem and haw until he checks with public relations. Inquire about a new product: he'll sidetrack with "Our marketing boys say it is terrific"!'

In my own research I was repeatedly left with the sense that most of the people I contacted in the billion-dollar-size corporations were more constricted in their responses than people in medium-size or smaller companies. This applied even to psychologists. A psychologist working for a very large corporation called me from his home on a Saturday to explain something he said he hadn't wished to put in a letter which he had written the day before. My correspondence from people in the giant-sized companies tended to be much more guarded and formal.

Three other results of the impact of the typical large-corporate environment on the human managers involved are worthy of note:

1. The intense, near-total commitment expected of the man by the company tends to keep him so absorbed in company affairs that he becomes isolated from the viewpoints of others; and then when he finds himself confronted in the outer world with differences in viewpoints he tends to react with hostility, suspiciousness, or bewilderment.

2. The growing feeling of helplessness of many of the people caught up in the seemingly endless layers of authority of a really giant corporation should also concern us. Many develop the resigned feeling that the situation is bigger than any of us and that it has become futile to hope they can be among the few managers in ten thousand who arrive near the top.

This raises seemingly unanswerable questions about how big a corporation should be, since most of them keep growing relentlessly. Annual mergers and acquisitions nearly tripled in the fifties. The economic reasons – including tax losses and other financial manipulations – for further growth of multi-billion-dollar conglomerates may seem irresistible but what, one might ask, are the human implications of ever more growth into the indefinite future?

3. Finally there is the fact that the aspiring executive's system of values tends to go dangerously askew when he is expected, as increasingly he is, to make a total commitment to the promotion of goods or services that are frivolous, of dubious social value, or perhaps even harmful. In the corporate value system, products of least utility deserve as much dedication as products and services that contribute significantly to the quality of life. In fact, the more frivolous

products often receive the most lavish advertising attention. Seemingly countless millions of dollars are devoted to selling the least useful products (cigarettes, whiskey, cosmetics, and the like). An enormous amount of executive energy and ingenuity goes into marketing such items as electric toothbrushes and leg shavers that have the built-in light for milady.

Or consider the matter of the many executives training their ingenuity to promote the cigarette-smoking habit among young people. Tobacco advertising placed in college newspapers despite what many scientists called 'damning' evidence that heavy smoking apparently leads to cancer, heart attack, and many chronic diseases. Surely it is pertinent to ask what this kind of huckstering does to the young huckster?

But aspiring executives are not supposed to wonder why when the sales manager hammers the table and shouts, 'We've got to increase sales' or 'We've got to have something new!'

The private corporation is unquestionably the best institution yet devised for filling the material wants and needs of a society that can afford a great variety of life's amenities. But ideally, from a philosophic if not an economic viewpoint, one would think that somehow a great nation's most talented businessmen should be encouraged to apply their best creative efforts to projects that make some sort of significant contribution to their countrymen's way of life.

CHAPTER 23

Some Large Questions About Executive Assessment Techniques

Despite our growing knowledge of manipulative skills . . . there is no demonstrable or even desirable way of creating sound interpersonal relationships on any basis but sincerity, honesty and mutual esteem. Philip R. Kelly, American Cyanamid Company

The people-processing techniques modern corporations have developed during the past decade to assess and 'develop' ambitious managers are being viewed with increasing scepticism. There is doubt about the validity of many of the techniques now being so widely and eagerly used in industry. There is uneasiness over the spectacle of 'professionals' appraising strangers like merchandise. And there is some dismay at the sight of second-rate people playing God on appraisal sheets based on personal characteristics.

M.I.T.'s Douglas McGregor in his *The Human Side of Enterprise* (1960), which seems destined to become a classic in management literature, virtually dismisses as nonsense the predominant mid-century concepts used in executive development. He feels that management has wandered far off the path in its arid, mechanistic approach to the problem.

'There is almost no relationship,' he says, 'between the amount of formal programming and machinery of management development and the actual achievements of the organization in this respect. I sometimes think the correlation may be negative! Programmes and procedures do not *cause* management development, because it is not possible to produce managers the way we produce products. We can only hope to grow them, and growth depends less on the tools we use than on the environment which is created.'

McGregor and Chris Argyris, author of the sharply analytical *Personality and Organization*, stand as the two boldest and most respected of a number of recent challengers of the conventional thinking about executive development and effective superior-subordinate relationships. Some serious students of management go so far as to suggest that executive development in the U.S., at least until very recently, has become largely bankrupt.

Among companies, General Electric is one of several major institutions whose current managements are having grave second thoughts about the value of the assembly-line approach to 'developing' executives through rotating, teaching, periodic checking of personality traits, and similar routines. When G.E. invited outside interviewers to ask 300 top managers what had been most important to their development, 90 per cent said: 'It was working for So-and-So at such-and-such a place' – some inspiring mentor in an exciting environment. G.E.'s Moorhead Wright has decided that 'rating sheets based on personality traits generally fail in actual application. Time and again men who rate poorly turn out to be good managers, and vice versa. Even such a faithful standby as education is a poor measurement.'

Another popular concept that G.E. has rejected is the practice of singling out the promising men early and giving them an exclusive chance to travel the road to the top. Out of curiosity its officials checked up on 143 men who had been singled out for special grooming ten years earlier. Only a little more than a third of them were fulfilling their early promise.

The conventional annual or semi-annual appraisal of managers on the pyramids of authority has also come under increasing attack as disillusionment has spread. Some of the qualities (such as tact) assumed by the chart-makers to be important in assessing men are conspicuously absent in many outstanding men. Furthermore, how a man performs may be due almost as much to the superior as to the man himself.

Too, superiors doing the rating may over- or under-rate a

man for any number of unwitting or deliberate reasons, especially when asked to rate him on personal qualities. They may succumb to the strong temptation to play politics in their ratings; or they may differ, from superior to superior, in their interpretations of such words as *loyal*; or they may be poor judges of people, though they are highly effective in their own jobs; or they may just hate to give an adverse rating on anyone.

Still another criticism is that superiors may use the appraisal files to satisfy a natural curiosity to see acquaintances at the company stripped bare. One important management figure who would rather not be identified feels strongly that the inherent hazard in the appraisals that attempt to report on a man's way of life is that they stimulate 'the sadistic desire on the part of some people to find out what is wrong with other people for all kinds of reasons other than the most noble.'

Perhaps the most damaging feature of the conventional approach to executive appraisal is the conviction that the superior should follow up the appraisal by telling the subordinate where he stands and how he can improve. Behavioural scientists are generally appalled by management's bland assumption that subordinates want to know in detail the results of appraisals, and that in any case the subordinates should be 'counselled' on how to improve the ratings in which they are termed weak, and be appraised of a failing at appraisal time, which may occur many months after the behaviour being criticized.

Dr McGregor suggests that the effectiveness with which criticism can be conveyed to a person is 'inversely related to the subordinate's need to hear it.' He is sceptical that subordinates really want to hear criticism, even when they eagerly insist that they do. And he thinks it preposterous to expect any good to come when a man's judge slips into another robe and tries to become his counsellor.

The Institute for Social Research at the University of Michigan has studied at length the conventional 'performance review'. Rensis Likert of the Institute reports the conclusion that these reviews often do irreparable harm: 'The fundamental flaw in current review procedures is that they compel the superior to behave in a threatening, rejecting and ego-deflating manner with a sizeable proportion of his staff. . . .' Likert told of one superior in a major company who complained: 'What I would give to have that hour back! That discussion did more harm in my relationship with Joe than I can overcome in a year's time.' Dr Likert feels strongly that if a company is to get the best performance out of a man, his superior must play a supportive role, which contributes to the subordinate's sense of personal worth and importance.

Now we come to the sticky, perplexing, and highly controversial question of the widespread fascination with psychological counsel and testing in the appraisal of executives.

More than a thousand psychologists have been serving business organizations in one or another aspects of company affairs. Psychologists themselves have been among the most uneasy about some of the misuses of psychology in executive selection. Much of the overemphasis by companies has been against the warnings of psychologists.

Dr Harry Levinson comments: 'The speed with which psychological services have been accepted by industry – especially clinically derived techniques – has not been an unmixed blessing to psychology as a profession or to the managements which have sought its help.' He said many psychologists are concerned about the ethical problems involved in the adaptation of clinical techniques to business settings and 'the number of people offering psychological services who are ill-prepared to render them.'[1]

A few of the leading psychological consulting firms have been de-emphasizing testing. They place the major emphasis upon the psychologist rather than on his tools. Those who have growing doubts about psychological testing tend to be particularly wary of the use of so-called personality testing.

From an ethical standpoint, a distinction can also be made between pre-employment testing and on-the-job testing. It is more difficult to justify imposing tests on a man already employed than it is to ask a man outside the company who is under consideration for a job to submit to probing. The outside candidate still has the option to refuse to cooperate.

Here are six of the more compelling criticisms of psychological testing:

1. *Users of tests often overrate accuracy of tests as predictors of future success.* There is no question that a number of the tests for mental ability, temperament, and the like will *tend* to separate the more promising from the less promising; but so would simple observation of a man for a few days by any perceptive superior. Even I, a most utter layman, could spend a few hours in social conversation with each of one hundred trainees and afterwards greatly improve on chances in separating comers from noncomers.

One large testing firm claims that it helps clients place men successfully in eight out of ten cases. Another testing firm claims 'correct' evaluations in '85–90 per cent of cases'. Yet I found many knowledgeable people sceptical of such claims. S. Vincent Wilking, vice-president at Barrington & Company, has concluded that test information is the least important of the ways to assess an executive or would-be executive. He explained that test results are 'only right six times out of ten, or a little better than chance.'

Dr McMurry, who has considerable experience with testing, now is most sparing in the use of tests. 'There is probably no greater racket in industry than many psychological testing programmes,' he says. 'The ethics committee of the American Psychological Association has not faced up to the fact that many of the psychologists using tests in industry have not validated the measures they use for the specific purposes for which they are being employed.'

One of the most massive validation studies of aptitude tests ever undertaken is reported in *Ten Thousand Careers* by Dr Robert L. Thorndike and Dr Elizabeth Hagen. Its conclusions should produce humility in would-be testers. A study was made of 10,000 men a decade after they had taken aptitude tests during the Second World War. The authors concluded that the results 'would suggest that we should view the long-range prediction of occupational success by aptitude tests with a good deal of scepticism.'

Some knowledgeable observers contend that tests are more effective in weeding out incompetents than in identifying the inspired leaders of the future. It has been charged that no existing test will tell how hard a man will work or how reliable his judgement will be, or how much intellectual curiosity he has. Some critics say that at best you can try testing for only one third of the factors that contribute to a man's success.

In coming years substantial advances probably will be made in developing instruments with higher theoretical predictive value. But we can also assume that as more tens of thousands of managers are introduced to test-taking their capacity to survive test-screening will also improve. The self-rating tests at least can be faked. As time goes on one of the main abilities the testers will be testing is the subjects' capacity to perform in approved ways on tests.

And, even granting the possibility that test-makers do devise instruments which can guess right eighty-five times out of a hundred, it still seems a raw injustice that the other fifteen would be removed from consideration because of the errors of an impersonal test battery.

2. *Test results tend to demean even a good man by magnifying his weaknesses.* When the psychologists tabulating test results begin making their inventory of a man's psyche they frequently list weaknesses as well as strengths, even for a highly rated subject, which seems to make such test reporting essentially destructive. Recruiter William Clark commented: 'The report may say that Bill Clark is a fine prospect but he has a tendency to be impulsive or gregarious to an extent that might impair his viewpoint. Now the president of the client company reads this report and says "Gosh, I guess Bill *is* gregarious," and he will start watching out in the future for gregarious signs in Bill's behaviour, and will in fact begin reading gregariousness into his behaviour. And with this he'll assume impulsiveness.'

3. *Testing tends to standardize the breed that succeeds in the*

corporation. The tendency is, as Crawford Greenewalt of Du Pont states, to 'assume a standard or a personality pattern against which candidates can be calibrated . . .' Dr Lewis Ward found from assessing results of a 1960 survey of attitudes of executives that many were convinced that testing contributed to conformity.[2] One executive commented: 'All tests measure from a base [norm]; therefore if you use tests for part of the promotion process, you will tend towards this norm, thereby tending towards carbon copies of the norm.'

4. *In testing, there has been too much use of clinical tools by people not competent to interpret them properly.* Dr Harry Levinson of Menninger commented: 'Though projective techniques are used widely in evaluation and selection of executives, in my judgement no psychologist is capable of interpreting these instruments without a wide range of clinical experience, and a thorough grounding in personality theory. Too many people who are using these techniques in industry have neither.' He believes that any company employing a psychological consultant should assure itself that the consultant is certified by the American Board of Examiners in Professional Psychology.

5. *Testing intrudes into a manager's life further than a company has any reasonable right to intrude.* Companies of course profess that they are only interested in factors which will affect a man's performance as an executive. But when you are dragging the bottom of the ocean, as any fisherman knows, you can't be sure what is going to come flapping up in the net. One psychologist said to me: 'Of course we come up with some things that are none of our business. We always find more than we need for a specific job. A lot of the stuff we find does not go into the report. We confine the report to what we feel the client has to know to work with the person. . . .' It takes a strong will for a psychologist not to demonstrate his virtuosity to his corporate client when he ponders how much to reveal.

British business managements tend to be considerably less willing to employ personality tests than U.S. companies and generally less enthusiastic about appraisal forms. They do believe in getting to know a prospective employee personally and in studying his record with considerable care.

6. *Test findings can be damaging to the self-respect of the individual involved*, just as appraisal reviews can be damaging. The code of ethics of psychologists requires that they 'do no harm' to the person they attempt to understand, yet they are often expected to 'feed back' their findings to the men they have probed.

Graduate students at the Harvard business school who made a study of the role of the psychologist in executive selection covered this puzzle by saying simply: 'The individual candidate should be given an opportunity to read his report and to discuss it with the psychologist. Some judgement must be used, however, if the information contained in the report would be likely to prove destructive or permanently damaging.'[3] But what is 'destructive or permanently damaging'? A man could be 'permanently damaged' by reading a psychologist's report stating that while he is a swell fellow in many respects, he is only average bright.

Timed tests which a subject rarely finishes in the allotted time are particularly demoralizing, since failure to finish is often interpreted, erroneously, as proof of failure.

Psychologists certainly have a very important contribution to make in helping to develop more effective executives. A first-rate Ph.D. in psychology can use his wisdom about human behaviour to improve greatly the calibre of executives and help create for them a healthier environment in which to function within the company.

But if the promise of psychology in management is to be fulfilled, the psychologists must function as professionals, not peddlers. And it is urgent that the practitioners become much more prudent about the free-and-easy use of such intrusive tools as screening devices on people who have no reasonable alternative to submitting to them.

Psychologists – and psychiatrists – can make their best contribution to the executive and the company by individual counselling. The psychologist can help the man to be more effective and to solve personal problems that may be disrupting his efforts. James Farr, who has interviewed several thousand executives, mentioned such a case. This executive had reached a very high level rapidly and had six departments under him. He made a tremendous first impression, and everyone agreed he was earnest, hard-working, conscientious. But he was in such trouble that there was great pressure at headquarters to get rid of him.

Farr described the man as an anxious conformist and perfectionist who was 'so concerned with doing the right thing and in reaching his goal that he lost all sensitivity. And in controlling his own anxiety façade he came out a cold person. He was concerned about the right clubs and he was even concerned about calling cards being correctly engraved. When he picked up my calling card the first thing he commented was: "It's not engraved – you ought to get your cards engraved. They make a nicer impression." '

The man wanted so much to be right that he couldn't make decisions. Virtually everyone under his jurisdiction – even department heads – complained that he checked in detail everything they did and often treated them like flunkeys. Dr Farr relates: 'I fed to him the kind of impact he was creating with other people. I had forty spontaneous comments mentioned by subordinates.' The man agreed something had gone wrong, and began having sessions with Dr Farr over many months. Dr Farr meanwhile also worked on the people below this executive 'to get them ready to accept any change that might come. I got him to agree to start having staff meetings; and I got the guys on the staff to work to make sure that the staff meetings, once started, would be successful so that they would have what I call a "success experience." '

Dr Farr said that the man, though much more relaxed and effective, still gets into trouble occasionally, but he now has enough insight to call to tell the psychologist he needs advice on a situation. Dr Farr added: 'Now we can talk and he can fix it.'

Another way psychologists can be helpful is in offering general guidance to management on the kinds of men that are needed. And they can make an important contribution by working to improve interpersonal relations in executive ranks by talking individually to all the people involved. Psychological testing is most valuable and most justifiable if it is used as an aid to psychological judgement rather than as a sole device.

Ideally, the relationship between the psychologist or psychiatrist and the executive should be a completely confidential one. A man could freely and joyously submit to all tests and probings that the counsellor felt might be useful if he could be certain that they were confidential. The results of such evaluations then might be valuable in helping the man plan his career and so improve his usefulness to the company. If the company insists on being privy to the evaluations, the professional should insist on rendering an oral report, and keep all test results locked in his own files.

The director of one psychiatric clinic which has worked with companies advised: 'We render no reports, even if the company pays the bills. We discovered that just as soon as you start reporting on anybody you are in a hell of a mess all around.'

CHAPTER 24

Efforts to Develop More Leaders of Breadth

A great society is a society in which its men of business think greatly of their functions. Alfred North Whitehead

As executives demonstrate their dedication to the problems of their particular world, a great many of them not only become oblivious to society at large but also remain uninformed or predictably misinformed about national and world affairs. On current-affairs tests executives come out approximately the same as students en route from high school into college. Their attitude towards literature, music, art, and studies of the nature of man is likely to be either scornful or indifferent.

They speak proudly of the staggering amount of reading they do each day. It is true that they shuffle through papers stacked high in the IN basket. And they read their trade journals and to some extent read newspapers and magazines. A more realistic test of their enthusiasm for reading, however, would be their book-reading, especially serious book-reading. Here there is a startling drop in interest. *Fortune* reported one survey that showed most executives read less than one book per month, and a high percentage of this book-reading was mysteries and management books. In short, the little that they do read tends to be escape literature or management materials which reinforce the values of business and tend to heighten their isolation. Seymour Freedgood found in his investigation of the homes of top auto executives in Bloomfield Hills that although there may be a five-car garage 'there is no library; the typical Bloomfield Hills family reads magazines, not books.'

The head of an executive-development programme at an Ohio university told me of his discouragement in putting out books for the executives to take home to read. He said: 'These guys aren't reading. They won't pick up most of the books. They are interested only in books clearly related to their job. In talking, they come out with the most naïve things.' A trade association in heavy industry which invited me to give a talk to its members – many of them heads of companies – sent me beforehand a briefing memo which included this sentence: 'They are well read in newspapers and periodicals; not so well read in books.'

One sophisticated executive offered this comment about his associates in his company's Mahogany Row: 'I'd guess that only two out of the top fifty men might reasonably be called broad-gauge types.'

It has been my impression that British executives are considerably more sophisticated intellectually than their American counterparts, broader in their interests, and gayer in their after-hours relaxatnio. In comparing notes with Dr McMurry, who frequently visits England, I find that he agrees in general. He attributes their greater breadth of interests to their education, which places more emphasis on cultural than on technical subjects, and to the fact that they are generally more travelled and have had to be more international in their outlook.

Executives may argue, as they do, that too much interest in being a sophisticate of the world – or being compassionate about one's fellow man – might well detract from a man's effectiveness as an aspiring executive. Still, in our rapidly changing society, it seems dangerously shortsighted to have only two broad-gauge men out of fifty at the top-management level of a major national institution.

The United States is going through an upheaval – in both its socio-economic make-up and its value systems – that has been matched few times in its history, and the rate of change is accelerating. Business leaders who cling to the concepts which proved so reassuring in the twenties and thirties are becoming as badly outdated and alienated from the main body of American society as the pitiful Marxists who keep predicting an uprising of hungry, downtrodden U.S. workers.

Our times call for corporate leaders who can be effective

agents of change. Such a leader must understand the social and political environment in which he operates and the motivations of the people upon whom he depends for success. As a minimum target, he must prevent an alienation of his institution from society. As an optimum goal he can help lead his institution and society in a direction that best serves the long-range interest of everyone. Dr Lewis Ward stated the need thus: 'One of the functions of the executive of any organization is to lead his organization in the changes that are occurring . . . a failure of an executive at any one point in his career may not seem too serious, but I would suggest that failure to lead the organization to fit better into its environment is indeed a failure.'

Americans in general are demonstrating a great upsurge of interest in cultural matters and showing increasing respect for intellect. Dullness and narrowness of interest are no longer esteemed – even in the most eminent.

Furthermore, our business leaders should perceive that the continued growth of their often already gargantuan institutions is likely to bring demands that their institutions be made more clearly responsive to public interest as expressed at the ballot box. Corporate leaders may find cheer in the fact that Americans have come to accept big organizations as inevitable for their way of life, and the fact that Americans find less and less appeal in any share-and-share-alike philosophy, Marxist or otherwise, for their personal lives. Still, many Americans find it hard to understand what is 'private' about a multibillion-dollar corporation employing hundreds of thousands of people, having hundreds of thousands of stockholders, and capable of exerting great impact on the national economy and style of living.

On a revenue basis General Motors is already vastly larger than any state in the Union and is still growing. On the same basis the fifty largest U.S. corporations are considerably larger than the fifty states.

It seems preposterous, for example, that national institutions which are so gigantic still run their executive suites as if they were social clubs and for all practical purposes bar all prospects that are not male, college-bred *WASP*s. Such companies are left with a pool of less than 3 per cent of U.S. adults from which to find their high-level leaders. This obviously not only deprives the managements of a vast amount of talent in leadership and of a colourful richness in tone; it also serves to promote the narrowness of outlook, aridity, and stuffiness common to so many of today's executive suites. Also, one could add, it makes the giant corporation a far more inviting target when the cold winds of criticism start blowing. Corporations have in the past fifteen years fallen far behind the general U.S. community in moving towards the concept of equality of opportunity and in appreciation of the values of diversity.

One thoughtful executive commented: 'The corporation lives only through the toleration of the people. The closer the views and behaviour of the corporation are to the views and value systems of the people the more the people will like the corporation. The more estranged the corporation becomes from the majority of people the more likely is the corporation to be the goat when someone wants to make political capital.'

For these reasons men with wide-ranging interests – since school days – in the humanities and the behavioural sciences seem to make especially effective corporate leaders in today's fast-changing world. That widely respected elder statesman of industry, Clarence Randall, has suggested that broad cultivation of the mind brings 'the wisdom, the tolerance, and the intellectual fortitude which are the hallmarks of distinguished industrial leadership. . . . In my own case,' he says, 'chance plunged me into the steel industry without warning. Looking back from the high plateau of retirement, I am glad it happened that way. Had I even dreamed that steel might be my career, I would have concentrated on metallurgy, chemistry, mechanical engineering and geology and would have missed Shakespeare, philosophy, economics, prose composition, public speaking and law. No amount of technical training, for example, would have served to help me play my part in dealing with labour problems of my generation; but law, and learning how to speak and write the English language, did.'[1]

How does one gain breadth of perspective? For a number of top executives it comes naturally. They explore horizons outside their business world every day. Stanley de J. Osborne, president of Olin Mathieson Chemical, has been writing a history of Spain. Crawford Greenewalt not only has written a definitive study of the hummingbird but is a widely read student of Roman history. Robert McNamara, while still president of Ford, found his stimulation by soaking up such books as *The Phenomenon of Man* and *The Western Mind in Transition* and he chose to live in Ann Arbor near the University of Michigan campus, rather than in either Bloomfield Hills or Grosse Pointe.

Every ambitious young man probably feels more confident in entering upon a career if he has acquired through intense study in school some speciality, whether metallurgy, law, finance, marketing, or nuclear physics. Such a speciality may well help him in his early years, but 'vocationalism' has its shortcomings for the long haul. In 1959 two reports, financed respectively by the Ford Foundation and the Carnegie Corporation, were both sharply critical of the overemphasis on vocationalism widely found in business education. Many observers feel the student of promise should devote, at the very least, half of his higher education – whether it lasts four or six years – to liberal arts. One's excitement in exploring the history of Western man, enjoying literature, pondering philosophy, learning languages, and plunging into the behavioural sciences for insights about his fellow man deepen his understanding of himself and the world in which he lives. Businessman William Benton has observed: 'The function of higher education is not to equip the student for his first job but rather to equip him with navigating instruments for the continuous voyage.'

William Gormbley, of Harvard's Advanced Management Programme commenting on the problem of determining what to teach the man who may well be at the top of his company ten years from now, said that one thing now seems clear. 'The broader the individual, the wider his ability to think, the less he is bound by technique, the more able he is to let his mind range and to cope with all kinds of problems,' the more chance the man has to be ready when he is needed.

A man is also helped in acquiring breadth as a person if he serves a part of his career outside business. Perhaps he does this by working with a university, with government, or with a foundation. Such a change in environment, at least once in a lifetime, adds perspective. It shakes the man up a bit, gets him out of parochial patterns or mental ruts he may have been in. Robert McNamara and Carter Burgess are two men who served in both government and university before becoming presidents of their companies. Many executives are too busy in business to pay more than token attention to public affairs until after they have retired from the pinnacles of their companies. Russell Kirk has observed, however, that there are disadvantages to society in being led by 'emancipated slaves'. It is of greater value both to the man and to his company if the executive can gain his public service before the culmination of his business career.

One executive of a giant corporation observed: 'If I could direct the policies of our corporation I would say that every man, before he becomes a vice-president, should spend at least two to three years working on national problems. He would never be the same afterwards and it would make him a better leader for his company. It would introduce him to the problems of the majority of the people, and reduce his isolation.' French managements are much more respectful of experience in national problems than U.S. managements are. In France, it is not uncommon for a man to spend a decade or so in government service before entering industry at the vice-presidential or presidential level.

Several observers have recently urged that corporations start offering sabbaticals to executives so that they can spend six months or more, with pay, every seven years, travelling reading, studying, writing.

Presently the favourite method used by corporations to help their more promising executives gain breadth of viewpoint is to invite them to go away to a school or special course for a while. This often happens when the man is at the point in his career of moving from being a specialist to being a generalist in management.

The approaches vary but almost all have one interesting aspect in common. They seek to *shake up* the executive, throw him into a new, permissive environment and into new ways of thinking. Some of his classmates may be executives from faraway lands or non-businessmen.

The setting, typically, is a 'cultural island', a distant campus or retreat. One way of getting the businessman to think broadly, in the opinion of William Gormbley, 'is to make him think outside his area. . . . Get him to think in areas where he has no preconceived concepts. Make him think of society and of art and drama, and of functional aspects of business in which he is not an expert. This forces new patterns of thinking.' In these cultural islands, it is usually possible for the man to let off steam, be critical. He can even wear a bow tie and short socks.

A number of colleges have been offering executives an immersion in the humanities to help combat their narrowness of viewpoint. The most ambitious projects of this nature have been sponsored by companies in the Bell Telephone System, which found that too many of the younger men rising to high office appeared to be overspecialized and might well lack the breadth that would make them good leaders – or good advertisements for the company. Over a period of seven years approximately 130 executives (average age thirty-seven) were packed off with their families to the Institute of Humanistic Studies for Executives at the University of Pennsylvania. For ten months they read Proust, Mann, Joyce, de Tocqueville, Dreiser, Sophocles, Dante; they visited museums or attended symphonies or chamber-music concerts every week; they heard poetry readings by John Ciardi; they studied ethics, international relations, the social sciences, and logic. The one thing they did not do was study anything directly relating to corporate management.

I spent a few days with these executives. Many of the men seemed to be dutifully trying to prove they could be more enthusiastic about Proust than the next man as they pursued the cultural programme carefully organized for them. But at the very least the experience did seem to give them practice in dealing with imaginative ideas – and ideas critical of business, an absolutely new experience for many of them. They also got practice in pulling together unrelated and unfamiliar facts to get a harmonious whole, which should help them in over-all management. And to some extent they got practice in thinking for themselves.

The ten-month institute at Penn has now been discontinued (it cost a Bell company about $12,000 to maintain a man at the Institute), but meanwhile shorter comparable eight-week programmes have been launched under Bell sponsorship at Northwestern University, Dartmouth, and a number of other colleges.

These organized efforts by managements to unfreeze and broaden their earmarked men by shipping them off to cultural isles at least represents an awareness of inadequacy. And they undoubtedly do result in some change (how permanent it is difficult to say) away from narrowness of outlook. They are no substitute, however, for what the man should be doing for himself every day if he wants to live a full life.

Another approach to shaking up an executive is to send him to an institute specifically geared to helping him become more aware of his own motives and the motivations of others. Anybody who occupies positions of power over people ought to seek to become more aware of his own self and of human behaviour generally. The Menninger Foundation conducts seminars on human motivation for high-ranking executives.

Perhaps the most celebrated and controversial of the efforts to promote awareness of self and others in executives is what has come to be known as 'sensitivity training'. The fountainhead of sensitivity training is the National Training Laboratories in Group Development, headed by Lee Bradford, who was associated with Kurt Lewin, pioneer in group dynamics. N.T.L. is affiliated with the National Education Association.

Its laboratories in sensitivity training for executives are held in many 'cultural islands' throughout the country, most particularly in Bethel, Maine, and at Columbia University's mountain-top Arden House. Many of the nation's largest companies spend approximately $750 so that an executive can be immersed in sensitivity training for two weeks.

Despite the plush settings, the course is no country-club outing. For many, sensitivity training is a jolting experience, a sort of group psychotherapy. The executives are shaken up in their modes of thinking in a way they will never forget. The heart of the system is the T-Group (T for training), a unit of about ten with a staff trainer. What most baffles and upsets the executives is that the trainer does not take charge, set up an agenda, or form committees. Instead he just acts tongue-tied for a while. This creates a power vacuum that causes many executives to fret. Some move in to take charge. The trainer then suggests that they discuss the behaviour and motives of the man who has made the move to take charge. The behaviour of those who rush in to criticize or analyse is in turn analysed. Everyone is urged to be completely frank. And so they examine their own and each other's behaviour, and in the process not only become more aware of themselves and others but learn something about group cohesion and constructive use of authority as well.

Sensitivity training of course has its critics. If a man is mal-adjusted to start with, the experience, some say, can be down-right distressing. On the other hand it has many enthusiastic supporters, including its alumni. Dr. Argyris (who is on the board of N.T.L.) relates: 'I went to some sessions in the early fifties and vowed I would never go back because there were all sorts of séances. I came back in 1954 and felt that much had been learned and many effective changes had been made. After my own experiences in research and consulting I am convinced that laboratory education – or sensitivity training – is one of the best ways to tackle some of these problems.'

The American Management Association has developed its own version, called 'Executive Action', and sends all its staff men on the Executive Action programme to N.T.L. for training. More than 1,500 executives have had experience in seeing themselves as others see them at A.M.A. sessions. They role-play and then analyse each other's behaviour not in terms of judgement but rather in terms of feeling. One A.M.A. executive exclaimed: 'Executive Action is the greatest thing that has come along in fifty years!'

Executive Action sessions are one of the few kinds of A.M.A. activity in which participating executives are not assigned to groups according to rank. And it is the only A.M.A. course in which the participants do not put their titles on their badges. They are identified only by their names. That in itself can shake up a man.

CHAPTER 25

Experiments in Rediscovering the Individual

The blunt fact is that we are a long way from realizing the potential represented by the human resources we now recruit into industry. Douglas McGregor, Massachusetts Institute of Technology[1]

The problem of the appropriate role for the individual who finds himself enclosed in a gregarious society – which so troubled Henry David Thoreau even in a much earlier era – takes on ever-increasing pertinence and urgency with the continued growth of private and public bureaucracies.

In the United States the proportion of the adult population that works in large organizations continues to increase, and there is no prospect that the trend will reverse in the foreseeable future. A recent check of the forty-seven billion-dollar corporations showed that in terms of sales nearly three quarters of them have been growing faster than the economy as a whole, as reflected in the gross national product.[2] Another study, by the Census Bureau, shows that in the decade ending 1958 the nation's 200 largest manufacturers raised their share of total national output from 30 per cent to 38 per cent.

Three characteristic features of life within a large bureaucracy are impersonality of treatment, an elaborate system of rules, and a proliferation of differentiations by hierarchical layers. All can seem oppressive to the individual who cherishes his dignity and independence of mind. The relative impingement of private bureaucracies against that of public bureaucracies has never, to my knowledge, been measured. It does appear to be true that the private bureaucracies have recently become more intrusive in their personal demands on the individual at the managerial level and more manipulative towards that individual. In any case, when organizational thinking is in full sway, the individual typically reacts either by fighting the organization or by adapting himself to it, thereby becoming both passive and dependent.

Some observers have called for an all-out fight against the organization as the only hope of salvaging the individual. Others argue that, realistically, the greater hope lies in trying to increase the potential for individual growth within a framework of cooperative effort in the organization. Douglas McGregor, Chris Argyris, and Harry Levinson are three who have come to this viewpoint. In fact, Professor McGregor contends that a really effective managerial group 'provides the best possible environment for individual development.' And Dr Argyris believes that the conflict between the individual and the formal organization, though it usually leads to decay in the individual, can in fact be a source for growth.

What can be done to increase the individual human's potential for growth and personal fulfilment in large organizations? Dr Levinson suggests that, as a very minimum to assure sound mental health, any jobholder *anywhere* should be able to find in his work:

A sense of shaping his own life activities.

A sense of participation with dignity in both the task and the decisions which affect him relating to it.

A sense of status, worthwhileness, recognition.

A sense of creative contribution – of giving something of himself for the betterment of his fellows.

If the human potential is to be optimized in large business organizations it is obvious that their managements must build in mechanisms for the expression of dissent and criticism. Free society at large has such means for an honest voicing of dissent without fear of penalty, but most of the billion-dollar private bureaucracies do not. Individuals within these organizations must usually be content to hear critical thoughts about corporate practices only in the washrooms and read them in such journals as *Fortune* and the *Harvard Business Review*. Some of the recent excesses in trait-rating, for example, surely would have been avoided if managers had had an honestly open forum.

Cornell economist Ernest Dale contends that 'the greatest single bane of management today is its growing absolutism, its refusal to discuss or listen to different opinions. Management must encourage free discussion' in its own ranks. Dr Argyris suggests that the manager needs to have opportunities to 'question the very "guts" of the company's make-up.'

Another minimum requirement is that the business organization wholeheartedly commit itself to glorying in and encouraging the unique capacities of each individual, despite its felt need for uniformity. The organizations must be convinced that the 'executive development' most worth encouraging is the man's own programme for self-development. Such a philosophy was splendidly voiced by Victor H. Pomper, vice-president of H. H. Scott, Inc., when he said: 'My major contribution is to help create an environment that stimulates disparate individuals within our organization to try new things, to take risks, to make decisions, and so to stretch and grow by learning from those mistakes inevitably attendant to things that are new.'

A few companies are starting deliberately to install mavericks and needlers in their ranks. The head of a petro-chemical company in Indianapolis will hire as executives only men with clear records of 'maverickism'. The highly unconventional Murray D. Lincoln, long-time head of Nationwide Insurance, has argued that every big organization needs one 'vice-president in charge of revolution' who needles, questions, keeps everything stirred up.

We must recognize, however, that much of the recent interest in the New Maverickism does not go beyond the ghost-written proclamations of corporate spokesmen. What is commonly wanted by corporate leaders is the appearance of individualism by basically polite, well-broken-in team players. The only recognition of individualism that will have any real meaning as a signal to wary managers will be that which is accompanied by bold example and thorough and emphatic shaking up of established conformity-imposing practices.

If a spiritually tolerable relationship between man and the large business organization is to be attained, man must set up some ground rules defining the conditions of his cooperation – and he must act to protect his independence. Some years ago Dr Clark Kerr, now president of the University of California, made an eloquent appeal entitled 'What Became of the Independent Spirit?' He urged that the individual in self-protection 'avoid total involvement in any organization,' resist the organization's efforts to 'absorb' him, and 'give himself to many organizations rather than to one.'[3]

It is odd, incidentally, that while executives talk about the professionalization of their role, one can find no national professional association of consequence that effectively promotes the interests of the individual executive as a man apart from his company. Women executives have their own association, and local plants of large companies have their semi-independent associations. And of course there are many associations executives join as company representatives. But executives need a national association which would examine the terms of their existence as individuals and promote their legitimate interests in the way that doctors, lawyers, architects, authors, and engineers have their individual interests promoted.

An association of executives could suggest to its members where reasonable cooperation with the corporation ends and where exploitation begins. It could examine current practices in such controversial matters as company policies in moving executives about the landscape, the ethical issues posed for executives by many companies, the common practice of interviewing executives' wives, the lock-in techniques in setting compensation, the widespread practice of subjecting executives to non-confidential psychological testing, and the usual practice of rating executives on a form which the executives themselves had no part in shaping.

A gain in respect for the individual has been occurring in this last area. Although in the great majority of companies the superior still fills out his periodic report cards on his flock, a rapidly growing minority of companies are throwing up their hands at such paternalistic intrusiveness. They're getting out of the character-judging business and starting to appraise a man (not 'rate' him) by the *results* he attains. Standard Oil of Ohio is one of the larger companies that is getting 'out of the psychiatric business' and back to judging a man by his job performance and results.

Lawrence A. Appley, president of the American Management Association, feels that important progress is being made in this area. Under this new philosophy, he notes, appraisal work is restricted to actual performance evaluated in terms of results and methods. The personal relationships, difficulties, characteristics, qualifications that may conceivably affect the man's performance are left to skilled specialists who are made available to the individual, ideally on a confidential basis. Mr Appley points out that this 'removes from management the embarrassment of discussing personal shortcomings with individuals. . . . Management provides help without knowing what help or whether help is needed.'

Some companies are dispensing entirely with long appraisal sheets and are going by a few general but penetrating questions that bear on how the man is doing, what he and the company can do to help him develop faster, what his long-term potential is. More interesting, other companies are inviting the man being judged to share in the appraisal process. Both the superior and subordinate appraise the subordinate's performance against the objectives they set for the job a year earlier. General Electric is one of the companies that has used this approach of dual appraisal in some of its operations. It has been found that a man usually assesses himself more critically than his superior does.

Perhaps the most heartening present development is the demonstrable growing awareness that there are many ways in which people can work together for a common economic purpose. The authoritarian hierarchic pyramid is only one of the most obvious systems for organizing cooperative effort –

and may not be the most logical or desirable for the affluent, enlightened society we have today.

People of talent have sufficient opportunities to make a basic living in the opulent and many-faceted U.S. economy to free them to look beyond the financial terms of employment to the possibilities of personal fulfilment and other non-material satisfactions. They can afford to favour the enterprise which treats them as a colleague rather than as a cog in a chain of command. Management by direction and control is losing its sureness in motivating men.

Captains of industry and their counsellors still heavily favour the older tried-and-true benevolent autocracy as the most appropriate (and easiest) way to organize cooperation in the corporation. But a revolt is in progress, and some of the revolters are at the highest levels.

Questions about the appropriateness for today's world of the command hierarchy based on the pyramid are being raised more and more insistently. It is granted that any sizeable organization is likely to end up with a hierarchical structure; and it is recognized that the pyramid is highly efficient for handling decisions that don't take much ability or are routine or must be taken under conditions of severe stress.

But even from the company's standpoint the pyramidal power structure has obvious shortcomings. William T. Brady, chairman of the board of Corn Products, has complained that when power and decision are concentrated at the top you get a sterile system and an important loss in innovation. You also tend to get cliques of yes-men, he says, and an unhealthy environment pervaded by anxiety.

Barrington & Company, one of the nation's leading management-consulting firms, has concluded that authoritarian leadership limits the possibility of growth both for the company and for its managers. When power of decision is restricted to the top alone, the organization can never become any better than the men at the top. But conversely, an organization that surges with vitality and creativity all the way down can become better than the sum total of all the people in it.

Dr Argyris feels that the power pyramid is inefficient from management's standpoint because it can't solve problems in such a way that they stay solved. On the pyramid, feelings tend to get suppressed so that there is a loss of openness and authentic relationships. No one is willing to upset the top authorities by giving them unpleasant facts. There is the constant tendency to keep one's head down, a reluctance to experiment, take risks. After observing executives in action on hundreds of occasions Argyris has concluded that such factors lead to less effective decision-making, deeper organization 'increasing inputs of human energy to achieve its objective, maintain itself internally, and adapt to its external environment.'[4]

It strikes him as curious, he says, that many managements that send their bright young (and middle-aged) men off to executive-development programmes at universities explain that the men need unfreezing and exposure to fresh viewpoints. 'This implies that the internal organization as it is presently constituted freezes people. If this is true, why not build a "defroster" system *within*, and as an integral part of the organization?'

Another complication produced by the usual pyramidal approach is that executive personnel tend to hang on to old responsibilities and authority as they go to higher and higher positions in the pyramids. At one billion-dollar company a top vice-president still carries his slide-rule. Years ago he was an outstanding engineer.

A final shortcoming from management's viewpoint, of course, is that getting any kind of action out of a larger power pyramid is likely to be time-consuming, as memos go up and orders come down the channels, through many, many layers.

The shortcomings of the corporate power pyramid from the viewpoint of the individual manager seeking personal fulfilment are, as we have seen, numerous. Most crippling, perhaps, are the continual dependence upon a superior for favour and the leading of a frequently passive existence interpreting directives. By tight structuring the management determines for the managers what is to be done and how it is to be done. And both rewards and punishments are likely to be impersonal.

Robert V. L. Wright of Barrington & Company has concluded that authoritarianism in business is out of date and should be viewed as a bankrupt concept. 'In recent years the evidence has been coming in in overwhelming proportions,' he contends. 'The study of organization behaviour brings us to the conclusion that the formal organization with its emphasis on formal authority, traditional superior-subordinate relationships, and subordinate dependency is in effect the enemy of the free, constructive expression of the individual.'

Wright is only one of many calling for experimentation in forms of cooperation and integration within the corporate environment. Most of the experiments I've encountered involve broadening the base of real decision-making, modifying the traditional superior-subordinate relationships and enhancing the self-reliance of the rank-and-file manager.

Those who would modify the traditional authoritarian mode of decision-making at the top naturally have their critics and sceptics. These include Dr McMurry, who said: 'Sure, I'm against sin too. I'm not arguing that this is not highly desirable. I just say it won't work in practice. It disregards people's real human nature.' In general the critics' arguments tend to take one of these lines: most rank-and-file managers don't really want independence and responsibility. Or: they have limited potential for development. Or: they are lazy. Or: spreading responsibility would probably produce chaos. The advocates of change insist they are marshalling evidence which proves otherwise. Many of these hold that while corporate hierarchies today, by and large, have many of the characteristics of a jungle inhabited by jungle fighters, this need not be so, and that there are more effective ways to run enterprises if the managers do not need to be jungle fighters. Here are four of the more notable approaches to giving below-the-top managers more responsibility to act. The fourth, I believe, is the most exciting and noteworthy.

One mild approach to modifying the traditional pyramidal

power structure is to change from the usual functional structure (sales, finance, manufacturing, etc.) to a product structure (radios, vacuum cleaners, refrigerators, etc.). Under this
concept each product line has its own pyramid with a president and a complete organization for sales, finance, and the
rest. Each product president is held responsible for profits.
This at least tends to give the men at the tops of the divisions
more sense of running their own enterprise.

A second approach is to flatten out the pyramid by giving
each man a great many subordinates instead of the traditional
few. This has been tried with success, for example, at Sears,
Roebuck, which has been highly successful in developing
leaders. An executive at Sears may find he has forty managers
reporting to him. The traditionalist will exclaim that it is impossible to supervise properly the work of forty managers –
which is the whole point. James C. Worthy, former Sears vice-
president, has explained that there are positive advantages in
this overloading 'precisely because it tends to *avoid* too close
supervision and control. The amount of time these superior
executives can devote to any of their subordinates is, on the
average, limited. Under these circumstances the only possible
way for them to accomplish [their] jobs . . . is to have people
in the subordinate positions who can take responsibility, who
can be trusted to use good judgement, and who can move
ahead on their own without having to clear everything in
advance.'[5]

A third approach is to give some rank-and-file representatives a voice in top management. This concept was pioneered by McCormick & Company, one of the world's largest
spice companies. McCormick inaugurated a 'multiple management' setup to supplement its regular line management. A
number of rank-and-file boards (The Factory Board, The
Sales Board, The Junior Board, etc.) were established and
had the power at least to make recommendations to the
regular Senior Board of Directors.

The fourth and most dramatic approach, and one that is
presently exciting most interest, is the concept of overhauling
superior-subordinate relationships at every level of manage-

ment in order to produce greater individual responsibility and improve the environment in which managers work. It focuses on creating an environment that will encourage a deep commitment from managers to the company's objectives.

Each man sits down with his superior and defines his area of responsibility. They agree on objectives and ground rules consistent with company objectives. Once this is done the man is advised 'This is your baby.' And he knows it is. This is not the usual 'delegating', so widely proclaimed, where the subordinate must keep reporting back. This man is actually free to act. He has responsibility without strings. Proponents of this approach are convinced that any reasonably intelligent and stable man who operates on the basis of self-control is far more dependable and committed than the man who operates by remote control imposed from outside.

Dr Charles A. Myers, director of M.I.T.'s Industrial Relations Section, told of asking men to name the one boss for whom they had worked best in their lives. Nine out of ten, he found, would say in effect when asked to explain why they named the man they did: 'He gave me responsibility. He wasn't always checking on me and breathing down my neck.' Dr Myers would then often ask: 'Well, if it worked so well with you why don't you treat your own subordinates in that way?' He adds: 'They would see the light.'

Some sceptics say: 'What if a man down the line muffs a decision? Doesn't this leave the company more vulnerable?' Proponents reply that it is actually safer to leave decisions within a man's agreed area of special competence to him than to pass the problem up through several layers of command to a generalist at the top who must act on the basis of fourth-hand information. Furthermore, if the results of the actions of this manager-on-the-spot are bad, he can soon be relieved because he has agreed at the outset on the objectives he should be achieving. The occasional incompetent manager seems to offer no serious problem. He washes out much faster than he would in a more paternalistic setup where frightful incompetence is often tolerated from those who continually demonstrate their loyalty and deference.

Under this concept of responsibility-without-strings, the superior's role is something like that of a lawyer with a client. Instead of being the daily order-giver and super-decision-maker, he plays a supportive role in helping the subordinate to do his job by offering counsel, helping define problems, and making resources available. This is quite different from the usual idea that the subordinate is the superior's helper. In operating terms, this concept may mean that the superior will stroll to the subordinate's office rather than hold court in his own. They usually work together on the basis of mutual confidence rather than on the more traditional basis of authority.

The superior's main function here is not to control people but rather to control the climate – or environment – in such a way that his people are able to grow. In this ideal climate, his group will function on an informal, relaxed basis. They will respect each other but not be disturbed by the appearance of disagreements. And group decisions most commonly will be made on the basis of a general, informal consensus.

Among the larger companies that have introduced this concept experimentally in at least some part of their operation are Union Carbide, I.B.M., Corn Products, A. T. & T., Maytag, West Virginia Pulp & Paper, Hotel Corporation of America. The introduction is usually guided by an outside consultant. It seems to work better that way.

In all there may be twenty men in the entire United States now actively working as consultants in introducing some variation of this concept in a large organization. The movement is so new that these pioneers have never had a joint conference (though there is much individual conferring). All draw upon the recent findings of behavioural scientists regarding human motivations and human behaviour in group situations. Some seem to be putting primary emphasis upon transforming the tone of the inter-personal relationships; others are working primarily on the mechanics of relationships to assure more autonomy at each level. But the goals are much the same.

The man generally regarded as the father of the research

which led to this concept was the late Kurt Lewin of M.I.T., a pioneer in the study of group dynamics. I spent a few days with Dr Lewin in the forties and recall him as an intense, wiry, modest, marvellously wise man. He was then testing ways to use group interaction to reduce irrational prejudices against strange foods and minorities. Some of his insights, it turned out, had application to the development of effective managers and management teams.

Among the leaders currently introducing the concept of overhauling superior-subordinate relationships in U.S. business institutions are Douglas McGregor of M.I.T. (a former president of Antioch College and colleague of Lewin), Chris Argyris of Yale, Rensis Likert of the Institute for Social Research at the University of Michigan, Vice-President S. Vincent Wilking and his associate Robert V. L. Wright at Barrington & Company, the first major management-consulting firm to make the break to this new concept; and the consulting team of Bennett E. Kline and Norman H. Martin, social scientists who wrote an early delineation of the concept.

The concept still has no agreed name. Lewin used one obvious word, *democratic*, to describe the approach. But *democratic* is scarcely a word to attract the interest of old-line order-oriented authoritarians running most of the nation's large corporations. Perhaps it smacks too much of wild-eyed egghead chaos. McGregor simply calls it Theory Y to contrast with his Theory X, which embodies the traditional carrot-and-stick concept of motivation. The heart of Theory Y is that 'man will exercise self-direction and self-control in the service of objectives to which he is committed' and that in the modern business world the promise of commitment can itself be an important reward.

Barrington & Company uses the phrase 'Freedom within Law' to describe the managing process through which real commitment tends to occur. Others call it 'Management by Objectives'.

In pondering the movement I searched for a phrase that would describe both its mood and its mechanics and concluded that *Relaxed Autonomy* is as descriptive as any, and herewith submit it.

Sceptics will ask how this concept works in actual practice. They may even repeat a favourite notion of authoritarians that you can push decision-making down but it won't stay down. Certainly it is true that it won't stay down in a company working on the conventional pyramidal principal of authority. Or they may cite the alleged Goldwynism: 'I want you guys to tell me candidly what's wrong with our operation – even if it means losing your job!'

Ideally, the introduction of the concept needs to start at the top. Robert Wright of Barrington has been devoting full time for two years to introducing this new philosophy to the entire management group of a large division of one of the nation's largest companies. The vice-president in charge of the division has strongly supported it in a speech. About 500 men are involved. Wright meets with about twenty at a time. They come together to discuss a problem that involves them all. It may be a pricing problem or it may involve salary administration. Working only with real problems, Wright seeks to re-educate them gradually to the new approach. When a superior slips – perhaps unwittingly – into the old way of solving problems by taking charge, Wright calls him on it: 'If you act like the boss, all you are going to get is the old subordinate-type reactions – "Yes sir! That's right, sir." '

He added to me, 'Most superiors think they are getting obedience and compliance when actually they are only getting the appearance of obedience and compliance.'

Wright makes sure that three levels of management are always present when he has one of these sessions to consider a problem. Having three levels present has facilitated remarkably the process of wiping out the old power arrangements. He had discovered that 'an *A*-level man will usually try to buffalo a *B*-level man out of habit – but he won't do it in front of a *C*-level man. And I've found that a *B*-man will never be dictatorial to a *C*-man when an *A*-man is present.' Wright has estimated that if he works with only two levels at a time he can be only 20 per cent as effective as he can when working with three levels!

Chris Argyris reported on a week-long session he shared at a vacation retreat with ten top executives of the largest division of one of the nation's giant companies. The group, with Argyris encouraging and supporting, told the president of the division that he was a 'problem'. Argyris recalls: 'Everyone was startled. They were needling the president. They and I watched him as he reacted. As one man said later, "When I realized that he was not wearing his shoulder boards I felt that I was safe in this setting." ' (Some experimenters call this needling process 'the dither effect'.)

The president wanted to know *why* he was a problem. Members of the group gave him a number of reasons. He managed by crisis. He managed by detail. He managed by fear. The president said, 'Who, *me*?' and insisted that he did not. He asked for specifics and the other nine men gave him many examples. The president responded by saying: 'I have to. I don't know if I can trust you sometimes.' And he told them frankly of the problems he had with them. (In such an unfrozen environment executives can also face up to inhibiting corporate practices such as the maintenance of barriers against non-*WASP*s.)

This week-long session had taken place seven months before I talked with Argyris. 'It is interesting,' he told me, 'to see how much change there has been in their relationships. The whole thing has gone quite rapidly. There has been a levelling and a growth in openness and in risk-taking among them. Their effectiveness as a group has gone up with amazing speed. They find they can cut corners in ways they never did before because they are out in the open and trust each other.'

In addition to staging such unrestrained discussions with the top executives of this division, Argyris has also attended more than fifty high-level meetings as an observer. His report on his work with this company, *Interpersonal Competence and Organizational Effectiveness*, is one of the most impressive executive studies in recent decades. Nine months after the original session he held a seminar with the ten executives and found that all of them, including the division president, felt that the laboratory experience had had a constructive impact upon their work life. One of the men said that 'my job has been made easier by a magnitude of five'. Another said, 'It is a wonderful feeling when you no longer have to be on guard.' There was general agreement that subordinates down the line now have considerably more influence, for example in shaping the budgets under which they must operate.

Argyris stresses that simply unfreezing a man in his personal behaviour and relationships is far from enough. If the process stops there, the unfrozen will eventually freeze again. In the long run, he contends, what is necessary are new kinds of organization structure, job design, and new policies and practices in hiring, firing, rewarding, penalizing, and evaluating people which will reinforce, sanction, and expand this interpersonal unfreezing.

Such changes can best be introduced gradually over several years on a multi-stage basis. Argyris is convinced that the enlightened organization of the future will vary managerial strategy (and thus its structure) according to the kinds of problems it faces, with all members of the group sharing in defining the rules for determining which pattern is most appropriate.

For some kinds of decision, the old action-from-the-top method may still be considered most appropriate, as when the company faces a sudden emergency. Other decisions may be reserved for superiors, with the understanding that they are acting as *representatives* of the subordinates. Still other kinds will be left to a particular individual, whatever his position, who is the best qualified man in the company to act upon a problem. Some decisions will be reserved for action by all members of the group, arriving at these by consensus – for instance, decisions regarding the criteria used for making promotions, apportioning the money available to the department for salaries, or establishing a production objective for the department. Those managers who don't really want more responsibility presumably can elect to leave most of the decisions to higher authorities – but at least they will now share in defining the structure within which they will operate.

Prof. Harold J. Leavitt is another respected theorist who has arrived (by a somewhat different line of thinking) at the conviction that in the future we will see much more adjustment of type of management to the task at hand. As business organizations become more diversified and spread out, it becomes increasingly implausible to try to maintain the tidy uniformity of procedure that systems-planners so dearly cherish.

Under the concept of relaxed autonomy as it usually works, the superior must be prepared to see a project carried out in a way he might not have thought of or chosen himself. At the same time, he is the final judge of the ultimate results. Do the results measure up to what he and the subordinate originally agreed should be obtained?

The superior is measured (and promoted) largely on the basis of how much his subordinates have grown in their jobs and achieved in their objectives. From time to time the subordinates and his superior jointly assess the results the subordinate has been obtaining.

In the view of some of the pioneers, under a relaxed autonomy the superior's traditional duty of nominating men to fill openings at a higher level remains the same as in older management frameworks. A man who has done a fine job of delivering in his present job may or may not be the ideal man for a specific opening above. Wright points out that 'in baseball you don't necessarily make the home-run king a manager. They have two different jobs.' But under a relaxed autonomy the superior has got to know the qualities and abilities of his subordinates far better than he could have learned them in an authoritarian scheme. Argyris feels that each individual should participate in decisions regarding promotions and salaries affecting his area, at least to the extent of helping establish criteria.

In any case, Wright believes strongly that managements should abandon routine hoarding of information, including secretiveness about job openings, and follow the practice of the U.S. federal government and of British industry of posting notice of job openings on bulletin boards.

From his experience Wright has concluded that most U.S. corporations are top- and bottom-heavy with paper-shuffling executives, and that by adopting this new concept they could, if so inclined, eliminate up to a third of their levels of management. Furthermore, the companies can move much faster into new opportunities and out of perilous situations with this freer kind of operation.

One critic of the approach, a management consultant, suggests that the good results often claimed may have another explanation. He contends that managers who can easily turn responsibility over to subordinates tend to be stronger and more self-reliant people than their more authoritarian colleagues 'who seek to conceal weakness under the manners of a martinet.' He adds that a strong, self-reliant manager is an efficient productive manager *no matter what system of leadership he employs* – an interesting interpretation. Proponents of the relaxed-autonomy approach contend that the newer way will produce more such 'strong, self-reliant' managers in the future.

The relaxed autonomy approach has been considered more successful in some places than in others. Procedures for introducing it are different and still evolving and the preconceptions of those doing the judging are also difficult to evaluate. But even those most stubborn in refusing to concede that such an approach is more productive economically generally concede that it does afford higher job satisfaction.

The chairman of one large food company has stated flatly that the concept has helped his company make money *and* has contributed to his own effectiveness. Wright still is enthusiastic after two years of front-line experience: 'In eight out of ten cases we've gotten the kind of results we hoped we would get, always realizing that changes of this kind take time.' And his boss at Barrington, vice-president S. Vincent Wilking, comments, 'We have people who say they see this as a better way to work. They are getting more done. They are much happier. It is fun. And they are getting decisions made more quickly.'

This concept – or something like it – is certainly badly needed in practice if we are to humanize the business corporation in the face of organizational giantism and growing technological complexity. Today the lingering authoritarianism among those who direct the economic life of most of us stands high in our society's list of unresolved challenges.

The philosophy of broadening responsibility and increasing self-determination in the modern corporation is certainly consistent with what we know about human behaviour and psychological needs. It is consistent with the need of a democratic society to cherish and strengthen the individual. The idealism behind the concept is heartening in itself. *And* it appears to be consistent with the need of business to make a profit.

Such a philosophy of management promises to make the individual manager in the corporate hierarchy a more independent, mature, self-controlling, creative, and committed person.

For life on the pyramids, that is quite a promise.

Notes

CHAPTER 1

1. Arch Patton, *Men, Money and Motivation* (McGraw-Hill, 1961), p. 191.
2. 'Does Big Business Breed Conformity?', *Dun's Review and Modern Industry*, March 1959.

CHAPTER 2

1. Crawford H. Greenewalt, *The Uncommon Man* (McGraw-Hill, 1959), p. 21.
2. C. Wilson Randle, 'How to Identify Promotable Executives', *Harvard Business Review*, May–June 1956.

CHAPTER 3

1. Frances M. Fuller and Mary B. Batchelder, 'Opportunities for Women at the Administrative Level', *Harvard Business Review*, January–February 1953.
2. Harold J. Leavitt, 'Management in the 1980s', *Harvard Business Review*, November–December 1958.
3. *The Committee Reporter*, October 1960; published by the Institute of Human Relations of the American Jewish Committee.
4. Seymour Freedgood, 'Life in Bloomfield Hills', *Fortune*, July 1961.

CHAPTER 4

1. Lewis B. Ward, 'Putting Executives to the Test', *Harvard Business Review*, July–August 1960.
2. Alan Harrington, *Life in the Crystal Palace* (Cape, 1960).

CHAPTER 5

1. 'The Hullabaloo over Executives' Wives', *American Business*, August 1957.
2. Osborn Elliott, *Men at the Top* (Weidenfeld & Nicolson, 1960).

CHAPTER 7

1. *Executive Selection: How Psychologists Can Help*, a special report to management by graduate students of the Graduate School of Business Administration, Harvard University (Cambridge, Mass.: Management Reports, 1959), Appendix, Exhibit 8.

2. Ernest Dale and Alice Smith, 'Now Report Cards for Bosses', *The New York Times Magazine*, 31 March 1957.
3. *Executive Selection*, Appendix, Exhibit 4A.

CHAPTER 8

1. George J. Kienzle and Edward H. Dare, *Climbing the Executive Ladder* (McGraw-Hill, 1950), p. 19.
2. Perrin Stryker, 'Is There an Executive Face?', *Fortune*, November 1953.
3. 'Businessman's School for Good Behaviour', *Newsweek*, 10 October 1960.
4. Cameron Hawley, *The Lincoln Lords* (Michael Joseph, 1961).
5. William B. Terhune, 'Brief Psychotherapy with Executives in Industry – The Emotional Checkup', in *Progress in Psychotherapy* (New York: Grune & Stratton, London: Heinemann, 1960).

CHAPTER 9

1. Edmund P. Learned, David N. Ulrich, and Donald R. Booz, *Executive Action* (Boston, Mass.: Division of Research, Graduate School of Business Administration, Harvard University, 1951), p. 48.
2. 'What Would a Psychologist Tell You?', *Chemical Week*, 17 May 1958.
3. Learned, Ulrich, and Booz, p. 60.

CHAPTER 10

1. Arch Patton, 'What Is an Executive Worth?', *Harvard Business Review*, March–April 1961.
2. Lewis B. Ward, 'Do You Want a Weak Subordinate?', *Harvard Business Review*, September–October 1961.
3. Thomas W. Harrell, *Managers' Performance and Personality* (Cincinnati: South-Western Publishing Company, 1961).
4. Jerome C. Beam and John D. Drake, *The Organization Approach to Decision and Action;* scheduled for publication by Prentice-Hall.
5. Douglas McGregor, *The Human Side of Enterprise* (New York: McGraw-Hill, 1960), p. 181.

CHAPTER 11

1. Lyman W. Porter and Edwin E. Ghiselli, 'Self-Perception of Top and Middle Management Personnel', *Personnel Psychology*, Winter 1957.
2. Lewis B. Ward, op. cit.
3. Robert N. McMurry, *Management Clinic* (Batsford & Business Publications, 1960).

CHAPTER 12

1. Frederick J. Gaudet and Ralph A. Carli, 'Why Executives Fail', *Personnel Psychology*, Spring 1957.
2. Harlan Byrne, 'The New Bosses: Prince Revives Armour by Preaching Profits, Swells His Own Wealth', *The Wall Street Journal*, 25 January 1962.
3. 'Managing Your People', *Nation's Business* booklet (Washington: Chamber of Commerce of the U.S.).
4. C. Wilson Randle, op. cit.

CHAPTER 13

1. C. Northcote Parkinson, 'The Art of Being No. 2', *Fortune*, September 1961.
2. William R. Dill, Thomas L. Hilton, and Walter R. Reitman, *The New Managers: Patterns of Behaviour and Development* (Prentice-Hall, 1962), p. 2.
3. Roy Lewis and Rosemary Stewart, *The Managers: A New Examination of the English, German and American Executive* (New York: Mentor, 1958), p. 88.

CHAPTER 14

1. 'Inside the Executive Mind', *Motivations*, January 1957; published by the Institute for Motivational Research, Croton, New York.
2. 'Great Aspirations: Career Plans of America's June 1961 College Graduates', National Opinion Research Centre Report No. 82 (Chicago: The University of Chicago, 1961).

CHAPTER 15

1. Norman C. Miller, 'The New Bosses', *The Wall Street Journal*, 2 January 1962.

CHAPTER 16

1. Francis X. Sutton, *et al.*, *The American Business Creed* (Oxford University Press, 1956), p. 105.
2. Two recent Jennings books are *An Anatomy of Leadership* (1960) and *The Executive* (1962), both published by Hamish Hamilton.

CHAPTER 17

1. Arch Patton, *Men, Money and Motivations*, p. 35.
2. *Executive Recruiting: How Companies Obtain Executive Talent*, by students of the Graduate School of Business Administration, Harvard University, 1960; copies available through Executive Reports Associates, Lake Forest, Ill.

3. William E. Henry, 'Conflict, Age and the Executive', Michigan State University *Business Topics*, Spring 1961.

CHAPTER 18

1. 'Status Symbols Termed Legitimate Incentives', *Steel*, 29 February 1960.

CHAPTER 20

1. Perrin Stryker, *The Men from the Boys* (Hamish Hamilton, 1961).
2. *Toward Understanding Men*, transcript of a seminar for industrial executives (Topeka: The Menninger Foundation, 1957).

CHAPTER 21

1. William B. Terhune, 'The Emotional Checkup for Executives', a paper presented at the 42nd annual session, American College of Physicians, Miami Beach, 8 May 1961.
2. 'Nervous Tension Starts at Home', *Nation's Business*, January 1961.
3. 'How to Live with Job Pressure', *Nation's Business*, September 1956.
4. Seymour Freedgood, 'Life in Bloomfield Hills', *Fortune*, July 1961.

CHAPTER 22

1. Eugene E. Jennings, *An Anatomy of Leadership*.
2. Kienzle and Dare, *Climbing the Executive Ladder*, p. 36.

CHAPTER 23

1. Harry Levinson, 'The Psychologist in Industry', *Harvard Business Review*, September–October 1959.
2. Lewis B. Ward, 'Problems in Review', *Harvard Business Review*, July–August 1960.
3. *Executive Selection: How Psychologists Can Help*.

CHAPTER 24

1. Clarence B. Randall, 'The Myth of the Specialist', *Dun's Review and Modern Industry*, November 1960.

CHAPTER 25

1. McGregor, *The Human Side of Enterprise*, p. vi.
2. 'Rate-of-Growth Analysis of 801 Leading Corporations', *Sales Management*, 16 December 1960.
3. Clark Kerr, 'What Became of the Independent Spirit?', *Fortune*, July 1953.
4. Chris Argyris, *Interpersonal Competence and Organizational Effectiveness* (Tavistock Publications, 1962), p. 131.
5. James C. Worthy, *Big Business and Free Man* (Harper, 1959), p. 109.

Suggested Reading in Specific Areas

THE EXECUTIVE'S PLACE IN SOCIETY

Bowen, Howard R., *Social Responsibilities of the Businessman* (Harper, 1953).

Dalton, Melville, *Men Who Manage* (Chapman & Hall, 1959).

Dale, Ernest, 'The Social and Moral Responsibilities of the Executive in the Large Corporation', *American Economic Review*, May 1961.

Henry, William E., 'The Business Executive: Psychodynamics of His Social Role', in Robert Dubin, *Human Relations in Administration* (Prentice-Hall, 1951).

Jennings, Eugene E., *An Anatomy of Leadership* (Hamish Hamilton, 1960).

Kirk, Russell, 'The Inhumane Businessman', *Fortune*, May 1957.

Newcomer, Mabel, *The Big Business Executive* (Oxford University Press, 1955).

Selekman, Benjamin M., 'Businessmen in Power', *Harvard Business Review*, September–October 1961.

Warner, W. Lloyd and James C. Abegglen, *Big Business Leaders in America* (Harper, 1955).

THE GROWTH OF EXECUTIVES

Advanced Management, 'Is Management Development Worth the Cost?', November 1960.

Andrews, Kenneth R., 'Is Management Training Effective?', *Harvard Business Review*, January–February and March–April 1957.

Argyris, Chris, 'Executive Development Programs: Some Unresolved Problems', *Personnel*, July 1956.

Bradford, Leland P., 'A New Look At Management Development', *Advanced Management*, October 1958.

Business Week, 'G.E. Institute Nears End of Run – Now What?', 4 March 1961.

Business Week, 'Are B-Schools on the Right Track?', 13 April 1959.

Dill, William R., Thomas L. Hilton, and Walter R. Reitman, *The New Managers: Patterns of Behaviour and Development* (Prentice-Hall, 1962).

Goldwin, Robert A., and Charles A. Nelson, *Towards the Liberally Educated Executive* (New English Library, 1960).

Klaw, Spencer, 'Two Weeks in a T-Group', *Fortune*, August 1961.

McMurry, Robert N., 'Executive Development: Dollars down the Drain?', *Dun's Review and Modern Industry*, August 1960.

National Opinion Research Center, Report No. 82, 'Great Aspirations: Career Plans of America's June 1961 College Graduates' (Chicago: The University of Chicago, 1961).

Nation's Business, 'Graduates Assess Executive Schooling', September 1958.

Pamp, Frederic E., 'Liberal Arts as Training for Business', *Harvard Business Review*, May–June 1955.

Pierson, Frank C., *et al.*, *The Education of American Businessmen* (McGraw-Hill, 1959).

Silk, Leonard S., *The Education of Businessmen* (New York: Committee for Economic Development, December 1960.)

Taylor, Erwin K., 'Management Development at the Crossroads', *Personnel*, March–April 1959.

Wright, Moorhead, 'Seven Keys to Successful Executive Development at G.E.', *Management Review*, April 1957.

THE ASSESSMENT OF EXECUTIVES

Appley, Lawrence A., 'A Major Breakthrough', *Scratchpad*, The American Management Association, April 1961.

Executive Selection: How Psychologists Can Help, A Special Report to Management by graduate students of the Graduate School of Business Administration, Harvard University (published by Management Reports, P.O. Box 136, Cambridge, Mass., 1959).

Gardner, Burleigh B., 'What Makes Successful and Unsuccessful Executives', *Advanced Management*, September 1948.

Gaudet, Frederick J., 'A Study of Psychological Tests as Instruments of Management Evaluation', American Management Association, 1957.

Henry, William E., 'Identifying the Potentially Successful Executive', *Personnel Series*, No. 127, American Management Association, 1949.

Heyel, Carl, *Appraising Executive Performance* (New York: American Management Association, 1958).

Kelly, Philip R., 'Reappraisal of Appraisals', *Harvard Business Review*, May–June 1958.

Levinson, Harry, 'The Psychologist in Industry', *Harvard Business Review*, September–October 1959.

Merrill, Harwood F., 'It's Time to Overhaul Appraisal', *Management News*, December 1960.

McGregor, Douglas M., 'An Uneasy Look at Performance Appraisal', *Harvard Business Review*, May–June 1957.

Personnel Journal, 'How 47 Companies Measure Their Executives', July–August 1957.

Ward, Lewis B., 'Putting Executives to the Test', *Harvard Business Review*, July–August 1960.

THE IMPROVEMENT OF EXECUTIVE PERFORMANCE

Argyris, Chris, *Interpersonal Competence and Organizational Effectiveness* (Tavistock Publications, 1962).

Bower, Marvin (ed.), *The Development of Executive Leadership* (Oxford University Press, 1949).

Bursk, Edward Collins, *How to Increase Executive Effectiveness* (Oxford University Press, 1953).

Drucker, Peter F,. *The Practice of Management* (Heinemann, 1955).

Gaudet, Frederick J., 'Why Executives Fail', *Personnel Psychology*, 1957.

Jennings, Eugene E., *The Executive* (Hamish Hamilton, 1962).

Learned, Edmund P., David N. Ulrich, and Donald R. Booz, *Executive Action* (Boston: Division of Research, Graduate School of Business Administration, Harvard University, 1951).

Leavitt, Harold J., *Managerial Psychology* (Cambridge University Press, 1958).

McMurry, Robert N., *Management Clinic* (Batsford & Business Publications, 1960).

Moore, Robert F., *How Am I Doing?* (New York: Forbes, 1952).

Nation's Business reprint collections 'Managing Your People' and 'Managing Yourself', (Washington, D.C.: Chamber of Commerce of the U.S.).

Rowland, Virgil, *Improving Managerial Performance* (Harper, 1958).

Stogdill, Ralph M. and Carroll L. Shartle and associates, 'Patterns of Administrative Performance', Research Monograph No. 81, Bureau of Business Research, Ohio State University.

Stryker, Perrin, *The Men from the Boys* (Hamish Hamilton, 1961).

THE SEARCH FOR EXECUTIVE CHARACTERISTICS

Argyris, Chris, 'Some Characteristics of Successful Executives', *Personnel Journal*, June 1953.

Business Week, 'National Industrial Conference Board Says Lists of Executive Virtues Are Little Help in Picking Talent', 27 July 1957.

E.I.M.P., Summary report of the Early Identification of Management Potential research project at the Standard Oil Company (N.J.), prepared by the Social Science Research Division, Employee Relations Department, Standard Oil Company (N.J.), August 1961.

Fox, Sol, 'Do Our Military Leaders Make Good Executives in Industry?', *Printers' Ink*, 6 December 1957.

Ginzberg, Eli (ed.), *What Makes an Executive?* Report of Round Table on Executive Potential and Performance. (Columbia University Press, 1955).

Harrell, Thomas W., *Managers' Performance and Personality* (Cincinnati: South-Western Publishing Company, 1961).

Huttner, L., S. Levy, E. Rosen, and M. Stopol, 'Further Light on the Executive Personality', *Personnel*, March–April 1959.

Motivations, 'Inside the Executive Mind', published by the Institute for Motivational Research, January 1957.

McMurry, Robert N., 'How to Pick Capable Men', *Nation's Business*, February 1960.

O'Donovan, Thomas R., 'Can Executive Success Be Predicted?', *Advanced Management*, October 1961.

Porter, Lyman W., and Edwin E. Ghiselli, 'Self-Perception of Top and Middle Management Personnel', *Personnel Psychology*, Winter, 1957.

Randall, Clarence B., 'The Myth of the Specialist', *Dun's Review and Modern Industry*, November 1960.

Randle, C. Wilson, 'How to Identify Promotable Executives', *Harvard Business Review*, May–June 1956.

Rosen, Ephraim, 'The Executive Personality', *Personnel*, January–February 1959.

THE STRATEGIES OF SOME EXECUTIVES

Business Week, 'Executive Coaching Catches on,' 9 March 1957.

Ewing, R. H., 'The Gentle Art of Channel-Jumping', *Supervisory Management*, September 1958.

Industrial Marketing, 'Which Way to the Top – Marketing or Production?', August 1958.

Jennings, Eugene E., 'You Can Spot Office Politicians', *Nation's Business*, December 1959. Also: 'Power: How to Use It', ibid., December 1960.

McDonald, John, 'How to Get a Raise', *Fortune*, December 1953.

McMurry, Robert N., '16 Ways Executives Dodge Decision-Making', *Sales Management*, 20 December 1957.

Moore, David G., 'Why Some Win, Others Lose', *Nation's Business*, October 1960.

Printers' Ink, 'Are More Marketing Men Getting the Top Posts in Management?', 20 May 1960.

Stryker, Perrin, 'How Executives Get Jobs', *Fortune*, August 1953. Also: 'How to Fire an Executive', ibid., October 1954.

Ward, Lewis B., 'Do You Want a Weak Subordinate?', *Harvard Business Review*, September–October 1961.

THE RECRUITING OF EXECUTIVES

Business Week, 'When a Company Wants Brass, Executive Searchers Go to Work', 5 December 1959.

Cony, Ed., 'Executive Hunters', *The Wall Street Journal*, 29 November 1960.

Executive Recruiting: How Companies Obtain Management Talent, prepared by nine students at the Graduate School of Business Administration, Harvard University. Published by Executive Reports Associates, Lake Forest, Ill., 1960.

Gunther, Max, 'Men Wanted: $25,000 a Year', *Saturday Evening Post*, 2 February 1957.

Management Digest, 'Executive Recruiting Firms', October 1960.

The New Yorker, 'Commodity', 6 April 1957.

Stryker, Perrin, 'The Pirates of Management', *Fortune*, June 1961.

THE INDIVIDUAL IN A HIERARCHICAL STRUCTURE

Argyris, Chris, *Personality and Organization* (Harper, 1957). Also: 'Organizational Health and Executive Development', *Advanced Management*, December 1959; 'Top Management Dilemma: Company Needs *vs* Individual Development', *Personnel*, September 1955; 'The Integration of the Individual and the Organization', paper presented at University of Wisconsin School of Commerce, May 1961.

Bennis, Warren G., 'Leadership Theory and Administrative Practice: the Problem of Authority', *Administrative Science Quarterly*, December 1959. Also: 'Revisionist Theory of Leadership', *Harvard Business Review*, January–February 1961.

Boulding, Kenneth E., 'The Jungle of Hugeness', *The Saturday Review*, 1 March 1958.

Brady, William T., 'The Management of Innovation', *Advertising Age*, 4 December 1961.

Dun's Review and Modern Industry, 'Does Big Business Breed Conformity?' (President's Panel), March 1959.

Greenewalt, Crawford H., *The Uncommon Man* (McGraw-Hill, 1959).

Harrington, Alan, *Life in the Crystal Palace* (Cape, 1960).

Katz, Robert L., 'Toward a More Effective Enterprise', *Harvard Business Review*, September–October 1960.

Kerr, Clark, 'What Became of the Independent Spirit?', *Fortune*, July 1953.

Kline, Bennett E., and Norman H. Martin, 'Freedom, Authority and Decentralization', *Harvard Business Review*, May–June 1958.

Lawrence, Paul R., *The Changing of Organizational Behaviour Patterns* (Boston: Graduate School of Business Administration, Harvard University, 1958).

Likert, Rensis, 'The Motivational Approach to Management Development', *Harvard Business Review*, July–August 1959.

McCormick, Charles P., *The Power of People* (Harper, 1949).

McGregor, Douglas, *The Human Side of Enterprise* (New York: McGraw-Hill, 1960).

McMurry, Robert N., 'The Case for Benevolent Autocracy', *Harvard Business Review*, January–February 1958.

Miller, J. Irwin, 'The Dilemma of the Corporation Man', *Fortune*, August 1959.

Odiorne, George S., 'Is the Organization Man Obsolete?', *Michigan Business Review*, March 1960.

Stessin, Lawrence, 'Needed: Executives Who Talk Back', *Forbes*, March 1957.

Whyte, William H., Jr, *The Organization Man* (Cape, 1957).

Worthy, James C., *Big Business and Free Man* (Hamish Hamilton, 1959).

THE EXECUTIVE WAY OF LIFE

American Business, 'This Hullabaloo over Executives' Wives', August 1957.

Chappell, Russell, 'Sizing up Executive Wives', *Newsweek*, 13 May 1957.

Editors of *Fortune*, *The Executive Life* (Garden City, N.Y.: Doubleday, 1956). Also in *Fortune*: '1700 Top Executives', November 1959.

Elliott, Osborn, *Men at the Top* (Weidenfeld & Nicolson, 1960).

Fuller, Frances M., and Mary B. Batchelder, 'Opportunities for Women at the Administrative Level', *Harvard Business Review*, January–February 1953.

Freedgood, Seymour, 'Life in Bloomfield Hills', *Fortune*, July 1961.

Heckscher, August, 'Executive Leisure', *Harvard Business Review*, July–August 1959.

Johnson, Harrison R., 'The Office Caste System', *Modern Office Procedures*, June 1960.

Management Methods, 'How Your Wife Can Back You in Your Job', August 1958.

O'Meara, J. Roger, 'Membership in Outside Organizations: a Survey of Company Practices', *Management Record*, July–August 1960.

Porter, Sylvia, 'Bias in Industry', *The New York Post*, 3 May 1961.

Taylor, Duncan Norton, 'Why Don't Businessmen Read Books?', *Fortune*, May 1954.

Vartan, Vartanig, report on American Management Association survey of backgrounds and living habits of 335 corporation presidents, *The New York Herald Tribune*, 16 December 1957.

THE EUROPEAN EXECUTIVE

Business Week, 'In Europe, the Perks Add Up', 13 August 1960, and 'French Brass Returns to Class', 1 December 1956.

Granick, David, *The European Business Executive* (Weidenfeld & Nicolson, 1962). Also: *The Red Executive* (Macmillan, 1960).

Lewis, Roy, and Rosemary Stewart, *The Managers: A New Examination of the English, German and American Executive* (New York: Mentor, 1958).

Stewart, Rosemary, 'Executive Development, British Style', *The Management Review*, February 1957.

THE REWARDS OF THE EXECUTIVE

Business Week, 'What the Top Brass Is Making' (annual survey of executive compensation based on proxy statements filed with Securities & Exchange Commission), 19 May 1962.

Dun's Review and Modern Industry, 'Presidents View Executive Pay', November 1960. Also: 'The Fringe Binge, How Long, How Costly?', May 1960.

Journal of Taxation, 'Items in the Tax-Sheltered Package, a Checklist', May 1958. Also: 'Compensating the Corporate Executive Presents Various Tax Problems', January 1958.

Patton, Arch, *Men, Money and Motivation* (McGraw-Hill, 1961). Also: 'What Is an Executive Worth?', *Harvard Business Review*, March–April 1961.

Steel, 'Status Symbols Termed Legitimate Incentives', 29 February 1960.

U.S. News & World Report, 'Now It's Fringe Benefits for Big Executives', 17 January 1958.

Ziegler, Edward W., 'Payment by Status', *The Nation*, 12 November 1960.

THE ETHICAL PROBLEMS OF EXECUTIVES

Austin, Robert W., 'Code of Conduct for Executives', *Harvard Business Review*, September–October 1961.

Baumhart, R. C., 'Problems in Review' (survey on business ethics), *Harvard Business Review*, July–August 1961.

Childs, Marquis, and Douglas Cater, *Ethics in a Business Society* (Harper, 1954).

Cubbedge, Robert E., 'The Ethics of U.S. Industry', *Newsweek*, 24 April 1961.

Finkelstein, Rabbi Louis, 'The Businessman's Moral Failure', *Fortune*, September 1958.

Fuller, John G., *The Gentlemen Conspirators – The Story of the Price-Fixers in the Electrical Industry* (New York: Grove, 1962).

Norris, Louis William, 'Moral Hazards of an Executive', *Harvard Business Review*, September–October 1960.

Smith, Richard A., 'The Incredible Electrical Conspiracy', *Fortune*, April and May 1961.

Sullivan, A. M., 'Men, Morality and Management', *Dun's Review and Modern Industry*, October 1960.

THE STRAINS OF EXECUTIVE LIFE

Business Week, 'Faster in-and-out in Top Jobs', 26 November 1960. Also: 'How a Mentally Ill Executive Can Get Treated and Work Too', 19 January 1957; and 'Now the Brass Is Always Roving', 26 January 1957.

Cassels, Louis, 'How to Live with Job Pressure', *Nation's Business*, September 1956.

Farnsworth, Dana L., 'Health under Pressure', *Harvard Business Review*, November–December 1957.

Kissock, Joyce, 'So Your Husband's Being Transferred?', *Reader's Digest*, January 1961.

McMurry, Robert N., 'The Executive Neurosis', *Harvard Business Review*, November–December 1952.

Menninger, William C., 'Prescription for the Executive', *The Menninger Quarterly*, June 1958.

Nation's Business, 'What Can You Do about Stress?' (interview with staff members of the Menninger Foundation), June 1958.

Packard, Vance, *The Status Seekers* (Longmans, Green, 1960).

Page, Robert Collier, 'What You Should Know about Health', *U.S. News & World Report*, 15 July 1955.

Sheehan, Robert, 'We've Been Transferred', *Fortune*, July 1957.

Smith, Richard Austin, 'The Executive Crack-up', *Fortune*, May 1955.

Spencer, Lyle M., 'Ten Problems that Worry Presidents', *Harvard Business Review*, November–December 1955.

Stewart, Nathaniel, 'Friendship Can Ruin Your Business', *Nation's Business*, January 1959.

Terhune, William B., 'Brief Psychotherapy with Executives in Industry – The Emotional Checkup', from *Progress in Psychotherapy* (Heinemann, 1960).

THE EXECUTIVE'S CHANGING CORPORATE ENVIRONMENT

Anshen, Melvin, and George L. Bach (eds.), *Management and Corporations*, 1985, Symposium held on occasion of 10th anniversary of Graduate School of Industrial Administration, Carnegie Institute of Technology (McGraw-Hill, 1960).

Argyris, Chris, 'The Organization: What Makes It Healthy?', *Harvard Business Review*, November–December 1958.

Dale, Ernest, 'Executives Who Can't Manage', *Atlantic*, July 1962.

Drucker, Peter F., 'The Next Decade of Management', *Dun's Review and Modern Industry*, December 1959.

Leavitt, Harold J., 'Unhuman Organizations', *Harvard Business Review*, July–August 1962.

Management Review, 'Impact of Automation on the Executive's Job', March 1958.

Maurer, Herrymon, *Great Enterprise: Growth and Behaviour of the Big Corporation* (New York: Macmillan, 1955).

Myers, Charles A., 'The Challenge of the 1960's: Manpower Management', *Personnel*, May–June 1959.

Randall, Clarence B., 'The Myth of the Organization Chart', *Dun's Review and Modern Industry*, February 1960.

Index

*Other Pelicans by Vance Packard
are described overleaf*